WRITING PANCHO VILLA'S REVOLUTION

WRITING PANCHO VILLA'S REVOLUTION

Rebels in the Literary Imagination of Mexico

MAX PARRA

UNIVERSITY OF TEXAS PRESS
Austin

Requests for permission to reproduce material from this work should
be sent to:
    Permissions
    University of Texas Press
    P.O. Box 7819
    Austin, TX 78713-7819
    www.utexas.edu/utpress/about/bpermission.html

∞ The paper used in this book meets the minimum requirements of
ANSI/NISO Z39.48-1992 (R1997) (Permanence of Paper).

LIBRARY OF CONGRESS CATALOGING-IN-PUBLICATION DATA

Parra, Max.
    Writing Pancho Villa's revolution : rebels in the literary imagination
of Mexico / by Max Parra. — 1st ed.
        p.   cm.
    Includes bibliographical references and index.
ISBN 0-292-70697-9 (cl. : alk. paper) —
ISBN 0-292-70978-1 (pbk. : alk. paper)
    1. Mexican prose literature—20th century—History and
criticism.   2. Mexico—History—Revolution, 1910–1920—Literature
and the revolution.   3. Villa, Pancho, 1878–1923—In literature.
I. Title.
    PQ7207.M48P37   2005
    868'.60809358—dc22

                                                    2004030856

A la memoria de
Benjamín Parra Banderas (1917–2000),
que se amanecía leyendo novelas de la revolución.

CONTENTS

ACKNOWLEDGMENTS

Writing a book is as much a social enterprise as it is an individual endeavor. Strictly speaking, no one writes a book alone: the invisible presence of others, like the submerged mass of an iceberg, is always there. Society furnishes critical traditions, conventions, and emerging trends that frame and condition, to a greater or lesser degree, how and what can be written; financial sponsors enable or facilitate research and the writing process; and no less important are the informal intellectual networks that often surround and nourish the otherwise solitary task of producing an original work.

I am grateful to UC-Mexus for providing a timely grant in the last stage of the writing process and to my colleagues in the Spanish Section of the Department of Literature at the University of California, San Diego (UCSD), for their unfailing support during the years I worked on this project. In the early stages of my research, Prof. Irene Matthews of Northern Arizona University, Flagstaff, generously allowed me to read two chapters of her book manuscript "Nellie Campobello: La centaura del norte," which was subsequently published in Mexico City. I am most appreciative to her. An exchange of letters with Mexican poet, novelist, and critic Jorge Aguilar Mora, now at the University of Maryland and a Villista scholar, proved intellectually valuable, as did his writings. In addition, Aguilar Mora made available to me difficult-to-find material by Dr. Ramón Puente. Two outstanding UCSD graduate students, now scholars in their own right, Brian Gollnick and Kenia Halleck, followed my musings in independent and graduate seminars on subalternity and intellectual culture in Mexico. Their incisive comments and questioning helped clarify my ideas during the writing of this book.

In Mexico City, critic Evodio Escalante was openly receptive to my ideas and suggested bibliographical references. Art historian Laura González Matute revealed the existence of the Fondo Campobello, at the Biblioteca del Consejo de las Artes, and shared journalistic material from her personal files on the Campobello sisters. Prof. Edith Negrín, of the

Universidad Nacional Autónoma de México (UNAM), read and provided useful comments on Chapter 2. Jesús Vargas Valdés, a specialist in the history of the state of Chihuahua and organizer of Villista conferences, patiently answered my questions during numerous lengthy conversations on the Villista movement and regional history. I deeply appreciate his encouragement and disinterested support. Herzonia Yáñez graciously provided room, board, and unfailing hospitality during many of my visits to Mexico City and kept me updated about news directly or indirectly related to my research.

I would like to thank the Centro de Estudios Literarios "Antonio Cornejo Polar" (CELACP) for granting permission to publish segments of my article "Memoria y guerra en *Cartucho* de Nellie Campobello" (*Revista de Crítica Literaria Latinoamericana*, Sem. 1 [1998]: 167–186). An abridged, and slightly modified, version of Chapter 2 was published as "Villa y la subjetividad política popular: Un acercamiento subalternista a *Los de abajo* de Mariano Azuela" (*Foro Hispánico* 22 [2002]: 11–26).

This book was originally written in Spanish and placed in the hands of a professional translator. Dissatisfied with the results, I came to the conclusion that I would have to rewrite the manuscript in English. In the process, I expanded Chapters 1 and 3, completely rewrote Chapters 4 and 5, and added Chapter 6. I was fortunate to receive critical input and encouragement from two outstanding individuals. Anne R. Archer, of New York City, read the entire Spanish manuscript and my first draft in English. A most lucid reader and a supportive ally throughout, she provided thoughtful comments, editing suggestions, as well as keen interest in the material, particularly on Campobello. Prof. Aníbal Yáñez from California State University, San Marcos, proofread the entire manuscript and spent countless hours correcting and discussing with me subtle matters of style and nuance. Whatever imperfections this book may have they are less numerous, I am sure, than they would have been without his help; my debt to him is most profound. My wife, Consuelo M. Soto, read the manuscript and suggested corrections at different stages of my writing. Her support and insightful comments made me rethink, for the better, the connection between Mexico's cultural politics and history.

Finally, I would be remiss if I did not mention my father, Benjamín Parra Banderas, who died after a long illness before the book was completed. In fact, caring for him and writing the book will always be inextricably linked in my mind. An avid reader despite a limited education, my father instilled in me a love of knowledge and curiosity about the world around me. His passion for books became mine and set me on the path that led me to write this book. I am forever grateful.

WRITING PANCHO VILLA'S REVOLUTION

INTRODUCTION

HISTORY

On March 6, 1913, Francisco Villa and eight followers crossed the border into Mexico from El Paso, Texas, with the aim of overthrowing the dictatorship of Gen. Victoriano Huerta. They had nine rifles and nine horses, "500 cartridges per man, two pounds of coffee, two pounds of sugar, one pound of salt."[1] By the end of that year, Villa's forces had swelled to several thousand well-equipped men. The former social bandit was now chief commander of a loose coalition of revolutionary forces known as the Division of the North and controlled most of the state of Chihuahua.[2] Six months later, Villa's Division of the North crushed the federal army in the city of Zacatecas, in central Mexico. After a brief truce with competing revolutionary factions from other regions, Villa and his army continued their advance south, unopposed, to Mexico City.

The impressive rise of the Villistas from a grassroots movement to the undisputed masters of the country in the period 1913–1914 is a military phenomenon still being unraveled and debated by historians.[3] There is general agreement that no other revolutionary mobilization in Mexico had "the popular intensity and mass following" of Villismo, nor did any other arouse such feelings of pride and power among the rural poor.[4] The unmistakable message of Villa's military success was that the years of living in fear were over. The time had come to take by force what rightfully belonged to the historically disenfranchised. This had a profoundly liberating impact on the psychology of the downtrodden. The rural masses' bold acts of social transgression, unimaginable a few years earlier, became commonplace.[5]

The change in popular mentality stunned the wealthy landowners and the "decent people," those who "dressed well, were rich, and were not too dark."[6] The colonial structures of Mexican society, still in place even after a century of independence from Spain, were shaken to the core. Arturo Warman summarizes the new social reality: "The ethnic barrier was torn down. To be a dandy or to look like one ceased to be a privilege and became a risk. The revolutionaries killed some citizens because of their manners and appearance. Skin color, attire and manner had been instruments of oppression that, to a certain degree, functioned as a dividing line between the opposing groups."[7]

Historical time accelerated in a matter of months. The rural oligarchy abandoned its haciendas in the countryside and moved to the cities or left Mexico altogether, seeking a safe haven abroad from the ragged armies of hungry campesinos. Members of the rural oligarchy sensed that the revolution was as much an attack on the city and urban culture as it was a war against the dictatorial Huerta government. Well-to-do city dwellers, terrified by the news of revolutionary soldiers looting stores and residences, barricaded themselves in their homes. Few images better illustrate the dramatic changes taking place than the photograph of Villa seated in the presidential chair in Mexico City's national palace alongside Gen. Emiliano Zapata, the legendary agrarian leader from the south. Widely reproduced in newspapers, the photograph of the uneducated but astute revolutionaries was an eloquent statement of the people's empowerment, a visual reminder that the social order had been turned upside down.

Villa's remarkable rise to national prominence, however, was short-lived. During the course of the civil war that ensued among various revolutionary factions after Huerta's fall, Villa's military power and social appeal were severely eroded. Villista defeats in central Mexico (the Bajío region) during the spring and summer of 1915, as well as defections and betrayals within his own camp forced him to retreat to his home base in the northern states of Chihuahua and Durango.

Back in Villista territory, the former cattle rustler and social bandit disbanded what was left of his once-powerful Division of the North. A few hundred faithful soldiers, determined to continue fighting, followed him to the mountains. Taking advantage of Villa's enviable knowledge of the terrain, they waged a bloody guerrilla war against the newly installed revolutionary government of Venustiano Carranza.

Villa's weakened and regionally confined military activities diminished his influence in national affairs, but his daring guerrilla actions and popular appeal continued to have a formative effect on the country's social and cultural imaginary. In March 1916, Villa crossed the border into the United States and raided Columbus, New Mexico, in a calculated move to exact revenge against a former ally (the United States) that now sided with the popular leader's foes and officially recognized Carranza. Washington reacted to the attack on Columbus by organizing the so-called Punitive Expedition to search for and capture Villa in Mexican territory.

After ten months of fruitless searching, the U.S. expeditionary force withdrew, and the legend of the indomitable Villa continued to grow. The Hearst newspapers in the United States portrayed Villa as a symbol of south-of-the-border lawlessness and made him and Mexicans in general a target of racist commentaries.[8] In Mexico, however, Villa's raid on Columbus made him a popular symbol of nationalism, forcing President Carranza to intensify his campaign to discredit the rebel leader.[9]

In 1920, Venustiano Carranza was assassinated while fleeing a military revolt by his own forces. With the death of Villa's personal enemy and unrelenting persecutor, the Villistas agreed to an armistice. The new regime gave the "Centaur of the North," as the Mexican press had christened him, the hacienda of Canutillo in the northern part of the state of Durango. Although occasional statements to the press continued to make the Mexican government uneasy about his intentions, Villa lived peacefully in Canutillo for the next three years.[10] On a July morning in 1923, he was ambushed and killed along with his escort in the nearby city of Hidalgo del Parral. Personal and political enemies, with the acquiescence and support of prominent government officials, were behind the assassination (perhaps including Pres. Álvaro Obregón himself).[11]

Henceforth, Villa's place in the history of the revolution and the military and cultural legacy of the Villista movement would not be disputed on the battlefield, but on the terrain of the discursive and ideological struggles of the postrevolutionary period.

POLITICS AND CULTURE

The meaning of Villa's rise and fall, the vicissitudes and ultimate neutralization of Villismo, were hotly contentious issues in the politics and culture of postrevolutionary Mexico. The official government version of events discounted Villa as a revolutionary leader. His marginalization was due in part to the new ruling elite's unwillingness to rehabilitate a military enemy they had personally fought. According to Ilene O'Malley, however, the decisive factor behind the official neglect of Villa was his popularity.[12] Popularity "carried in it reminders of the power of the popular classes when mobilized," undermining the regime's quest for hegemony.[13] The public's enthusiasm for Villa irritated the country's rulers, and they reacted by shrouding his name in silence, an act of "implicit denial of Villa's importance" and "the only means to counteract his fame."[14]

The popular revolutionary leader was, indeed, regarded by all segments of Mexican society as a vivid and forceful expression of the people's power, pride, and resilience. Even those who opposed him took delight in mythologizing his controversial life and military feats, and the postrevolutionary regimes' slight did little to diminish Villa's massive appeal.

Banished from the official memory of the revolution, it was in the realm of culture, not politics, where Villa's political and symbolic meaning for the Mexican nation would be appraised and discussed. The government's dismissal left the field open for Villa's "image to be shaped more by popular tastes, fiction writers, and journalists than by official propagandists."[15] The Villistas' legendary violence and terror inspired curiosity, fear, and admiration among the urban population, and the print media gleefully exploited these sentiments. Tall tales ranging from the critical to the folkloric, from the bizarre to the sympathetic, fueled the public imagination. Hyperbolic accounts proliferated about Villa's days as a social bandit, about his arbitrary killings, brutal popular justice, unexpected generosity, or improbable survival. His famed ruthlessness and charisma along with his followers' deeds and excesses were recounted in the oral culture of legends, corridos, and popular myths.[16]

The collective fascination with Villa and Villismo was fruitful for literature. The epic spectacle of warfare and Villa's adventurous life and rise from poverty and banditry to revolutionary leader inspired novels, novelized memoirs, short stories, and biographies. In the 1920s and the 1930s, decades of national reconstruction, over twenty books on Villa and Villismo were published, an unprecedented number in a country characterized by the paucity of its publications. The peak year was 1931, when five works appeared—one biography, three novels, and one collection of short stories.

Villista literature was, by and large, the work of educated people who had witnessed the revolution at close range and wrote about it based on personal memory. Yet, more often than not, writers created their own authoritative discourse and mythology about Villa and the revolution by drawing on information from elite and popular sources, such as testimonials, oral culture, military reports, and newspaper articles.[17] These accounts were written in a style accessible to the common reader; nevertheless, they were, to greater or lesser extent, elite versions of the historical agency of subaltern groups that had participated in the revolution.

Representations of Villa's grassroots insurgency and of his personality articulated different and, at times, competing views about the class and cultural "Otherness" of the rebellious masses. These views, in turn, were symptomatic of a larger cultural war taking place: a war fought over the dead, over how the Mexican people should remember their fallen revolutionaries at a time when the meaning of the war, and therefore its legacy for the present, was still unresolved. How should the dead be remembered? What was the meaning of popular violence? Whose memory would prevail? These were critical questions because the answers touched on issues of societal restructuring (e.g., the place of the uneducated masses in the new order) and political legitimation (who has the right to speak for the nation). Villista literature participated, directly or indirectly, in this cultural war.

Violence was a recurrent, often dominant, theme for Villista writers. Their work, unlike other writings on the revolution, called attention to the brutalities of war and the emotions associated with it: fear, anger, hate, revenge, guilt, denial, and so on. "There is no record of the culture of violence and disruption in the many monographs dedicated to the revolution, although it is registered in a masterly way in the novels, stories and memoirs of the writers," notes Enrique Florescano.[18] Villista literature, then, furnishes a privileged site from which to explore the popular revolution's culture of violence and how it was represented, debated, and incorporated into postrevolutionary culture.

This book examines the cultural and political construction of Villismo in postrevolutionary literary discourse. It focuses on narratives that highlight the different aesthetic and ideological positions taken toward the movement during the years of national reconstruction (1925–1940), when literature became another battlefront in the social struggle for hegemony. A dominant concern throughout the book is the treatment of popular consciousness, understood as "politicized forms of knowledge and popular identity."[19] How did writers represent popular consciousness? What role did these representations play in discursive and ideological wars of the period? What did they do for the creative process of imagining a nation's collective identity?

My strategy engages theories of identity as they relate to subaltern positionalities and relates them to larger issues of cultural and political history. Recent critical developments in the social sciences and humanities have reopened the question of popular politics in rural movements. These theories are grounded in the idea that the inner workings of rebel

identity and the modes of expression of cultural politics are far more subtle, culturally bound, and contentious than previously acknowledged. By
stressing the internal logic of popular movements and thus recognizing
the intricate nature of subaltern epistemology, these revisionist trends
critique the conventional images presented by liberal rationalist currents.
This often-patronizing tradition portrayed a popular movement beset by
intellectual naïveté, political anarchy, and arbitrariness. This book's emphasis on questions of local identity, subaltern positionality, and popular
politics is therefore intended to problematize *idées reçues* about popular
violence and political consciousness. The book also reexamines the position of intellectuals vis-à-vis popular culture and social movements in
Mexico's modern history.

SUBALTERN AND REGIONAL PERSPECTIVES

Subaltern studies is a revisionist trend in the social sciences and the humanities toward reassessing the historical agency of subaltern groups,
particularly in times of social upheaval. It provides a broad, useful framework for the themes addressed in this study.[20] Subalternist scholars are
concerned with the "analysis of how subalternity was constituted by
dominant discourses."[21] They try to explore the "fault lines" of dominant
discourses as a way to generate alternative accounts of popular rebellion.
Ranajit Guha, a prominent member of this school, has specifically studied what he calls "the domain of subaltern politics" in popular rebellions.
Guha's research on rural insurgencies in nineteenth-century India focuses
on the semiotics of transgression, that is, on the rebels' radical rupture
with the basic code that organizes relations of domination and subordination in society. Some historians have contemplated the applicability of
this approach to the study of the Mexican Revolution.[22]

   This book is also informed by the renewed interest in regional historiography. Traditional studies on revolutionary literature implicitly
privilege the conceptual framework of "nation" and modern nationalism
(identification with national space and a centralized state apparatus). This
is the case with the so-called literature of the Mexican revolution (Castro
Leal, Dessau et al.). I distance myself from such currents by emphasizing
"region" as opposed to and in dialogue with "nation."

   The concept of "region" is a critical component in the study of Mexican history and culture. As Eric Van Young has explained, "the varied
and difficult topography of the country . . . produce[s] an enormously
complex arrangement of climatological zones, micro-ecologies, subcul-

tures, and local histories. This luxuriant and confusing variety has played a central role in the evolution of Mexico's history and in the consciousness of Mexicans as portrayed in their politics, art, social thinking, and *mentalidad.*"[23] During the revolutionary war, regional and local identities, more than explicit political affiliations, were key unifying factors behind popular mobilizations. The concepts of region and regionalism (a self-conscious, cultural, political, and emotional attachment to a specific territorial homeland within the space of the nation, sometimes called *"patria chica"*) are therefore useful analytical tools in that they place subaltern insurgencies in their own unique revolutionary dynamic, rooted in local historical processes and cultural practices. These concepts are critical to understanding how regional rebels define themselves and their participation in the war. For example, an examination of the geography and history of the northern Mexican region that became Villista territory reveals that even before the revolution there existed a violent tradition of frontier culture with its own valued forms of social identity.

Subaltern studies and regional historiography have different agendas. The former is openly political, speculative, and liberationist in its objective; the latter falls, for the most part, within the confines of conventional historical scholarship. Both overlap, however, in their effort to highlight the importance of primary networks of sociability (kinship, territoriality, local cultures) in the construction of collective identities and in understanding the epistemology of popular mobilizations.[24] Regional historiography is interested in studying the array of local identities that resist or try to negotiate their integration into the larger community of the nation on their own terms.[25] Subaltern studies, on the other hand, includes discourse analysis and takes a critical distance from the ideology of nationalism.

My work on Villismo does not strictly adhere to either school. Both provide a critical horizon that has stimulated my thinking on the cultural politics of popular rebellion and on how subalternity is represented in cultural discourse. I have found Guha's methodology for reading dominant narratives "against the grain" particularly useful in examining the cultural construction of popular subjects in canonical works written by liberal-minded authors, such as Mariano Azuela.[26] Regional historiography brings to the discussion a historical specificity that has been lacking in the study of revolutionary literature. This facilitates the scrutiny of how certain subaltern practices are culturally processed—how and why they are highlighted, reworked, deemphasized, or silenced in literary discourse.

My approach to Villista literature engages critical and theoretical discourses that position subaltern and regional subjects as central foci of analysis. I concentrate on literary works that represent the key positions and narrative strategies adopted by authors who wrote about the theme of Pancho Villa and the Villista armed movement in the age of reconstruction. Villista literature during these years can be divided into three periods. The works of all three periods express the distinct ideological and aesthetic positions toward Villismo at the time during which they were published and illuminate the status of the debate and the evolution of the dominant cultural politics toward popular revolutionary subjects.

The first opens the debate on Villismo in the nation's literature during the presidency of Plutarco Elías Calles, from 1924 to 1928. Mariano Azuela's *Los de abajo* (The Underdogs, 1916; 1925) and Martín Luis Guzmán's *El águila y la serpiente* (The Eagle and the Serpent, 1928) are thematic and stylistic breakthroughs that, I will argue, are nevertheless still enmeshed in the intellectual mores of the prerevolutionary period in terms of their portrayal of the rural masses. Both Azuela and Guzmán, I contend, wrote works that in the act of representing rebel subjectivity simultaneously tried to control and suppress it by employing a social philosophy anchored in notions of private property, individuality, and bourgeois nationhood. Azuela and Guzmán represent two modalities of urban, liberal, postrevolutionary thought (populism and elitism, respectively).

The second stage, from 1929 to 1935, the years of the Maximato (when General Calles, no longer the president, remained Mexico's strongman), signals a shift toward a more radical view of Villa and the revolution and draws heavily on the popular myths of regional culture. Rafael F. Muñoz's *¡Vámonos con Pancho Villa!* (Let's Ride with Pancho Villa!, 1931) and Nellie Campobello's *Cartucho: Relatos de la lucha en el norte de México* (Cartridges: Tales of the Struggle in Northern Mexico, 1931; 1940) are the two works from this period that illustrate this new emphasis, despite their different objectives and styles.[27] Unlike Azuela's and Guzmán's early work, these writers' work explicitly makes Villista forms of cultural and political community the centerpiece, albeit for very different purposes: Campobello, to defend a regional identity under siege (popular regionalism); Muñoz, to enhance and capitalize on the brutalities of war (market-oriented sensationalism). Both, however, delve into the internal conflicts, contradictions, and limitations of what one critic has called the "alternative rationality" of subaltern culture.[28]

The third period covers the presidency of Lázaro Cárdenas, from 1934 to 1940. Villista literature during the Cárdenas years was in many ways a by-product of the state's populist cultural policies and attempted to incorporate Villa into the official memory of the nation. Martín Luis Guzmán's "new" Villa in the monumental (and apologetic) *Memorias de Pancho Villa* (Pancho Villa's Memoirs), and Celia Herrera's reaction to the official effort to institutionalize Villa, *Villa ante la historia* (History Judges Villa), are contrasting narratives representative of this stage.

The relationship between literary production and historical context is critical to my analysis of the cultural construction of popular subjects. Because of this, I present as much as possible of the circumstances under which each author wrote. This is particularly necessary since I do not study the works in strict chronological order: I pair Azuela with Campobello and Guzmán with Muñoz in order to highlight the contrasting alternative narrative strategies and positions vis-à-vis popular subjects.

Chapter 1 locates the production of Villista narratives in the context of the social struggles for hegemony during Callismo. It summarizes the Callista politics of national reconstruction and its contradictions, with an emphasis on the Mexican state's endorsement of the social leadership of the emerging middle class and the importance of official nationalist cultural policies in shaping the literary trend toward social and revolutionary themes. I discuss Villa's regionalist, anticentralist politics and how, after the revolution, his position (antagonistic to Calles's) continued to be a fundamental point of contention in the debates over the incorporation of the rural population into national life.

Chapter 2 provides a revisionist reading from a subalternist perspective of Mariano Azuela's *Los de abajo*, one of the classic novels on revolutionary Mexico. I begin by briefly discussing the "discovery" of this work by Mexico City's intellectuals in 1925 and synthesize the conventional reading of the novel. I then assess the contribution made by Azuela's novel to the process of suppressing popular political subjectivity in the dominant discourses of the postrevolutionary period. In the last section of the chapter, I read the novel "against the grain" in order to examine marginal areas of knowledge as they bear on the domain of popular politics. By exploring textual spaces that reveal the presence of an alternative popular politics centered on General Villa, I critically reassess Azuela's thesis regarding popular subjects' lack of political rationality.

Nellie Campobello's approach to Villismo in *Cartucho* differs from that of Azuela in that her narrative style re-creates a vision of the past that is not external to the world of the characters themselves. In Chapter 3, I argue that three subaltern perspectives are at work in *Cartucho:* the regional (as opposed to the national); the domestic/maternal (as opposed to the public/male); and the child's (as opposed to the adult's). These interlocking perspectives reinforce each other and reaffirm, albeit not without contradictions, the collective identity of a community under siege by supraregional military forces. A key element discussed in this chapter is the author's elaboration of a discourse that counters the ideology of centralism through the use of poetic devices that originate in oral culture.

The focus in Chapter 4 is the reconstruction of authority in elite culture through the description of subaltern themes and subjects in Martín Luis Guzmán's *El águila y la serpiente*. My analysis focuses on the author's aesthetic approach to the revolution (*atelismo*) and his use of the "civilizing code" as a narrative strategy of domination, which, I argue, produces overdetermined pronouncements about subaltern subjects. A second section examines the dual construction of Villa: as the necessary "low-Other" on whom the narrator constructs his own self-identity and status; and as the epic hero whose legendary attributes represent "positive" qualities associated with a popular Mexican identity. Insofar as the epic Villa is defined by his antagonism to the Mexican state, he represents a contradiction to the narrator's civilizing project. Yet this contradiction is rearticulated and ultimately deflected by subordinating the stories of the epic hero to the dominant discourse of integrative nationalism.

¡Vámonos con Pancho Villa! by Rafael F. Muñoz is a by-product of urban readers' demand for blood-and-glory tales about the revolution in newspapers and magazines. The author's narrative strategy, based on the exaggerated treatment of soldierly male bonding, was designed to appeal to the reading public's craving for morbidly violent anecdotes. The process by which Muñoz put readers vicariously in touch with a world that was both "uncivilized" and "natural," and the relevance of this Otherness to the formation of the country's cultural identity, are the subjects of Chapter 5. Like Martín Luis Guzmán, Muñoz exploits the military mythology of Villismo to shock and horrify his readers; unlike Guzmán, however, Muñoz approaches and judges General Villa in this novel through the eyes of Villa's soldiers, thereby placing the logic of violence within the region's radical military culture and mythology. In doing so, Muñoz is able to move beyond Azuela and Guzmán's liberal views on violence and introduce popular images of frontier war culture that will be integrated as valued features in the cultural construction of "Mexicanness."

Chapter 6 discusses the role of Cardenismo in the efforts to rehabilitate General Villa. This provides the context for analyzing Martín Luis Guzmán's monumental *Memorias de Pancho Villa* and Celia Herrera's *Villa ante la historia*, both outgrowths of Cardenista policy. I study the stylistic qualities that make Guzmán's apologetic *Memorias* the greatest piece of populist literature of the period and contrast the author's "new" Villa with the "old" and more critical representation of him in *El águila y la serpiente*. The chapter ends with a brief review of Celia Herrera's *Villa ante la historia*. This work, originally written to prevent Villa's institutionalization and as a response to Guzmán's *Memorias*, summarizes the anti-Villista views of a regional middle class and is an important domestic source of Villa's black legend.

The final chapter discusses General Villa's fate in official historical memory after 1940 and summarizes my subalternist-regionalist reading of Villista literature. I conclude that representations of subaltern subjects in this body of work reorganize our understanding of the past in that they oblige us to reconsider forms of identity and community that have been partially suppressed or discredited in the process of modern nation-building. These forms are particularly relevant, in the age of globalization, to the collective task of reconceptualizing Mexico's identity, culture, and politics. I also propose that this conceptualization of Otherness produced two distinct narrative genealogies in postrevolutionary Mexico—one canonical, the other marginal. The latter needs to be further explored if we are to have a more comprehensive understanding of Mexican literature and its evolution.

The Calles era, the years when Gen. Plutarco Elías Calles ruled Mexico, first as president, from late 1924 to 1928, and then as the behind-the-scenes de facto ruler of Mexico between 1929 and 1935, was a period of transition and turmoil. The general faced the formidable task of rebuilding a country devastated and divided by war, and this became the single overriding concern of his rule. For him, reconstruction and the entry into modernity meant imposing the regulation and order of a centralized government and the development of a capitalist economy. In many ways, this was a continuation of the national project of the prerevolutionary period (the Porfiriato). Unlike what happened in the previous era, however, the new project did not—or could not—exclude the rural masses and sought to incorporate them.

To establish state hegemony, Calles had to contend with several impediments, such as the continuing peasant revolts in the countryside and the regional power of military caudillos. He succeeded in neutralizing the caudillos by appointing them to military governorships and other administrative posts, where they had access to the state coffers and could retain local power and privilege. Calles's move to reorganize and take control of the country's unions and certain regional agrarian movements was, however, met with severe opposition. To deal with the independent labor movement and with the Cristero movement (in the Bajío region) from 1926 to 1928, he had to resort to violence.[1]

Economic reconstruction originally reflected the Liberal dream of creating a country of small, productive landholders. Land distribution in the form of communal property (or ejidos) was a first step, or transitional form,[2] as Calles put it, to prepare for a society of small landowners.[3] After he took office, however, his position on economic reconstruction came to mean the protection of landowners and the abandonment of agrarian reform. A growing emphasis on productivity favored the agricultural-capitalist approach of large estates over the self-sufficient practices of the small farmers and prompted Calles to turn toward a more conservative agrarian policy.[4]

As had occurred in the Porfirian era, President Calles's push toward industrialization had a disorganizing impact on the peasantry, but helped consolidate the rise of the social protagonists of modernity: the new bourgeoisie; a growing working class; and the middle class in the cities. The middle class was particularly favored in the regime's reconstruction efforts, for it carried the values of economic individualism and social mobility as well as the urban manners and literacy necessary to implement the project of capitalist development desired for the nation. During the presidential campaign of 1923–1924, candidate Calles repeatedly singled out the middle class as having a progressive leadership role in the transformation of the country. The middle class was the "third" and, in many ways, the ideal class because, according to Calles, it had the "cultivated talent of the capitalist" and the "decisiveness and character of the proletariat."[5] The model class to be emulated by the rest of society, it was urged to take its rightful place at the forefront of the new Mexico.

The social and cultural implications of the future president's call were profound and far-reaching. Mexico's rural masses, who provided the bulk of the revolutionary fighting forces, would be displaced as the principal force in the creation of the new order. The middle, and not the lower, class would be the primary beneficiary of the government's policies.

The masses, however, refused to be dismissed so easily. Years of violence, partial victories, and complex negotiations on the part of the masses in the economic, social, and cultural spheres would follow before the government was able to incorporate this segment into the project of modern nationhood.

A cornerstone of the Calles presidency and perhaps its most enduring ideological legacy was the redefinition of the relationship between the revolutionary regime and the people. Calles represented the emergence of an explicitly elitist ideology in the ranks of the revolution. This elitism can be perceived in the official idea of the revolution. Until Calles's rise to power, the revolution had been associated with the popular uprising and the war itself. Calles's predecessor, for example, Pres. Álvaro Obregón, had been the supreme commander of the constitutionalist forces and a revolutionary hero. He did not need to justify his position as chief of Mexico's revolutionary state because he embodied, figuratively speaking, the revolution. Calles, on the other hand, a secondary military figure in the revolution, did not enjoy Obregón's public recognition. His presidency required the creation of a populist ideological apparatus to help legitimate his tenure in office.[6]

Calles catapulted the idea of "the revolution" to the future, Guillermo Palacios has argued, to stress the actions to be taken by the government *for the benefit of the people*. This shift in the semantics of revolutionary rhetoric relegated the masses to the essentially passive role of being mere recipients of the government's populist policies. The revolution was what was to come, a constructive phase. The past, or destructive phase, should cease to be the primary source of the revolutionary government's legitimacy.[7] Thus the Mexican state would be "popular" not because of its social origins but because of its tendencies and dedication to social progress.

The rationale behind this exercise in directed democracy under the guidance of the new political elite was the old class-bound assumption that the rural and urban poor were unprepared to participate judiciously in the direction of the country. The new concept of the revolution involved a top-down effort (which eventually succeeded) to reestablish relations of subalternity in which class and culture again played a pivotal role in societal restructuring. Callista ideology, in short, proclaimed and justified the separation of the revolutionary ruling group from its "popular" base.[8]

A key shift in revolutionary rhetoric, then, took place during the Calles regime. The "revolution" was conceptualized as a forward-looking process, an ongoing movement of tasks and commitments to be accomplished, open and potentially unlimited in its possibilities. The past, that is, the armed struggle, was to be treated by state ideologues as a fait accompli, a discrete historical period whose importance was to illuminate the inevitability of the new power.

Yet this revolutionary past was too recent and alive in people's consciousness to be erased easily. In the state's everyday struggles for legitimacy and power, there continued to be a need to invoke the popular rebellion. Thus the Calles regime oscillated between alliances with and celebrations of the revolutionary masses, on the one hand, and repression, on the other. This contradictory approach to the masses was imbedded in the discourse and praxis of Callismo, but was also an expression—one of many possible expressions—of the ideology of modernity itself advanced by Mexico's socially progressive forces.

Culturally, Calles followed his predecessor's policy of attracting writers and artists, garnering their cooperation, at times subsidizing them, to accelerate the creative process of locating, defining, and exhibiting the "soul" of the nation.[9] State-sponsored cultural nationalism was a key element in the reconstruction effort and was aimed at promoting the production of artistic and literary works that would arouse positive emotions of identity, pride, and lofty ideals among the population. Inspired in ethnic and vernacular motifs, it was meant to instill feelings of belonging and loyalty to the *patria*, or homeland, and to downplay class and regional cultural differences. Cultural nationalism encouraged collective unity and, consequently, became a powerful vehicle in the official effort to inhibit social practices hostile or antagonistic to the Mexican state.

The production of a nationalistic discourse was the work of state ideologues and supporters of the regime, but also of critics and challengers among the revolutionary elites;[10] thus, a multiplicity of opposing views proliferated. Ultimately, however, no matter how conflicting or critical, these views could all be integrated into the logic of nationalism and, therefore, benefited Calles's reconstruction efforts.[11]

In literature this trend in the cultural agenda took hold in 1925, shortly after the incoming minister of culture, José Manuel Puig Casauranc, called for the production of literary works that depicted the social reality of the country and the suffering of the people and encouraged readers to think about and search for "real reforms."[12] Literature, at this point, was expected to become an agent of national integration.[13]

The new literary policy had an immediate impact among writers and critics. In 1925, it triggered a polemic among Mexico City's intellectuals over the artistic merits of Mariano Azuela's *Los de abajo*, a novel about popular rebels during the revolution. At stake was the renovation of Mexican literature, a change in style and sensibility more conducive to the aesthetic appreciation of the country's social reality. The debate confronted the old literary guard with younger writers who tacitly enunciated ideas of revolutionary progress anchored in concepts such as "modern," "urban," "Mexican," "social," and "development."[14] The language of the debate, however, also included authoritarian and patriarchal expressions, such as the insistence on the desirability of a "virile" (i.e., popular, frank, epic, and revolutionary) Mexican literature and the repudiation of "effeminate" (weak, indecisive, and bland) forms of writing. The gendered language of the critics captured a unique phenomenon of the period: the rise of "machismo" as a socially acceptable expression of self-worth and (political) power. Because manly aggressiveness was associated during the war with popular resistance to oppression, it remained a positive (i.e., revolutionary) behavioral attribute after the war—a quality readily emphasized and exploited in the hero-cult discourse of the state and in the elaboration of the nation's cultural identity.

The polemic surrounding Azuela's novel was symptomatic of the rapid changes that took place in the literary world during Calles's presidency. The debate led to the republication of *Los de abajo* in 1925 and to the demise of "*colonialista*" literature, a trend in vogue in the early 1920s whose themes were inspired by the colonial era. The republication also marked the end of the "exercise of literature out of phase with the immediate historical reality."[15] From then on, a distinctive kind of realistic narrative, closer to popular speech and revolutionary themes and characters, would dominate literary production.

The debate over *Los de abajo* was also a debate over the immediate past (the revolution) and its outcome, and as such it signaled the moment when Mexican literature became another battlefront in the social struggles for hegemony. The ways in which literary discourse dealt with the revolutionary war and the rise of the masses projected the fitful and unresolved process of redefining social relations of power in Mexican society.

It is telling that the republication of the Villista novel *Los de abajo* occurred at a time when Mexico City was beginning to reconquer its former position as the nation's cultural center, from which it had noticeably slipped during the war. The reconstitution of the *ciudad letrada*, or "lettered city," to use Ángel Rama's term, a place which confers official recognition and prestige on cultural production, gained momentum when the elite, urban intelligentsia acknowledged and came to terms with the reality that the popular revolution was a valuable literary theme.

Ironically, between 1923 and 1924, there was a proliferation of Villa biographies published outside of Mexico. In Los Angeles, California, and San Antonio, Texas, homes to large numbers of Mexican exiles, Villa's brutal assassination in July 1923 sparked the production of these narrative works. Some of them would even undergo several reprintings. The biographies were hastily written and rushed into print in an effort to capitalize on the commotion in the Mexican exile communities Villa's death caused.[16] Most of these exiles lived along the U.S.-Mexico border, a region close to the revolutionary leader's field of military operations.

The assassination of president-elect Álvaro Obregón in 1928 triggered a political crisis that unexpectedly prolonged Calles's control of the military and political life of the country. A few months after Obregón's death, General Calles founded the National Revolutionary Party (Partido Nacional Revolucionario, or PNR), the official party of the revolution. Established as a coalition of diverse political interests, the PNR's raison d'être was to bring together those faithful to the government as well as disgruntled allies to negotiate the presidential succession and the distribution of political power throughout the country (governorships, etc.).[17] The founding of the PNR effectively defused, or at least weakened, attempts to destabilize the still-fragile postrevolutionary order.[18] Immediately after the birth of the official party, the campaigns for national unity intensified with the process of institutionalizing the revolution and centralizing power. Significantly, Villa was the only major revolutionary figure who did not benefit from the conciliatory spirit of the national unity campaigns in 1929 and 1930.[19] New elections were hastily arranged for 1929, and the PNR candidate won, albeit fraudulently.[20]

This inaugurated the period known as the Maximato, during which three presidents (hand-picked by General Calles) briefly occupied the national palace. But real power remained in the hands of the former chief of state, who assumed the role of *jefe máximo de la revolución* (supreme chief of the revolution). The Maximato is a complex transitional period in Mexico's modern history, molded as much by the internal dynamics of Mexican politics as by ideological and economic pressures from the outside world.

During this period, the *jefe máximo* reached the conclusion that land distribution (social justice) and commercial production (capitalist economic growth) were incompatible goals, because neither small private landholdings nor the ejido were economically efficient. Reluctant to break up productive agricultural estates, in 1930, Calles declared the revolution's land reform program a failure and threw his support behind market-oriented large landowners.[21] The Mexican government's reconstruction policy by the end of the Maximato had become one of growing social and economic conservatism. Intensified persecution and repression of workers (particularly Communists) were the order of the day.[22]

On the other hand, the constant mobilizations by independent peasants' leagues and workers' unions forced the government to try to incorporate them into the PNR or to weaken their demands. This pragmatic move enabled the regime to destroy "independent centers of power based on the organized support of the peasants and workers."[23] At the same time, however, agrarian leaders within the state itself (who had joined the official party) increasingly articulated peasants' needs and prevailed in keeping the discussion of agrarian reform alive and on the government's agenda.[24]

Events in the international arena also contributed to the radicalization of sectors of the PNR government. The establishment of a workers' state in the Soviet Union, the Roosevelt administration's New Deal in the United States, and the general crisis of world capitalism after 1929 weakened the case for the liberal ideology of individualism and laissez-faire free-market policies, already under siege.[25] The turn to a reformist-leftist ideology was most visible in the Ministry of Public Education (Secretaría de Educación Pública). There, a Marxist intellectual, Narciso Bassols—with the support of many state governors—successfully pushed a socialist education program grounded in basic notions of social justice and a militant anticlericalism.[26]

Thus, during the Maximato, Mexico's postrevolutionary regime was mired in internal contradictions and undergoing a process of self-definition that was being contested and negotiated from without and within the government itself. Conservative and radical positions coexisted under the wide banner of official nationalism, attesting to the fact that ideological positions had not yet completely hardened. Calles's procapitalist economic policies, however, increasingly collided with peasants' and rural workers' demands for land distribution and with the prolabor and anti-imperialist sentiments of the times.

VILLA AND THE POLITICS OF INCORPORATION

The convergence of several factors made the Calles era the most productive in terms of Villista narrative. On the one hand, Villa's tragic death in 1923 made him (i.e., the legend of his cruelty and violence, his daring military movements, the controversy surrounding his contribution to the revolution) the subject of public curiosity for years. His embodiment of many popular qualities and the "virility" valued in the emerging postrevolutionary culture no doubt inspired many writers. On the other, the government's literary policy of encouraging writers to deal with themes that promoted social awareness fostered, ironically, the production of Villista narratives at a time when his legacy was being silenced in the world of official politics.

Class and culture played a significant role in the shaping of Villa's image. Writers and journalists were mostly of urban, middle-class background. Unlike Villa, they "had only minor political grievances or social differences with the regime and its leadership." Therefore, "their treatment of Villa was broadly compatible with the regime's ideology and the dominant culture."[27] There were, of course, exceptions (as we shall see), but the norm was to concentrate—for purposes of dramatic effect—on the violent aspects of his personality. The political motivations behind Villa's actions were seldom emphasized, or were brushed aside. In postrevolutionary Mexico, particularly among the upper and middle classes (though also among some segments of the masses), politics was still perceived to be a matter reserved for "civilized" men. And Villa, a semiliterate, rough man from the countryside, did not belong in that category.

This was particularly true in the writings of middle-class intellectuals who supported and even joined the revolution but whose social mobility after the war was threatened by the growing political pressure of the lower classes. Prominent authors José Vasconcelos and Martín Luis Guzmán, for example, obliquely convey this social anxiety and spirit of competition in their assessments, and disqualification, of the two major leaders of the popular revolution, Emiliano Zapata and Francisco Villa. Vasconcelos writes: "After the death of Zapata, who was the disgrace of Zapatismo, there remained his best aides, the learned and the self-sacrificing; those who did not take land, or execute people with voluptuous pleasure, or participate in the excesses committed in the name of the revolution by so many."[28] And Guzmán: "Would he [Villa] put his force at the service of principles that either did not exist for him or were incomprehensible to him? This was the dilemma: either Villa would submit to the fundamental principles of the Revolution, and, if so, he and the Revolution would triumph; or Villa would follow nothing but his own blind impulses, and he and the Revolution would go down to defeat."[29]

Notwithstanding the differences in tone (Vasconcelos is openly scornful; Guzmán is condescending—condescension being a veiled form of contempt), in these passages Zapata and Villa are seen as obstacles—messengers of gratuitous violence, corruption, or naïveté—to be removed or subordinated if the revolution is to move ahead. Significantly, intellectual culture operates as a class instrument (invoked to sanction—implicitly—the desirable social hierarchies) in both examples. Vasconcelos and Guzmán, it follows, are voicing a conservative revolutionary (even counterrevolutionary) position wherein popular violence is condemned while class violence is wielded—at the discursive level—against those who made the revolution possible.[30]

Despite this dismissal of Villa, a study of his politics and *mentalité* is necessary to understand not only the Villistas, but also the different ways in which the movement was represented in the Calles era. Villa's regionalist approach to politics put him on a collision course with General

Carranza in 1914. Carranza wanted to reestablish a "strong, centralized, powerful Mexican state . . . [in order to] guarantee Mexico's independence and its development into a modern, capitalist nation."[31] Actions such as Carranza's effort to try to impose a governor of his choice in Chihuahua infuriated Villa and his followers, who were hostile to any outside control of regional politics. Before the war, during the Díaz dictatorship, "political centralisation was the necessary and immediate prerequisite of agrarian dispossession and concentration [of land]."[32] President Venustiano Carranza first and, subsequently, Presidents Álvaro Obregón and Plutarco Elías Calles all pushed for a centralized Mexican government in order to consolidate their power, better control the affairs of the nation, and implement a single project of economic development.

In contrast, the autonomy and interests of Mexico's regions were at the heart of General Villa's politics. At the height of his power in the fall of 1914, Villa proposed a "national solution of decentralization" ("una solución nacional de descentralización"). Friedrich Katz summarizes and comments on Villa's political thought:

> First each municipality, then each state, should hold local and state elections in order to establish local and state authorities. This accomplished, there should be elections for Congress and for president of the republic, who cannot be a member of the military, but a civilian. What was behind the Villista proposal was a broad project for the decentralization of political power; as an example of this, agrarian reform should be carried out in each state without a unified national project. In this sense, Villa is in some ways heir to nineteenth-century tradition, when the federalists, who sought a decentralized regime, fought the centralists. In part this reflected the fact that Villa's overriding interest was in his homeland, Chihuahua and Durango, the north in general, and he left it to others to make the decisions about the rest of the country.[33]

Instead of a centralized state, Villa envisioned a nation politically organized through horizontal alliances of relatively independent regions and local towns and villages. Founded on the decentralizing notion of *patria chica*, his program offered another way of "imagining" the nation's political community. It was an alternative project whose feasibility was attacked by the postrevolutionary regimes, which were struggling to centralize the control of politics.[34]

Villa's ideas on nationhood led him to oppose and fight any revolutionary plan that would weaken the autonomy of the *patria chica* and strengthen and expand the centralization of political power. His behavior regarding this matter was akin to what Alan Knight calls "peasant patriotism." This type of patriotic sentiment or primordial nationalism emerges from below and is expressed as loyalty to organic groups (the clan, the ethnic group). Peasant nationalism, writes Knight, associates the specific defense of the local community with the defense of the country itself, is hostile to state attempts at centralization, and, instead, seems to aspire to a "greater" homeland made up of a federation of "small homelands."[35]

For Villa, indeed, the first geographical source of identity with the *patria* was his home region; the nation in its entirety comprised a second circle of identity. The combination of concrete, local loyalties and the more abstract allegiance to the nation-state defined Villa's patriotic sentiment. From this perspective, the military defense of the home region was the most immediate and irrecusable form of nationalism.

During the reconstruction period, the Mexican postrevolutionary state was still in the process of formation and open to multiple pressures and proposals. Literature was one of the arenas where the viability, merits, and limitations of various ideological projects for nation building would be debated. Questions of class and culture (middle versus popular classes), territoriality (region versus nation), political ideology (centralism versus decentralization), and conflicting notions of nationalism (modernizing versus primordial) mediated the discussion. This web of contentious issues, critical points of reference in the investigation of Villista culture, frames my discussion of the literature.

MEXICAN LITERATURE DISCOVERS A SOCIAL CLASS

In October 1914, physician and novelist Mariano Azuela joined the troops of Villista general Julián Medina in Guadalajara with the rank of colonel. "I then satisfied one of my greatest longings," he wrote many years later, "to live together with the genuine revolutionaries, the underdogs, since until then my observations had been limited to the tedious world of the petite bourgeoisie."[1] The novelist's encounter with the "genuine revolutionaries," that is, the peasants who had taken up arms against the federal government, had a decidedly literary goal: to observe their world; to immerse himself in its atmosphere and language; and, eventually, to write a work that would reveal the human dimensions of the armed conflict. Azuela's contact with the Villista army also provided an invigorating spiritual antidote to the conventional and socially rigid world of which he was a part, and it proved to be a productive experience. A year later, in October 1915, a newspaper in El Paso, Texas, began publishing his campaign notes in installments under the title *Los de abajo: Cuadros y escenas de la revolución actual* (The Underdogs: Views and Scenes from the Current Revolution).[2]

Azuela's literary project was innovative. *Los de abajo* was not centered on the petite bourgeoisie, as had been most literary production during the Porfirian dictatorship.[3] Instead, Azuela focused on the popular classes, whose overwhelming presence during the revolution, especially between 1913 and 1915, had become a human reality that Mexico's dominant society could no longer ignore. This change in focus from one social group to another incorporated new social terrain, expanding the human register of the Mexican novel and giving it a breadth previously unknown.[4]

Azuela is credited with founding the "novel of the masses" in Mexico.[5] He accomplished this in three main ways. First, for the first time in the history of the Mexican novel, he assigned the role of protagonist to the "bajo pueblo," the rural lower classes. The construction of this collective character was unprecedented at the time in Mexico. It demanded innovative narrative techniques that used montage sequencing, quick cuts in action and setting, and a rapid, nervous tempo as the author moved back and forth from the affairs of the masses to those of individuals.

Second, Azuela was able successfully to re-create the language of the masses, which he collected during his months of campaigning with the Villistas. The great number and variety of colloquial expressions that appear in the novel are strongly rooted in the forms of popular speech.[6]

Third, Azuela's narrative offered a view of "a social division among the characters, between the guileless and the spontaneous (of rural extraction) and the opportunists and corrupt (of urban extraction)."[7] These three elements, along with the readily identifiable events that make up the historical background of the novel guaranteed its overwhelming truth effect.

Despite these elements and formal innovations, *Los de abajo* went largely unnoticed for ten years. The reasons for this neglect by Mexico's literary critics are not difficult to ascertain. Literary criticism, a precarious enough activity even under normal circumstances, was necessarily brought to a halt by the revolutionary war. This hiatus lasted through the early 1920s. In addition, the fact that Azuela was a writer from the provinces who was living outside the literary circles of Mexico City delayed the appreciation of his undeniable skill as a novelist. Finally, time had to pass for a new cultural climate to emerge in Mexico, one inspired by the social struggles of the revolution and stimulated by the state's cultural policy, before Azuela's *Los de abajo* could begin to receive the recognition it deserved. Beginning with Calles in 1924, the revolutionary governments began explicitly to favor the production of literary works with a social orientation and designed to contribute to an understanding of the recent conflicts and to instill in readers an awareness of the social problems facing Mexico.[8] This cultural policy was largely directed not at the rural classes but at an urban, middle-class population that needed to be educated about and "sensitized" to the terrible reality of abuse, exploitation, and violence that reigned in the countryside. Azuela's audacious look into the world of revolutionary peasants began to achieve renown in the context of this predominantly urban cultural project.

Critics have extensively analyzed the history of the discovery of *Los de abajo* by Mexico City's intellectual elite and its eventual acceptance as the quasi-official text of the revolution.[9] Briefly, the "discovery" happened in the context of a 1925 debate "that may be taken as the foundation of the revolutionary political and cultural project desired for twentieth-century Mexico."[10] Azuela's novel came into its own in the course of this controversy between the old guard of literary critics and a younger group of emerging middle-class intellectuals who were in many respects more attuned to the social and aesthetic changes taking place in Mexico and abroad. The old guard bemoaned the fact that no truly "virile" (i.e., revolutionary) literature existed, able to express the courage, epic spirit, suffering, and redemptive meaning of the armed struggle in Mexico. The new critics pointed to *Los de abajo*, at the time a little-known novel by an unknown writer, as evidence that such literature did indeed exist. A lively debate ensued for several months in Mexico City's newspapers.[11] As the novel gained notoriety, Azuela's focus on peasant rebellion became exemplary of the literary nationalism espoused by the postrevolutionary regimes, and his work eventually came to be regarded as *the* paradigmatic text of the revolution.

Three basic questions are posed by this gradual institutionalization of Azuela's *Los de abajo* within modern Mexican culture. First, what image does a Liberal writer molded by the positivist education of his time construct of the rebellious peasant, and what vision of society does this image support? Second, what are the structural factors that place ideological limits on Azuela's narrative? Third, is it possible to extract from the novel itself a subaltern perspective on the peasant revolution, a perspective that may even run contrary to the author's own ideas? A rigorous rereading of Azuela is required to answer these questions, paying particular attention to the symbolic dimension of Villismo in the novel.

The sociohistorical structure of *Los de abajo* parallels the history of the Villista movement in Jalisco between 1913 and 1915, as Stanley Robe has demonstrated.[12] Villismo is not, however, merely a historical point of reference. Mónica Mansour has observed that the distant, ethereal figure of Pancho Villa is the "implicit axis of the novel."[13] The cultural semiotics at work in this novel can readily be discerned by studying the construction of the figure of Villa as well as the attitudes of the characters and of the narrator toward him.

Two very different and antagonistic conceptions of the revolution fuel this semiotic. The dominant conception is that of the narrator and is articulated through a discourse that tends to distance itself from events. It rejects what Villa represents for the masses, that is, popular power as a valid revolutionary option. It tends to be explicit in the ironic commentaries of the narrator and in the voices of characters with a more sophisticated cultural background, forming a cohesive discourse that shapes the specific ideological attributes of the text.

The less-articulated conception is expressed primarily in the actions and the speech of the peasant characters, who offer the only real hope for social justice. It is made up of peasant actions and popular dialogue, is subordinated to the first, and is used to validate it. Thus, Azuela elects to circumscribe and resemanticize the different forms of popular revolutionary consciousness that enter into the elaboration of the plot.

The only possibility of glimpsing a subaltern perspective of the popular revolution, of even partially recovering "autonomous" peasant consciousness and political orientation, is to not get caught up in the novel's semiotic. This implies a reading that is more attentive to the cultural perspective of the characters represented in *Los de abajo*. A summary review of orthodox interpretations of the novel is in order, not to surpass or reject these interpretations, but to argue for new methods and forms of evidence that challenge or question the accepted readings and show their limits. A brief description of the novel's principal social actors, as well as the relationships between them, is also required, since it is through the characters that the author formulates the meaning he intends to assign to events. I shall discuss other historical and cultural references about peasant consciousness in order to examine the novel's ideological premises regarding revolutionary discourse. Finally, by drawing on recent subaltern studies regarding recovery of the voice and world vision of the oppressed and marginalized,[14] I shall develop an exegesis which argues for a broader understanding of the political subjectivity of the peasant inherent in the text.[15]

THE TEXT

Peasants

The novel's protagonist, Demetrio Macías, is a *serrano*, or mountain dweller, from Juchipila Canyon, a "pure-blooded Aztec" ("indígena de pura raza") who embodies the virtues and the limitations of the Mexican peasant.[16] Azuela uses him to present his ideas regarding the failure of the popular peasant movement. Macías cuts a heroic profile—he is fearless, proud, and unaffected. He is not moved to revolutionary action by political credos, about which he is almost completely ignorant, but by more basic principles: the right to live free of harassment; the preservation of his human dignity. In his instinctive struggle against injustice and his spontaneous armed rebellion, Macías is the incarnation of a prototype: the "unconscious" revolutionary. His rebelliousness derives from a hunger for justice, and this, not adherence to a particular political program, drives his actions.

In the first and longest section of the novel, the protagonist is the victim of political boss don Mónico, an abusive and unjust authority. Macías has to flee to the sierra in order to save his own life. He wages a guerrilla war against the federal army, which is pursuing him and his followers and fellow fugitives from justice—his compadre Anastasio Montañés, La Codorniz (Quail), Pancracio, El Manteca, Venancio, and others.[17]

A festive atmosphere reigns among Macías's troops in this first moment of regional conflict. Despite the risks, armed struggle has a liberating effect on them: it allows them to leave behind the misery of their everyday existence and to open the doors to adventure; it gives them the opportunity to reaffirm their worth and dignity as men, to act with great independence.

The pastoral, almost idyllic, existence of the *serrano* rebels is interrupted and transformed by the arrival of the upstart "Curro" (Tenderfoot), Luis Cervantes. Under his influence, Macías and his guerrillas join the Constitutionalist Army, distinguishing themselves on the field of battle. Macías is made a colonel and then quickly ascends to the rank of general. But military promotion carries a price: from the moment that the *serrano* rebels leave their home territory and enter into a revolutionary dynamic that is beyond their control, they lose their freedom of action. Spatial displacement takes a psychological toll, and the meaning of the struggle, which previously was so clear to them, becomes hazy and uncertain.

In the second section of the novel the peasant revolution undergoes a process of moral degeneration. The early skirmishes are relatively benign compared with the later abuses of popular power, a change that is registered in the behavior of the armed masses. With the defeat of the federal army, the underdogs' rise to power leads to looting, unruliness, promiscuity, and a thirst for collective revenge. Two new characters come to the fore, *güero* (blondie) Margarito and La Pintada (War Paint), each of whom personifies different aspects of the degradation and corruption brought on by the triumph of the popular revolution. Margarito symbolizes the barbarity and cruelty that are unleashed by war. Typical of his actions are his abusive and brutal behavior toward civilians and the sadistic way in which he kills a captive federal soldier.

La Pintada, on the other hand, represents a different phenomenon: the massive and brutal incorporation of women into the country's public life under the extraordinary circumstances of a popular, revolutionary uprising. In order to get ahead, to survive and to gain respect in a male-dominated world, La Pintada resorts to masculine behaviors typical of a war culture—bravery, arrogance, and self-sufficiency. Macías's troops, however, continue to see her as nothing more than a sex object.

Lascivious, impetuous, and violent, La Pintada is a complex figure. On the one hand, she is dependent on her "man," *güero* Margarito, although he is not her man all the time. On the other hand, she does exactly as she pleases, with little regard for the men around her, and leads a dissolute life. As a character, she stands halfway between the *soldadera* (the female soldier who accompanied men on the campaign but who also performed traditional tasks such as cooking and washing) and the independent woman, as Carlos Monsiváis, has noted.[18]

Using these two emblematic characters, La Pintada and *güero* Margarito, Azuela seeks to depict the popular rebellion's slide into moral degeneracy. Anarchy, chaos, and lack of conscience reign among the troops. Both characters disappear from the plot once their didactic function has been fulfilled.

The final and shortest section of the novel opens with an improbable letter that Venancio receives in the midst of the campaign. The reader learns that *güero* Margarito has committed suicide and that Pancracio and Manteca ended a dispute over a game of cards by stabbing each other. The message is clear: the revolutionary forces have entered a self-destructive phase as a natural consequence of the degenerative process that marks the peasant movement. After a looting incident, people from Macías's own region repudiate his troops. Macías and his men return to Juchipila Canyon transformed; they are wealthier but disoriented, and more estranged than ever from their land. Despite these setbacks, they maintain themselves as a combat-ready unit until they are all killed in an ambush.

The thesis of the novel, expressed in the demise of Macías and his men, is unmistakable: the peasants are the genuine revolutionaries, but their overwhelming ignorance, lack of formal education, and dearth of clear political goals precludes the possibility of a felicitous end to the armed struggle. The implication is that without educated leaders to formulate a political program from above that represents the will of the masses, the success of the revolution is doomed. Thus, the paternalistic populism of Mexico's postrevolutionary governments found in Azuela a convincing, if involuntary, spokesperson. Interestingly enough, despite Azuela's belief that the revolution would surely fail without educated leaders, the intellectuals portrayed in the novel are ineffectual; Azuela's deep-seated pessimism belies his convictions regarding their historical mission.

Intellectuals

A second group of more cultured characters from a different social class fulfills the ideological function that the rustic characters from the Juchipila Canyon region appear to be unable to realize. This second group provides a critical perspective on the revolutionary war that gives political, historical, moral, and aesthetic meaning to the armed uprising. The three characters who perform this task are Curro (Luis Cervantes), who uses his cultural capital for personal ends; Alberto Solís, who represents the Liberal tendencies of the middle-class revolutionary intelligentsia; and Loco Valderrama, who infuses that same Liberal thought with his own peculiar poetry and melodrama.

Cervantes is a former medical student and journalist who represents a different type of revolutionary. He belongs to the urban middle class and in many ways is the antithesis of Macías, the *serrano* leader. Curro deserts the federal troops and joins Macías and his men when he realizes that the balance of power is shifting in favor of the rebels. Ambition leads him to see in the revolution a unique opportunity for quick enrichment. Cervantes is central to the plot as the character that links Macías's regional rebellion with the national revolutionary war. But it is his own ambitious self-interest that dictates that he convince Macías and his men to join forces with the Constitutionalist Army. In a long speech, he explains to the peasant leader the meaning of his own military actions:

> You do not yet realize your lofty noble function. You are a modest man without ambitions, you do not wish to realize the exceedingly important role you are destined to play in the revolution. It is not true that you took up arms simply because of Señor Mónico. You are under arms to protest against the evils of all the caciques who are overrunning the whole nation. We are the elements of a social movement which will not rest until it has enlarged the destinies of our motherland. We are the tools Destiny makes use of to reclaim the sacred rights of the people. We are not fighting to dethrone a miserable murderer, we are fighting against tyranny itself. What moves us is what men call ideals; our action is what men call fighting for a principle. A principle! That's why Villa and Natera and Carranza are fighting; that's why we, every man of us, are fighting. (55–56)

Cervantes articulates the principles of the revolutionary movement for the guerrillas, providing Macías and his troop the national vision and consciousness they lack. In order to convince them to abandon their native soil and become part of a larger movement in which they will no longer be in control, Cervantes uses high-sounding rhetoric, weaving a verbal web around his audience. Cervantes begins his speech as an external onlooker ("you") and concludes by speaking from within the guerrilla group ("we"). On a discursive level, he identifies himself as an underdog rebel, even though he is not one of them and will abandon the peasant rebels when the time comes. Macías's reply to Curro's speech attests to the intoxicating effect that the latter's words have had on the popular leader's consciousness: "Hey, there, Pancracio . . . pull down two more beers" (56).

Macías decides to leave Juchipila and join forces with the Constitutionalists, and thus begins a successful military career that will eventually see him promoted to the rank of general following the key battle of Zacatecas. But as a result of his conversation with Cervantes, the protagonist also begins to express a sense of cultural inferiority: "Ain't it wonderful to be able to read and write!" (57), he exclaims, reflecting on Curro's words. These feelings of inferiority lead him to accept a division of labor within the revolution. Because of their lack of formal education and high culture, he and his men assume a strictly instrumental role that precludes genuine revolutionary agency. Thus begins his military subordination to other forces and other leaders.

Cervantes's motive in urging Macías to join the Constitutionalist Army is simply greed. He correctly anticipates the triumph of the revolutionaries and the spoils of war that will be theirs to pick and choose: "revolutionists or bandits, call them what you will, were going to depose the Government. Tomorrow would therefore belong wholly to them. A man must consequently be on their side, only on their side" (40). No other character comes close to Cervantes's exploits as a calculating thief. He leaves the country as planned, having reaped all possible economic benefit from the war.[19] Significantly, he will also be the only survivor from Macías's troops.

In addition to Cervantes, the upwardly mobile demagogue, another key figure in the novel is that of the idealistic revolutionary intellectual, a figure who stands for Mariano Azuela himself. The author, nonetheless, is present neither "as a character, nor as an axis of action but, rather, as an eye that sees through the lens of his ideal conceptions."[20] In order to express these "ideal conceptions," Azuela employs a literary technique typical of the nineteenth-century realist novel, whereby an incidental and passing figure becomes a central prophetic character. This transitory presence in the first part of the novel is Alberto Solís, the disillusioned intellectual. To a lesser degree, Loco Valderrama plays a similar role in the third section.

Solís plays the part of the prescient character, the one who is able to anticipate the course the guerrilla war will take and to diagnose the causes of its eventual demise, which he attributes to a lack of "ideals" (81). Before dying, Solís condenses into two words what he calls "the psychology of our race": *"Robbery! Murder!"* (81; original emphasis). Solís considers the Mexican peasant to be flawed for reasons of racial heritage. The underdogs' innate propensity for violence is symptomatic of the problem. Lacking the ideals that might mitigate what is presumed to be a congenital defect, the peasant is condemned to thwart the positive labors of the revolution. His self-destructive instincts are what condemn him to a subaltern position in society.[21] As events unfold, Solís's judgment about the masses' propensity to steal and murder is explicitly played out in the second and third parts of the novel. This is an unmistakable sign that this character's point of view is Azuela's own.[22]

The jester poet Loco Valderrama also makes a very brief but significant appearance in the novel. His allegiance to the revolution is due to its sublimity—for him it is an aesthetic rather than a historical experience. He likens the revolution to a "volcano in eruption"(136) and remarks: "What do I care about the stones left above or below after the cataclysm?" (136). His poetic image is echoed later by Macías when the leader's wife asks why they continue to fight. Macías throws a stone into a ravine and tells her: "Look at that stone; how it keeps on going . . ."(147). The rebel leader's identification with the stone suggests that he has become Valderrama's naturalistic image.

Solís's cynical disillusionment and Valderrama's political nihilism converge in a pessimistic view of the revolution characteristic of the intellectual middle class to which Azuela belonged.[23]

The centrality of Solís's opinions makes it clear that the prerogative to decide the meaning of the events narrated is assigned to the class that he represents, and that its version of history is to be seen as History itself. In this sense, the technique of postulating an image or behavioral norm for the revolutionary peasant and then having it unfold in the plot reveals that for Azuela subaltern characters are little more than stock figures, despite their apparent free will. The underdogs' raison d'être as a novelistic presence is to validate and personify the cultural expectations that the revolutionary middle class has of them. In this regard, it is useful to remember what Stanley Robe has to say about the novel's protagonist, Demetrio Macías. Reconstructing step by step Azuela's stint as a Villista from 1914 to 1915, Robe points out that Macías is less sophisticated than either Col. Manuel Caloca or Gen. Julián Medina, the two historical figures that Azuela used as models to create his character. "The political awareness of Caloca and Medina, the latter in particular, has escaped Demetrio completely."[24] The real historical characters' astuteness and political qualifications were inconsistent with the author's ideological plan.[25]

The Condensation and Negation of History

Through the personal story of Demetrio Macías, Azuela relates a condensed version of the history of the rise and fall of the popular revolution.[26] In fact, developments in the novel are historically situated by key events that symbolize stages of the revolution in each of the novel's three sections.

The first section of the book registers the initial, isolated outbreaks of popular rebellion. As these coalesce and are transformed into a single revolutionary force, they successfully confront the regime of the usurper Victoriano Huerta, who assassinated Pres. Francisco I. Madero. The uprising culminates with the defeat of the federal army in the decisive battle of Zacatecas (June 1914). Both historically and in the novel, this triumph marks the high point of the popular revolution.

The second section describes both the excesses of the revolutionaries once they attain power and the spectacle of the revolutionary forces split by internal divisions. Vying for power are the Villistas on one side and the Carrancistas on the other. Macías and his staff attend the Convention of Aguascalientes (October 1914), which is an unsuccessful attempt to resolve the differences between the revolutionary armies.

The third part of the novel marks the definitive decline of the popular movement and the gradual dispersion of the rebellious peasant armies. The historical referent in this case is Villa's military defeat at the hands of the Carrancistas in the battle of Celaya (April 1915).

Thus, the novel's social and historical framework captures the rise and fall of the popular revolution between 1913 and 1915. Another set of internal referents, however, contradicts the novel's own presentation of social and historical events. The failure of the struggle is attributed not to splits and divisions within the revolutionary forces but to deeper natural forces. This is a world in which everything is predetermined: "Beneath the appearance of historicity, Azuela's ideas are actually based on a naturalistic vision."[27] Violent images of the revolution that depict it as a tornado or a volcanic eruption render useless the efforts of the men fighting for social change.[28] Solís declares that the revolution is a "hurricane: if you're in it, you're no man . . . you're a miserable leaf, a dead leaf, blown by the wind" (73). With this image of a "dead leaf" the fighter is reduced to someone who does not govern his own actions. The poetic image nullifies the revolutionary's significance as a historical agent.

The circular movement of the plot is another element that reduces the popular uprising to a natural process. The novel begins and ends in Juchipila Canyon with almost the same cast of characters. In the end, however, the underdogs do not rise from the earth, "their legs and chests naked, lambent and dark as old bronzes" (19), but are reabsorbed into it, victims of enemy bullets. The lives of the characters are governed by cycles, like nature, like the seasons. The novel's naturalistic images obliterate any potential for transcendent human actions.

IDEOLOGICAL STRUCTURE AND THE
HEGEMONIC CULTURE OF THE REVOLUTION

Jean Franco has observed that meaning in *Los de abajo* is constructed through the roles or functions assigned to the characters within the narrative. The actions of the taciturn Demetrio Macías are in sharp contrast to the verbosity of Cervantes. Curro speechifies and preaches, he names Macías colonel, he articulates the ideals of the revolution, he invents. Franco points to the existence of a dichotomy between action and discourse that is borne out by the text's linguistic characteristics. Discourse is particularly susceptible to distortion and manipulation to the extent to which it can be abstracted from real situations.

According to Franco, the attributes of the other characters can also be reduced to binary oppositions: nature/culture; sincerity/corruption; spontaneity/calculation. Macías is spontaneous, sincere, and natural; Cervantes is calculating, corrupt, and learned; Margarito is corrupt and boorish; and so on. This system of oppositions and contradictions suggests that Azuela's novel is structured around the absence of an ideal synthesis: there is no character capable of combining the spontaneity and natural virtues of the peasant world with the prudence and rationality of the intellectual. These structural limitations rest on what for Azuela is an irreducible dichotomy: body-peasant/mind-intellectual. The novel, Franco concludes, precludes the Gramscian notion of the peasant as the organic intellectual of the revolutionary struggle.[29]

The idea that there is a fundamental contradiction between the very nature of peasant existence and the rationality of intellectuals was until recently an implicit axiom in historical studies of the Mexican Revolution. This idea, an outgrowth of modern ideological prejudices toward traditional societies, has shaped interpretations of the nature, motivations, and results of military actions that were not organically linked to the world of urban political culture. One of the foundational texts of modern Mexican historiography, Frank Tannenbaum's *Peace by Revolution* (1933), underlines this antithesis in its presentation of rural uprisings during the revolution: "The uprising itself . . . was not responsive to any plan. It was incidental. It was pragmatic. . . . It was essentially the work of the common people. . . . No organized party presided at its birth. No great intellectuals prescribed its program, formulated its doctrine, outlined its objectives. . . . There was not a Rousseau, a Voltaire, a Montesquieu, a Diderot in Mexico. . . . There is no Lenin in Mexico."[30]

Tannenbaum's analysis presents a Eurocentric perspective. Modern European history, with its political parties, intellectual leaders, doctrines, and objectives, becomes the norm for locating the peculiarities of Mexico's revolutionary phenomenon. This method affords Tannenbaum a closer understanding of his object of study and at the same time distances him from it. To the extent that he recognizes the relative unimportance of intellectuals (understood to be urban figures) as historical actors, Tannenbaum is obliged to focus his analysis on the reality of the peasant world. But insofar as the logic of this argument disregards the potential for peasant thought, there is no possibility of comprehending popular rebellions on their own terms. Within this interpretative framework, the U.S. historian ends up in agreement with Azuela. The armed rebellion is viewed as a natural force ("[u]nheralded and unguided . . . like a cyclone") and "spontaneous" in character (i.e., not premeditated).[31] Tannenbaum's vision, however, differs from Azuela's in that it offers an unequivocally positive evaluation of popular "spontaneity," finding in it the originality of the revolutionary forces that long to destroy the feudal and capitalist structures of the country. Despite this distinction, both authors share the same intellectual prejudice toward the peasantry, whereby their military actions are seen as unplanned, improvised.

A few years later, in 1939, Alfonso Reyes, member of the prestigious Ateneo de la Juventud and a prominent figure in the intellectual life of Mexico during the first half of the twentieth century, repeated Tannenbaum's thesis in an interpretive essay on Mexico's modern culture: "The Mexican Revolution sprang from impulse rather than from an idea. It was not planned by encyclopedists or philosophers, more or less conscious of the consequences of their doctrine, as was the French Revolution. It was not organized by the dialecticians of social warfare, as was the Russian Revolution."[32]

With Reyes it becomes clear that Tannenbaum's exegesis of the revolution was fully accepted and integrated into the intellectual discourse of Mexico's cultural elite. Years later, this hermeneutics would be strengthened and radicalized in another classic text on Mexican national culture, Octavio Paz's *El laberinto de la soledad* (The Labyrinth of Solitude, 1950). Paz's ideas have a similar slant, but his style is far more dramatic. He asserts that the difficulty of formulating "the confusing aspirations of the people in a coherent system become obvious as soon as the Revolution ceased to be an instinctive event and was established as a regime."[33] Paz elaborates: "The Zapatista and the Villista movements—twin factions, one in the north and one in the south—were popular explosions that proved almost wholly incapable of incorporating their truths, more felt than thought out, in an organic plan. They were a point of departure, an obscure and stammering expression of the revolutionary will."[34]

The antithesis between popular revolution and intellectual rationalism (or nature versus culture) in this canonical text once again establishes structural limits on how the revolutionary phenomenon may be interpreted. Paz refines the commonplaces implied in this contradiction: the campesino masses are an invigorating force, but they are not nor can they be the brains of the revolution. As a result, the deeper meaning of their military actions must be interpreted for them. Implicit in Paz's description is the following political program: Mexico needs a paternalistic political structure because the masses—Villistas and Zapatistas—are immature (their aspirations are "confused" and "stammering").

Paz's text, like those of Azuela, Tannenbaum, and Reyes, each covering a genre representative of high culture (essay, novel, and historical study, respectively), reveals a discursive practice that, with varying inflections, is part of the process of shaping a hegemonic culture. The view these intellectuals have of the popular revolution is akin to what Eric J. Hobsbawm calls archaic, "pre-political" movements. According to Hobsbawm, the lack of an explicit ideology, organization, or program reveals that these mass movements are composed of individuals or groups with little or no political consciousness, who have not yet found a suitable language to articulate their aspirations in the world.[35] This approach to rural uprisings has resulted in their being interpreted as spontaneous mass actions whose leadership, by definition, must depend on protagonists from outside of the peasant world (urban intellectuals, political parties, etc.).

Antonio Gramsci provides a useful counterpoint to Hobsbawm. Gramsci notes that pure spontaneity has no historical reality; that is, there are always traces of consciousness in unstructured mass movements.[36] Decades later, Ranajit Guha reexamined Gramsci's proposition. Guha affirms that the error of seeing peasant movements only in terms of spontaneity derives from two closely related ideas about organization and politics. The conscious character of a movement is associated with that which is "organized" in the sense of (1) "conscious leadership," and (2) well-defined objectives, with a program that specifies its particular components and the means for achieving them. The same equation holds if the term "politics" is substituted for "organization." Those who make that substitution, Guha argues, have the additional advantage of identifying consciousness with their own norms and political ideals. Activities of the masses that do not conform to those ideals can then be characterized as unconscious or, by the same token, as prepolitical.[37]

Gramsci's and Guha's writings can be productively applied in a revisionist approach to the Mexican Revolution, for they belie a steadfast cultural tradition that insists on the spontaneity of popular rebellions. In his assessment of intellectuals and the Mexican Revolution, Alan Knight, though not aligned with Gramsci and Guha's subalternist views, writes: "It is no longer possible to deny peasants intellectual and ideological attributes. . . . Numerous studies on peasants demonstrate that peasant consciousness is more complex, and contains more intellectual elements than was previously supposed. . . . In spite of what some observers of the period and later historians have said about popular leaders supposedly being manipulated like puppets by their scheming secretaries, evidence points to the contrary."[38]

Knight's commentary implies skepticism about the ways that "observers of the period and later historians" have represented peasant subjectivity. These representations, as I have already noted, are bounded by a structural dichotomy in which the space occupied by the peasant subaltern is determined by factors that contradict intellectual rationality: spontaneity, instinct, lack of political consciousness, naïveté, and therefore ease of manipulation. Azuela's text and the writings of Tannenbaum, Reyes, and Paz are different instances of an ambivalent cultural process that, at the very moment of representing the revolutionary agency of the subaltern peasant, proceeds to simultaneously and, to varying degrees, suppress it.

Given this context, the task of recuperating the political culture of the subaltern in a work such as *Los de abajo* is absolutely necessary for a critical reevaluation of postrevolutionary Mexican culture, but also an extremely complex undertaking. An entire intellectual tradition linked to the dominant ideology produced by the revolution itself and embodied in the logic of the plot works against such an act of recovery. As Knight suggests, however, it is no longer possible to adhere to the old interpretive schemes. It is necessary to break with them and develop new historical reference points as well as new reading strategies, both of which should aid in understanding Azuela's operative categories. The text is obviously a representation of the will of the author. As Guha writes in another context, referring to the various kinds of documentation available on peasant insurgencies, "these documents do not get their content from that will alone, for the latter is predicated on another will—that of the insurgent. It should be possible therefore to read the presence of a rebel consciousness as a necessary and pervasive element within that body of evidence."[39] Guha proposes new methods of reading that permit the reader to perceive within the text itself that Other will that the author would prefer to suppress. Reading against the grain implies a process of deconstruction that leads to questioning the "lines of power and hierarchy" of the documents.[40] In order to recover the cultural and political specificity of the peasant rebellions, it is necessary, first, to identify how subaltern culture, as represented by the official and elite culture, is distorted, and, second, to discover the social semiotics of the peasant insurgents' strategies and cultural practices.[41] Put another way, it is a matter of establishing which are the inherent alternative discourses that might be available to the reader in these hegemonic accounts of the rebellious peasants, despite the will of the author. This way of reading is especially useful for analyzing a realist, testimonial novel like *Los de abajo*. While not an official document, the novel is a canonical text within modern Mexican culture, sanctioned by the state, semiofficial and even didactic (in that it is required reading in the public schools).[42]

Los de abajo: TRACES OF A SUBALTERN PERSPECTIVE

Most interpretations of the popular revolution that began to be written in the 1920s were based on controlling and suppressing peasant subjectivity. I have already outlined the basic elements of this operation as they appear in Azuela's novel and in the writings of other postrevolutionary intellectuals. It is important to note, however, that this process of hegemonic formation does not consist of the simple, top-down imposition of a single point of view. In order to have the power of persuasion, the hegemonic process must also incorporate, co-opt, and rearticulate a number of potentially contradictory discourses. Therefore, we must be able to see through these discourses to find those instances that contradict the dominant ideology of the text. We begin from the general premise that, in spite of authorial intention, dominant versions of the revolution inherently contain remnants of alternative discourses. By locating these fragments, it should be possible to recognize the different types of subaltern agency that are at work in the text and use them to reveal the political forms and subaltern cultures that have been distorted or silenced.

In order to recover the subaltern perspective in *Los de abajo*, we have to identify and give new meanings to the traces of autonomous initiative of subaltern groups in the text. This is no simple matter, since Azuela's world view induces him to emphasize situations in which blind impulse prevails, especially scenes of looting and abuse, although these made up only a small portion of the popular armed actions during the revolution. Our assumption, nonetheless, is that these traces, even if occurring in a negative context, express the popular consciousness of revolutionary phenomena. That is to say, these fragments reveal politicized forms of understanding and identity that are not accessible through conventional political language (which belongs to the educated social sectors). They can be perceived in oral histories and in the body language of the characters, precisely the kind of details that Azuela the novelist knew how to capture so well. These scattered traces, however, because of their very fragmentary nature, do not coalesce into a coherent subaltern discourse. In 1915, when the novel was written, that clarity of vision had not yet been achieved either by popular movements or by the more educated sectors of the revolution. The most we can hope for is to reinterpret Azuela's portrait of the armed peasant movement and to point out a systematic process of suppression that has obscured a fuller and more evenhanded understanding of the popular revolutionary struggle and its motivations.

An indispensable strategy for this kind of analysis is to remain skeptical, to not regard the ideologies present in the text as natural and inevitable. Rather, they should be understood as artificial and motivated constructions.[43] Decentering ourselves as readers opens the door to the possibility of a reading that, up to a certain point, goes against the logic of the text. This also requires that we distance ourselves from conventional understandings of history as well as from received notions about the nature of politics and of intellectuals, as Florencia Mallon suggests in her study of the political and cultural practices of the subaltern.[44]

In terms of the plot, it is useful to recall the two functions that Roland Barthes proposes—*nuclei* (cardinal functions) and *catalyzers* (complementary functions)—in his discussion of narrative events and the logic connecting them.[45] Important events, or nuclei, form part of the hermeneutic code. They advance the plot and resolve doubts; they cannot be removed or substituted without disrupting the logic of the narrative, because "the action[s] to which [they refer] open (or continue or close) an alternative that is of direct consequence for the subsequent development of the story."[46] Minor events, or catalyzers, are not crucial in this sense. They can be deleted without altering the logic of the plot, although the omission will clearly impoverish the narrative aesthetically. They are what might be called necessary fillers, ancillary or circumstantial elements, or factors of verisimilitude responsible for the milieu, and so on.

The nuclei are narrative moments that produce critical junctures for the way events develop; they are the plot's hinges. In *Los de abajo* the most important narrative nucleus postulates the following problem: Demetrio Macías can continue to fight in his home region or choose to leave it and, along with his men, join forces with the Constitutionalist Army. The solution to the disjunction between the regional and the national struggle in the first part of the novel is crucial to the plot and to the novel's ideological message. It is therefore necessary to pause and consider closely how the author addresses it.

The framework in which this dilemma is introduced and resolved is a conversation between Macías and Cervantes (53–56), the most extensive dialogue in the novel. Cervantes urges Macías to join Gen. Pánfilo Natera's troops. The guerrilla leader's personal pride and his spirit of independence keep him from abandoning his home territory: "I don't like the idea of accepting orders from anybody very much. . . . Well that's all I want, to be let alone so I can go home" (54). Cervantes, however, finally persuades Macías to join the rebel army: "It is not true that you took up arms simply because of Señor Mónico. You are under arms to protest against the evils of all the *caciques* who are overrunning the whole nation. We are the elements of a social movement which will not rest until it has enlarged the destinies of our motherland" (55).

Cervantes's speech convinces the protagonist to leave the regional struggle and join the national revolutionary movement. It therefore marks a key moment of transition. José Joaquín Blanco, one of the most lucid interpreters of the novel, writes: "Luis Cervantes pushes him [Macías] to join the Villistas. . . . Cervantes is the channel that leads Macías to Villa."[47]

Other events of lesser importance, catalyzers, which are not part of the hermeneutic code and, consequently, are not meant to influence the course of events, contain information that complicates or contradicts rather than complements the preceding nuclei. Before his dialogue with Cervantes, the narrator explains that, while recovering from a bullet wound to his foot, Macías "was busy thinking of the best route by which to proceed to Durango" (43). The existence of an itinerary suggests that Macías was already entertaining the idea of leaving Zacatecas and entering Villista territory (the state of Durango, between Zacatecas and Chihuahua, the stronghold of Villismo). The existence of this plan is confirmed when the protagonist recovers completely from his wound and rejoins his men: "They began to discuss various projects to go northward where, according to rumor, the rebels had beaten the Federal Troops all along the line" (49). This suggests that even before hearing Cervantes's patriotic exaltations, and independent of them, the guerrillas were considering leaving their home region and taking up the struggle in the national theater.

What remained to be determined were the specific conditions of this participation, not the reasons for its undertaking. According to this narrative logic, the military isolationism Macías defends in his dialogue with Cervantes is either a contradiction in the novel's plot or signals a lack of confidence regarding the terms of participation. But this concern is very different from the limiting regionalist vision of the struggle that Curro seeks to attack in his speech. As catalyzers, however, the meaning of these passages—a plan of action collectively discussed, signaling subaltern political agency—is quickly lost from view as it is subordinated to a textual logic oriented toward the negation of autonomous initiative.

These passages raise the following question: What motivated Macías and his men to seek out the revolutionaries in the north? The answer can be deduced only from the subsequent behavior of the guerrilla fighters. But Villismo, both as a popular military movement and as a subjective phenomenon, clearly establishes the implicit ideological and emotional horizon for the rebels' actions. In this regard, Azuela maintains a curious duality. On the one hand, he insists on presenting Macías as a minor leader lost in the struggles between the political factions of the revolution. When he has to vote for a provisional president in the Convention of Aguascalientes, he does not know if he should take the side of Villa or Carranza: "President, what? Who in the devil, then, is this man Carranza? I'll be damned if I know what it's all about" (123).

On the other hand, the entire course of action of Macías and his men reveals an affinity—albeit one that is not altogether uncritical—with the Villista struggle. In fact, throughout the text, the actions, language, and psychology of Macías and his men indicate that the mythical persona of Villa is their main ideological referent for questions of cultural and class identity and forms of popular political knowledge.

The adherence to Villismo is shaken in the last part of the novel but not broken by the news of Villa's defeat at the battle of Celaya. At first, the guerrilla fighters receive the news with incredulity, and only Demetrio wrinkles his brow "as though a black shadow had passed over his eyes" (135). The confirmation of the defeat has a definitive impact on the consciousness of the characters. With the myth of the invincible Villa shattered, the promise of power and popular justice fades, and the morale of the troops begins to diminish. Codorniz pragmatically summarizes the new situation: "What the hell, boys! Every spider's got to spin his own web now!" (136). The Villista army begins to disband. The struggle continues, but with the fall of Villa, "they marched forward through the canyon, uncertain, unsteady, as blind men walking without a hand to guide them" (141). Macías's forces, however, remain loyal and die as Villistas on the road to Cuquío to fight the Carrancistas.

The profile of the revolutionaries in the novel cannot be dissociated from the populism of Villa's movement. It is therefore important to specify what Villa represents in the text and what social and political project he validates. During his first period of brilliant triumphs on the battlefield, Villa, the charismatic leader who attracted thousands of country people like him to his cause, acquired the attributes of an invincible warrior in the eyes of the disinherited masses. He came to symbolize a series of diffuse forces that converged in the revolution to put the people into power. In the first section of *Los de abajo*, the force of this myth is such that it even attracts some enemy soldiers serving under Gen. Victoriano Huerta. They are attracted by the possibility of exacting revenge against the federal army, which drafted them against their will (the hated "*leva*"), or by the chance to acquire "shiny new silver coins" (34). Villa not only represents the prospect of righting injustice and poverty, he also becomes a canvas onto which the heterogeneous and contradictory desires of the combatants are projected.

The search for social recognition, the class hatreds, the desire for revenge, the hunger for authority, all converge on and become exaggerated in the popular construction of this patriarchal figure. *Güero* Margarito, the novel's worst example of the atrocities someone can commit in the wake of newly acquired power, appeals to the Villa myth while destroying bottles and windows in a cantina: "Send the bill to General Villa, understand?" (125), he tells the waiter.

Legendary stories that captivate and excite the popular imagination are woven around Villa. As one of Natera's soldiers says to Anastasio Montañés, "You ought to see Villa's troops! They're all northerners and dressed like lords! You ought to see their wide-brimmed Texas hats and their brand-new outfits and their four-dollar shoes, imported from the U.S.A. . . . They've got cars full of clothing, trains full of guns, ammunition, food enough to make a man burst!" (78). Among Macías's ragged soldiers, this exemplary tale of abundance, where all of the endemic needs of the lower classes disappear, responds point by point to what Macías's compadre demands at the beginning of the novel: "By God, if I don't own a Mauser and a lot of cartridges, if I can't get a pair of trousers and shoes, then my name's not Anastasio Montáñez!" (20). In Villismo, what one is meets what one wants to become; it is the point where reality and the desires of Macías's tattered troops meet.

Moreover, Villa and his movement lent social legitimacy to actions severely censored by a long tradition of respect for social ranking. Villa sanctioned the rancor and hatred accumulated during a lifetime of oppression and privation and their attendant contortions, excesses, and desperation; Villismo validated the joyous transgressions of privileged social spaces and hierarchies. La Pintada states: "Soldiers don't sleep in hotels and inns any more. . . . Where do you come from? You just go anywhere you like and pick a house that pleases you, see. When you go there, make yourself at home and don't ask anyone for anything. What the hell is the use of the revolution? Who's it for? For the folks who live in towns? *We're the fancy folk now, see?* Come on, Pancracio, hand me your bayonet. Damn these rich people, they lock up everything they've got!" (89; emphasis added). For Azuela, this statement (and many others like it) exemplifies the abuse of power and the arbitrariness unleashed by the triumph of the peasantry. His message is that the excesses of the revolutionaries are antagonistic to the revolution. Moral degeneration is inevitable. As Ruffinelli correctly observes, "This is not the way revolutionaries should act; this is how bandits act, according to the bourgeois code."[48]

At a remove from the bourgeois code, however, La Pintada's impetuousness hints at other glimmerings and shades of meaning that are profoundly motivated by race, class, and culture. Having grasped that authority is for once in the hands of "los de abajo," La Pintada launches a frontal attack on the sacred principle of private property. She embodies the drive to overturn the usual social hierarchies, the immediate, unstoppable, and abrupt desire for the redistribution of wealth. Her actions are consonant with the struggle for power. This political goal is made manifest in the violent transgression of privileged social spheres through actions that denote the negation and inversion of the established order; it is precisely this project which the narrator tries to discredit with the image of La Pintada. The crude, rudimentary way in which La Pintada articulates her hunger for power, however, does not invalidate it politically. Her actions and her declaration that "we're the fancy folk now, see?" (89) are a literal enactment of the collective aspirations incarnated in the myth of Villa. The narrator comments directly on this myth: "Villa the reincarnation of the old legend; Villa as Providence, the bandit, that passes through the world armed with the blazing torch of an ideal: *to rob the rich and give to the poor*. It was the poor who built up and imposed a legend about him which Time itself was to increase and embellish as a shining example from generation to generation" (77; emphasis added).

Characters such as Montañés and La Pintada make it possible to perceive how the Villista mission to redeem with pride the rights of the people was internalized. Also revealed are the contradictions that derive from personal temperament and the intoxicating effect that power has on the people, as in the case of *guëro* Margarito.[49] Note, however, that unlike La Pintada, the narrator does not share the point of view of the revolutionary masses. The elaboration of popular myths that exaggerate and end up distorting the real facts about Villa are to be deplored. The narrator offers an ironic assessment: "Events as they were seen and lived were worth nothing. You had to hear them narrating their prodigious deeds, where, immediately after an act of surprising magnanimity, came an extraordinarily bestial exploit" (77).

This critical view of the oral accounts, because of their propensity to distort the reality of events, marks the cultural and class limits of the narrator in his social representation of the underdogs. The narrator associates oral culture with illiteracy, ignorance, and social chaos. As a result, orality is rejected as a source of knowledge about the popular revolution. With this scathing, rationalist dismissal of the oral transmission of the events of the war and their impact on the collective psychology, the narrator misses an element crucial to a profound understanding of the mentality and cultural symbolism of the peasant revolution. On the one hand, the intellectual Solís, whose perspective complements that of the narrator, sees the soldier as a "miserable leaf," thus minimizing his importance as historical actor. For the soldiers, however, the myths forged by oral tradition, with their distortions and embellishments, fulfill a radically different purpose: they serve to invigorate revolutionary morale during the war. Oral tradition celebrates armed rebellion as a popular exploit. In this sense, it incites and mobilizes the masses; it encourages them to continue fighting and to feel that their actions are worthy of respect. An alternative revolutionary discourse emerges from these folk stories, a discourse that the narrator, located on "the other side of the division of classes, with the ideological measure of the bourgeoisie,"[50] is sensitive enough to reproduce, albeit in a fragmentary manner. He proves incapable of fairly evaluating it, however. Compare the narrator's dismissive commentary regarding the soldiers' stories of Villa's "prodigious deeds" with the animated account by one of Natera's soldiers, who celebrates his leader's unpredictability with surprise and admiration: "If General Villa takes a fancy to you, he'll give you a ranch on the spot. But it he doesn't, he'll shoot you down like a dog!" (78).

This account, of course, is inaccurate; it belongs to the realm of Villa's legend.[51] But it is of a piece with the instantaneous code of virtues and weaknesses established by the revolution, a code that differs from that of the narrator and is, to a certain extent, incomprehensible to him. Hence, it can only be partially stated in the novel. The soldier's anecdote foregrounds Villa's absolute power over his men's lives: by turns he is as generous or as terrible as a Greek god, subject to unfathomable passions. In the popular imagination, Villa personifies the extreme situations brought on by the convulsive context of the revolutionary war, where chance encounters become destiny, both good and bad. The meaning of the anecdote is simple and magnificently unsettling: with Villa we are thrust into the revolution as the realm of the unexpected. It is a vision of an unpredictable world of unknown reversals, strange bedfellows, unexplored social formations, vital social promiscuity, a world full of seductions and dangers that feeds on the masses' appetite for life. The unsettled narrator resorts to irony to undermine these war stories.

Again it is useful to call to mind the interpretation put forth by Solís, the intellectual who is able to prophesy the coming failure of the revolution and who portrays the revolution with metaphors that suggest a naturalistic vision. Villa's popular myth, on the contrary, suggests that nothing is "natural" or predictable in war. Everything is subject to the intensity of the moment, to tempestuous changes; the world becomes relative and life becomes precarious and volatile, full of capriciousness and fatal upsets, but also full of fortunate situations and unexpected possibilities, of great hopes and promises of social justice. This is a dual, carnivalesque world that enthrones and dethrones historical actors, freeing them or eliminating them. This popular version of revolution literally reveals an unscripted world, a world of that-which-is-not-written.

An alternative form of revolutionary consciousness emerges if we transfer this popular version of the armed rebellion—the unscripted world, with all its potentialities and contradictions—to the field of geography, the incessant movement of Macías's troops, their "nomadic existence: life beyond the civilizing institutions that oppressed them": "The unforeseen provides man with his greatest joy. The soldiers sang, laughed, and chattered away. The spirit of nomadic tribes stirred their souls. What matters it whither you go and whence you come? All that matters is to walk, to walk endlessly, without ever stopping; to possess the valley, the heights of the sierra, far as the eye can read" (148).[52]

The spatial displacements or movements of the troops embody a sense of freedom that does not correspond to an abstract conceptualization in Liberal political discourse but, rather, to a passion rooted in the daily lived experiences of the rural world: the ownership of the land. The dizzying growth of large estates during the reign of dictator Porfirio Díaz made landownership virtually impossible for the majority of the population. In this context, the soldiers yearn to possess the valley, the plains, etc., to roam the regional terrain, free of fixed paths or prohibitive barriers. This very movement corresponds to the founding of a long-yearned-for social order, one in which *los de abajo* are the masters of the land and of their own movements, physically and psychologically free from all oppression. This popular politics of space is explicitly stated in the only passage that alludes to a collective consciousness of the causes of the armed uprising: "They spurred their horses to a gallop as if in that mad race they laid claims of possession to the earth. What man among them now remembered the stern chief of police, the growling policeman, or the conceited *cacique*? What man remembered his pitiful hut where he slaved away, always under the eyes of the owner or the ruthless and sullen foremen, always forced to rise before dawn, and to take up his shovel, basket, or goad, wearing himself out to earn a mere pitcher of *atole* and a handful of beans?" (61).

By characterizing the masses as a "pueblo sin ideales" (people without ideals), Solís dismisses the prospect that they are capable of justice, liberty, and respect for human dignity. These ideals are nonetheless inscribed in the bodily movements of the characters. It follows that Macías and his men do not act according to the modern dichotomy of sense and intellect, which privileges analytical reason and the tendency to dissociate reflection from experience. Rather, the revolutionary behavior of these characters demonstrates an undivided sensory unity, where experience contains, expresses, and *is* a form of reflection. For this reason, the intellectual activity (and political consciousness) of *Los de abajo* is not expressed as a program or a slogan but as a way of acting whose vital dynamic breaks with the unjust social order, a rupture that longs to become permanent. This kind of thought in action is subversive, contradictory, and liberating, and it finds its greatest point of expression in the Villista movement. For this same reason, Villismo comes to embody a modality of political action and a popular epistemology with which the peasant characters in Azuela's novel can tacitly identify.

In *Los de abajo*, Azuela represents the unscripted world—the popular revolution—and subordinates it to the order of rational discourse. In the process, he controls and suppresses peasant subjectivity. But the traces of an alternative subjectivity that revolves around a historical experience of Villismo can be perceived in the characters' actions, their wanderings, their direct and colloquial language, or in the narrator's commentaries. The elements of the novel that guarantee its credibility and longevity reside in the revolutionary vitality of this "other" world, even when in the act of representing peasant subjectivity the author simultaneously tries to suppress it.

Azuela's greatest literary distinction, despite his lack of clarity and his moralizing, is to have captured the equalizing force of the masses, armed and on the move, tumultuous, disorderly, and destructive. The text reveals a world of intense passions, naked violence, looting and hatreds, the longing for recognition and for revenge, and deadly diversions and friendship spurred by alcohol, promiscuity, and libertine desires. And this despite the narrator's somewhat incongruent longing for moderation and order in the midst of the chaos of war. In this sense, the novel represents "a major step forward in [Mexico's] Liberal literature."[53] In effect, Azuela's novel, at times in spite of itself, confers on the anonymous masses of the revolution an epic face. This is the reason for José Joaquín Blanco's assertion that, notwithstanding the limitations of a writer loyal to the narrow national project of liberalism, *Los de abajo* constitutes an admirable attempt to break down class barriers within Mexican literature.[54]

Los de abajo served a fundamental role in the development of Mexico's modern narrative literature: it incorporated a complex and convincing version of peasant subjectivity into the national culture, a version acceptable primarily to the middle classes and the new intellectual elite.[55] This novel marks the rise of a new revolutionary narrative that identifies the interests of a modern, national society in the making with the subjectivity of the Liberal middle class. In the process, popular political subjectivity is reduced to a series of appealing archetypes that are repeated and imitated from 1925 on by the "novelists of the revolution." The actions of the rural masses are depicted as instinctive, spontaneous, naïve, and so on, through these stereotypes, and have predominated in Mexican culture with few changes until the present day.[56]

The objective of this chapter has been to question this cultural construct and reinterpret the political consciousness of the popular revolution in *Los de abajo*. With this in mind, I have attempted in the third section of this chapter to give a reading of the novel that runs counter to most accepted readings. The difficulty of this task resides in the fragmentary nature of the novel's representations of the motivations of the peasants. It affords us no more than glimpses of this popular political subjectivity. For the same reason, it is impossible to reach definitive or far-reaching conclusions. We know that Azuela's depiction of how the peasant fighters were manipulated by urban intellectuals is unsatisfactory; a subalternist, against the grain, reading helps reveal this by demonstrating the tensions between the internal logic of the novel and the disparate elements of popular revolutionary thought included in it. Such a reading signals the need, both cultural and political, to reevaluate the representation of the agency of subaltern groups in works that, as a genre, follow the paradigm of *Los de abajo*.

Azuela's ideological views cut off and constrain the political subjectivity of the popular rebels to fit the political and social philosophy of progressive middle-class intellectuals. Only with a new generation of writers, whose intellectual upbringing was affected—among other things—by the Villista movement itself, and who did not reproduce the narrative perspective of the middle-class intelligentsia, did an alternative and less-restricted construction of the fighters' subjectivity begin to be elaborated.

Chapter 3

RECONSTRUCTING SUBALTERN PERSPECTIVES IN NELLIE CAMPOBELLO'S *Cartucho*

Few towns during the revolution saw events as bloody as those that occurred in Hidalgo del Parral, a mining center in the state of Chihuahua that was one of the gravitational centers of Villismo. In the course of ten years, Parral suffered the violence of being taken no fewer than twelve times by contending revolutionary forces.[1] Its inhabitants lived through sieges, fierce battles fought street by street, acts of revenge, torture, executions, and the grotesque spectacle of mutilated bodies lying in the streets. The uncertainty of life, the daily deaths, the cruelty and hatred of the contending factions, exacerbated at times by the enmities of local blood feuds, left an indelible mark on the population. Years later, Nellie Campobello, who grew up in Parral, would turn to a storehouse of personal and family anecdotes and to collective memory to write *Cartucho*.

Campobello's *Cartucho* is neither a conventional novel nor a book of short stories; it is a collection of short narratives, a "blend of autobiography, history, and poetry" that powerfully evokes the extraordinary violence and devastation of the armed struggle,[2] and the psychological impact it had on the consciousness of the population. The work's forcefulness and originality largely rest on Campobello's unprecedented treatment of memory, on her unusual ability to reproduce how people try, in a manner consistent with their emotional needs and world view, to explain and make sense of the disturbing experience of war. By resorting to the narrative patterns of oral culture, the author effectively connects the act of remembering the past and the dead to the preservation of community in Villista territory.

Cartucho is a book about memory and identity, about memory and survival—individual and collective survival. The original edition contains thirty-three stories, all inspired by Campobello's childhood and family memories of the war. The basic structure is that of "an adult, now residing in Mexico City, who looks back, recalls, and . . . relives her childhood experiences."[3] The child's voice and point of view predominate, as does a narrative technique based on understatement. The stories the child heard or that were told to her by relatives and friends are an integral part of her own memories. Hence the narrator not only rescues her individual experiences, but also functions as a compiler of the intimate memories of other characters, whose tragic, incongruent, or, at times, humoristic recollections are registered in the text.

The stories are organized thematically into three sections: "Men of the North" (seven stories); "The Executed" (twenty-one stories); and "Under Fire" (five stories).[4] All sections depict the streets and places close to the family home in Hidalgo del Parral, which represents the slow accumulation of knowledge about the external world characteristic of childhood. A gallery of colorful and tragic Villista characters emerges from this limited visual field, all of them friends or acquaintances of the family (most of them Urbinistas, or followers of General Urbina). The events described are specific and local, assembled, at times, in an incomplete and fragmentary way; only the details that excite her childish imagination are mentioned. Thus the entire collection is never far removed from the family setting.

Cartucho is unique in that the events narrated are not subordinated to a value system that is external to the regional cultural world of the characters, as is the case with *Los de abajo*. Instead, they communicate an implicit and explicit empathy and solidarity with a view of the world "from below." How does Campobello convey this view and for what purpose? What are the limits and contradictions of writing about life in Villista territory in the context of the politics of reconstruction? To answer these questions, I propose a critical approach that focuses on three binary oppositions: the child's imaginative perspective as opposed to adult rationality; the female and the domestic sphere over the public, male sphere; and the restricted notion of regionalism in contrast to centralist or integrationist nationalism. These perspectives intertwine and reinforce each other in the narrative. The presence of one therefore implies the others and simultaneously conveys the personal and the collective experience of the war. For the purpose of my analysis, however, I examine these perspectives separately, privileging the notion of regionalism, for it is here that rebel subjectivity and the cultural politics of Villismo are most visibly at work. I read the child's perspective and the issue of gender closely in relation to region, as both support the ideology of the latter.

Before examining these perspectives, it is necessary to locate the writer and the production of the book in their proper historical and social context and to sketch some of the book's formal characteristics.

NELLIE CAMPOBELLO AND THE WRITING OF *Cartucho*

The struggle for survival—personal, social, and mental—is a central theme in Nellie Campobello's life and work. This struggle led her to explore her creative self and to go as far as to invent for herself a whole new persona. Her real name was María Francisca Moya Luna. She was born in Villa Ocampo, Durango, in 1900, to a family of small landholders.[5] When she was eight or ten years old, her family moved to Hidalgo del Parral, Chihuahua, a few miles north of her hometown. Francisca never received a formal education, but was taught to read and write by her aunt. Later in life she would claim to have written a short novel at the age of twelve.[6]

During the revolution, the Moya Luna family closely identified with the forces of Villista general Tomás Urbina, who came from the same locality in northern Durango. At the time, loyalty to homegrown fighters, primary networks of sociability (based on kinship, local origin, the compadre relationship between parents and godparents) determined revolutionary attachments more than did political affiliation.

Little is known of Francisca's adolescence and early youth other than that she witnessed appalling acts of violence and learned of the death of many family friends and acquaintances (mostly Urbinistas), a traumatic experience that would eventually fuel the writing of *Cartucho*. She had a child out of wedlock in 1919, and moved to Chihuahua City, where her only child died of pneumonia two years later.

Shortly after their mother's death in 1923, Francisca and her siblings moved to Mexico City. With the support of Stephen Campbell, her wealthy Anglo stepfather, Francisca and her younger half-sister Gloria joined the affluent life of the American community in the capital, where they were known as the Campbell sisters and studied classical dance.[7] In 1929, she published a book of poems, *¡Yo!* under the name Francisca.[8]

At around this time the sisters changed their last name to Campobello, a Spanish adaptation of Campbell. For some time they had been performing traditional Mexican dances in the capital and around the country under the sponsorship of the revolutionary government. The wave of postrevolutionary nationalism and the type of cultural work they were engaged in probably explain why they changed their Anglo surname. It is also true, however, that since her arrival in Mexico City the bright, artistically oriented María Francisca seemed determined to bury her past as a single mother and reinvent herself. The name changes, first from Moya to Campbell and later from Campbell to Campobello attest to a process of forging a new identity. The name Francisca also disappeared, to be replaced by Nellie, her family nickname.[9]

Irene Matthews and Blanca Rodríguez believe that the Campobello sisters traveled to Seville, Spain, in 1929 to perform as professional dancers. If indeed they made it to Spain, their stay was cut short for reasons that are unclear.[10] What is incontrovertible is that in the fall of 1929, the sisters were in Havana, Cuba, searching for work as dancers. They quickly came to dislike the "night club" milieu in which they had to perform, but had the good fortune of meeting José Antonio Fernández de Castro, a Cuban critic and journalist who knew everyone in Havana's cultural world. Fernández de Castro discovered that the temperamental Nellie was a poet and took a keen interest in her work, encouraging her to continue writing and publishing and promoting her.[11] Furthermore, he introduced the sisters to the African American writer Langston Hughes, who at the time was visiting Havana. Hughes and Campobello became friends, and he eventually translated some of her poems into English.[12] The Spanish poet Federico García Lorca, out of curiosity after Fernández de Castro showed him Nellie's book of poems, also met briefly with her during a visit to Cuba.[13] The sisters returned to Mexico in 1930, probably in the late spring or early summer.[14]

Nellie Campobello's stay in Cuba helped her define her new "self" and the kind of artistic endeavors she would undertake on her arrival in Mexico. Her plan was to open a dance school for poor girls and continue writing.[15] The public school she had in mind materialized in 1931, when she joined the state-sponsored Escuela Nacional de Danza (National School of Dance) as a founding member. *Cartucho*, the first book penned by "Nellie Campobello," was published that same year. Miss Campobello (la señorita Campobello, as she was called) had consolidated her new persona.[16] Thereafter she would be known as an independent woman, a writer, a dance instructor, and a choreographer.

Campobello initially wrote *Cartucho* to give her own account of the revolution in the north, which was different from the stories about Villismo that were circulating at the time. In the 1920s and the 1930s, when Plutarco Elías Calles ruled Mexico, it was not unusual for newspapers and magazines to publish chilling accounts of the actions of Villa and his soldiers during the revolution. "Francisco Villa," Campobello indignantly remembered in 1960, "was considered to be even worse than Attila. All his men were classified as horrible bandits and murderers."[17] These distortions, she said, drove her to write what she knew about the movement: "Because of that I had to write, to tell truths in the world of lies in which I lived."[18] Writing *Cartucho* was a moral and historical imperative: "It wasn't right not to speak out, knowing the facts. And so, although I had not overcome my fear, I began to write little by little, in my own way, and saving my notes."[19] A sense of obligation, then, to the dead Villistas was her guiding motivation.

It is difficult to establish when Campobello began writing *Cartucho*. A few sketches were probably written in Mexico City, although in her introduction to the 1931 edition, which is omitted in later editions, she mentions that the stories were written in Havana at the behest of Fernández de Castro, after he heard her relate personal anecdotes about the revolution.[20] These stories, she would recall decades later, were subsequently read by poet Germán List Arzubide, a member of the *estridentista* movement (an avant-garde poetic movement active in Mexico's cultural and political scene in the 1920s and the 1930s),[21] who had stopped in Havana on his return to Mexico from a trip to the Soviet Union. Impressed by the originality and intensity of the stories, the enthusiastic List Arzubide promised to have them published in Mexico.[22]

The first edition of *Cartucho* was produced by Ediciones Integrales, a publishing house based in Xalapa, Veracruz. The place of publication is significant. In 1931, Veracruz was a hotbed of radical revolutionary activity. The left-leaning governor, Adalberto Tejeda, had organized a powerful league of peasants armed to defend themselves against the landowners' private armies. Like many military caudillos, Tejeda was an ally of the central government, which, nevertheless, wary of his influence and power, would eventually move to divide and disarm his militias. It was with Tejeda's patronage in the early 1930s that a group of leftist intellectuals associated with the *estridentista* movement founded Ediciones Integrales, dedicated to the publication of antibourgeois, proletarian literature.

Cartucho, by the little-known Nellie Campobello, was the first book published by Ediciones Integrales. Although not an antibourgeois text in the Marxist tradition of social realism, Campobello's collection of stories was an unusual and highly original piece of "committed" literature. Each story operated within a social framework of ethical and aesthetic values that was "popular" and "localistic." The author's narrative style, elliptical and frequently grotesque, closely reproduced the oral sensibility and ironic outlook associated with traditional storytelling. List Arzubide, in the book's preface, which also served to introduce the new publishing venture, acknowledges the disturbing, subtle power of Campobello's writing style and perspective and, in a sly reference to his enemies in Mexico City, contemptuously contrasts it with the style of "revolutionary" writers.[23] He also quite insightfully declares that with *Cartucho* "we have learned to read with the eyes of the dead,"[24] that is, from the point of view of the vanquished.

The small world of Mexico City's intellectual community welcomed the publication of *Cartucho* and, according to Campobello, even the *jefe máximo*, Calles, read it eagerly.[25] Decades later, she wrote about the adverse reactions that her Villista sympathies had provoked in some quarters: "People who used to call themselves friends refused to greet me. They wanted nothing to do with the defender, according to them and their lies, of bandits. That is what the organized slander called them."[26] Nevertheless, the critical reception of the book was favorable. In 1935, Berta Gamboa de Camino, one of the pioneer scholars of the "novela de la revolución," praised Campobello for having written stories charged "with intense emotion, with energetic strokes, in a language freighted with tragedy. It is a sort of epic of the revolutionary novel, ingenuous, rough, sometimes incorrect, but alive and real, breathing, full of human feeling and deep pathos."[27]

Throughout the 1930s, after the publication of *Cartucho*, Campobello's visibility in the realm of public opinion grew considerably. She took it on herself to restore the revolutionary image of Francisco Villa, who at the time suffered from widespread political and cultural disapproval in urban Mexico. In 1932, on the anniversary of the guerrilla leader's death, Campobello published an article in which she unapologetically praises Villa's innate leadership qualities and his personal acts of violence. The article, according to the writer, aroused the ire of the country's strongman, Gen. Plutarco Elías Calles.[28] Several other articles would follow.[29]

Campobello campaigned for a state pension for one of the Villa's wives, Austreberta Rentería, and their children. In an interview with journalists arranged by Campobello, the widow revealed the existence of a 1914 memoir dictated by Villa to his secretary that was in her possession.[30] Furthermore, sometime before 1939, Campobello traveled north to interview Villista war veterans for a book on the military life of General Villa.[31] During this trip she also gathered folk legends from her home region and compiled a number of corridos, or ballads.[32]

At around this time, Campobello also made revisions to the original version of *Cartucho*, expanding it considerably. The second edition, published in 1940, drops one of the original stories ("Villa") and adds twenty-four new ones for a total of fifty-six. Whereas in the first edition the stories are based on her own and her family's immediate experiences during the war, the new stories draw from a wider range of sources, including material from her fieldwork on Villismo (e.g., testimonials from veteran soldier Ismael Máynez and from Austreberta Rentería [Betita], as well as from her compilation of regional legends and corridos).[33] In writing these stories, Campobello chose to pursue the artistic path rejected by Azuela in *Los de abajo:* to make the retelling and dissemination of the oral stories of the revolution the raw material of her literary endeavor. Hence they are not so much the product of a personal as of a social memory.

These new stories are distributed progressively throughout the second edition: one is included in the first section, seven in the second, and sixteen in the last. Consequently, as the reading advances, there is an increasing move from the domestic to the regional sphere, enabling the incorporation of "a greater number of characters from various social ranks, revealing the collective aspect of the struggle."[34] The "innocent" child's point of view of the first edition, while never disappearing entirely, gradually gives way to a broader awareness and perspective of the struggle.

The broadening of the narrative perspective, the epic quality of many of the new stories, and other changes and rearrangements were all intended to strengthen the book's pro-Villista (and therefore anti-Carranza) stance.[35] The second edition of *Cartucho* was for Campobello the final product of a decade of writing and rewriting stories about the Villista movement in northern Mexico. It marked, along with *Apuntes*, the culmination of a personal campaign to rehabilitate Villa in the public's memory.

My discussion of *Cartucho* follows the third edition, which comprises, with minor exceptions, the sum of the stories written expressly by Campobello for this book during the reconstruction period.[36]

THE NARRATIVE STRATEGIES OF POPULAR STORYTELLING

Campobello's narrative procedure is to reinterpret the memory of events within the framework of poetic writing that reproduces the strategies of oral culture. She uses several narrative techniques associated with orality. The first is to relate the circumstances under which the narrator becomes acquainted with the events being told, thereby transforming the act of storytelling into a shared experience of repeating stories told by others.[37] In *Cartucho* the main narrator incorporates into her own voice the voice of others—the mother, Severo, Pepita Chacón, the great uncle, "El Siete," the people, Chonita, and so on. Thus the narrator fulfills the social function of articulating other people's stories and ends up reproducing a collective world view in which she participates and to which she adheres. Individual and collective subjectivity converge, making it difficult to separate one from the other. At times, this cultural intersubjectivity is explicitly emphasized with commentaries that begin with an "I think," in which the narrator introduces personal views that expand on or corroborate the collective perspective of events.

Another technique is to eschew explanations, or at least to keep them to a minimum. Surprising or unexpected episodes of the war are recounted, but the psychological connections between one event and another are withheld. Thanks to this technique of understatement, what emerges is a latent pathos that surpasses the informational value of any given episode. This also plays well into the need to re-create the limited understanding of events characteristic of a child's mind.[38]

These stories are also marked by a poetic style based on the abundant use of colloquialisms from popular speech, such as redundancies ("Llegaron unos días en que dijeron que iban a llegar los carrancistas" [A time came when they said the Carrancistas were going to arrive (6)], and "uno de ellos dijo que le habían dicho" [one of them said he had been told (72)]), or archaisms ("cuando me trujieron la nueva" ["trujieron" is an archaic form of "trajeron": they brought]). A rhythmic prose and verselike structure reminiscent of the corrido meter is produced by poetic devices "such as parallel structures, repetition, and anaphora" ("Abelardo Prieto, un joven de veinte años, nacido en la sierra, junto a Balleza, en el mero San Ignacio" [Abelardo Prieto, a young man twenty years old, born in the mountains near Balleza, right in San Ignacio (81)]).[39] The poetic principle of phonetic attraction reinforces the rhythmic prose and stresses meaning ("a*dormeci*do *de do*lor recit*aba* una historia dor*ada* de b*ala*s" [numb with pain, he would recite a story gilded with bullets (54)], and "los ojos de mamá . . . *re/car*gados en el *cañ*ón de un *ri*fle de su *re/cuer*do" [Mama's eyes . . . resting on the rifle barrel of her remembrance (33)]).

These stylistic devices reveal an acute sense of rhythm and an appreciation for the materiality of language. The auditory function of the composition, so attuned to oral sensibility, is twofold. On a practical level, the use of mnemonic devices makes it easier to commit to memory the events being related. Aesthetically, these devices prove to be very powerful and evocative, allowing the storyteller to intensify the emotionality inherent in the telling of tragic stories.

At the core of Campobello's narrative poetics lies her penchant for the grotesque, which derives from the collision between the violent and the amusing in the accounts of mostly tragic incidents. The grotesque principle informs the entire collection and is a defining element in the construction of the author's ethical and aesthetic position, which is rooted in regional popular culture. The grotesque functions most visibly at the level of plot and imagery.

A recurrent and effective trope used to produce the effect of the grotesque in *Cartucho*, and one of the most recognizable of oral narratives, is metonymy. Campobello creates unusually charged, intense images by singling out one detail or aspect that condenses the exceptionality and pathos of the moment—a hand, a tray full of guts, a postmortem smile, an anthill, a kiss, and the like. The bizarre or hyperbolic quality of the images introduces a comical or festive element that stands, ironically, in sharp contrast with the frightening or tragic nature of the incident. The element of amusement aims to counteract and, ultimately, undermine and shield—psychologically speaking—the narrator from the horrors of war.

"Colonel Bufanda's Heart" is a case in point. The hated Colonel Bufanda dies when "someone—no one knew who—fired a shot that hit him near the left shoulder blade and exited through the pouch of his jacket, pushing his heart out with it" (26). Bufanda's body is thrown into the middle of the street, "where his shattered skull lay clinging to the rocks" (26). Yet his face, the narrator remarks, "had a look of satisfaction on it" (26). And she concludes: "Bufanda gave his best smile to those who were breaking camp. Everyone despised him, and they all gave him kicks. He kept on smiling" (26).

The collision between the crudely realistic description (killing Bufanda and then kicking his dead body) and the imagery (his undisturbed smile) produces a grotesque scene that serves the ambivalent purpose of highlighting the unexpected, horrendous, or macabre nature of the experience while humorously understating the shocking effect of witnessing such a brutal spectacle. The narrator's emphasis on an ironic detail (the smile) illustrates her seriocomic strategy for coping with gruesome events.

Campobello's metonymic technique is more than a personal strategy to deal with and cushion the psychological impact of violent incidents. The production of hyperbolic, memorable images is integral to the communication technique of oral culture. In societies where a cultural economy based on orality prevails, the accumulation, preservation, and transmission of notable events is not based on the written word. Therefore, a number of mechanisms that place an enormous weight on memorization have to be developed to ensure that the audience is able to retain and pass on information considered valuable by the community. In the telling and retelling of important events, "the storyteller and his audience have to be supported by multiple and peculiar mnemonic tricks, skills, devices."[40] One of these mnemonic strategies, consistent with an oral culture's need for narrative economy, is the production of shocking or disconcerting images capable of arousing the collective imagination and facilitating the mental retention of an incident. Campobello's production of memorable images takes its cue from this long-standing oral storytelling technique; in doing so, she assumes the values and world view that derive from this popular cultural practice. The grotesque is a reliable aesthetic and mnemonic instrument wherever the creation and storage of images is required, such as in societies where oral culture is still predominant. Connected to personal and collective survival and self-preservation, the grotesque contravenes the reality of horror; it has the liberating power of reaffirming and celebrating life through laughter in the midst of fear, suffering, and death.[41] Campobello's narrative poetics effectively conveys, through the grotesque, what has been called the "alternative rationality" of oral culture.[42]

HISTORICAL VIOLENCE AND
THE REGIONAL WORLD OF *Cartucho*

Popular movements are rooted in regional histories. This is particularly true for the Mexican Revolution, as proven by the lively debates among historians since the 1980s.[43] Villismo, for all its appeal and its impact on the course of national events during the revolution, never ceased to be a grassroots regional movement, though this became clear only after Villa's defeats in the battles of Celaya and León in the spring and summer of 1915. Most stories in *Cartucho* take place during the historical period between 1915 and 1919, when "the Villista 'core' reverted to its popular, serrano roots." Back in their home region, where they could count on the support and sympathy of the locals, the rebels staged a recalcitrant guerrilla war against the Carrancista government. "[O]nly gradually, as war-weariness increased, and the Villista popular base atrophied, were the guerrilleros forced to conscript and sequestrate, the social bandits obliged to lose many of their 'social' attributes."[44] Campobello's stories draw the reader into the military and human drama that took place in Villista territory at this time.

The geographical boundaries of this world can be inferred from the stories themselves. The numerous references, often couched in the formulaic manner typical of the oral raconteur whereby the place of origin of the protagonist is mentioned, to specific towns delineate the territory in question:

> Bustillo had been born in San Pablo de Balleza (9) . . .
> Bartolo came from Santiago Papasquiaro, Durango (10) . . .
> Antonio Silva, born in San Antonio del Tule, near Balleza (13) . . .
> José Rodríguez . . . had been born in Satevó (47) . . .
> Tomás Urbina was born in Nieves, Durango (48) . . .
> José Borrego came from the Indé District. Over by Mount
>   Gordo (67) . . .
> Pablo Mares was one of ours, from our land (76) . . .
> Ismael Máynez lives in the Allende valley, in the state of
>   Chihuahua (88).

This discourse of origins, at times invoked with genuine pride (Abelardo Prieto was born "en el mero San Ignacio" [right in San Ignacio (81)]), conjures up the image of a *patria chica*, or regional homeland. The territorial community evoked by these geographical references extended from northern Durango (Villa Ocampo, Nieves, Canutillo, Santiago Papasquiaro, etc.) to southern Chihuahua (Hidalgo del Parral, San Pablo de Balleza, Satevó, Pilar de Conchos, etc.).[45] The map drawn by the narrative roughly outlines a mining subregion that had as its head the town of Hidalgo del Parral, in the province formerly known as Nueva Vizcaya. Mining, it should be remembered, was the most important historical stimulus in the formation of Mexico's northern region, and Hidalgo del Parral was an active mining center (despite various economic downturns) until the twentieth century.[46] Hence Campobello's discourse of origins brings to the fore an awareness of the existence of a collective identity sustained by a deep-rooted sense of place. Even throughout the revolutionary period, the sense of belonging to and identification with the region continued to be strong, notwithstanding the newly constructed railroad, which accelerated the region's integration into the national economy.

Geographic location and history are keys to understanding the cultural contours of this world. From the colonial period until the close of the nineteenth century, the northern frontier was a no-man's land, violently fought over by Indians native to the area and immigrant settlers intent on making it their new home. The Spaniards, in their effort to colonize and take control of this region, established *colonias militares* (military colonies) and missions throughout Nueva Vizcaya. The Spanish colonial administration, and later the governments of Mexico's independent republic, distributed land and arms to any settlers willing to move there and wage war on the seminomadic tribes from the north, especially the Apaches. During this period, the settlers "acquired military skills, arms and the consciousness of constituting a special elite fighting against the 'barbarians.'"[47]

Geographical remoteness from Mexico City encouraged economic self-sufficiency and opened the way for semipolitical autonomy, making the region fairly independent from the rest of the country. Barry Carr points out that geographic isolation facilitated the "survival of certain semifeudal institutions such as private armies and the application of justice by private citizens, which continued to exist long after independence had been won."[48] In time, the violent struggle for territorial control created a warfare society where social honor was bound up with personal bravery and the ability to wage war; it also promoted, perhaps more than in other regions, respect for patriarchal values.[49] A long-standing bellicose tradition, regional political autonomy, a code of honor with aristocratic overtones—these were the factors that converged to shape the cultural consciousness of the region's inhabitants and their popular mythology.

The final defeat of the Apaches in 1886 dramatically altered the old privileges accorded to the military colonies. With the northern border fully secured, the Mexican government ended its policy of sinecures—land, arms, and autonomy—in the region. Construction of the railway was begun immediately, followed by economic development, particularly along the border with the United States. Land values quickly increased, and the great landowners of Chihuahua began to expropriate properties belonging to their former allies, the military colonists, with the tacit or explicit approval of state government. The colonists fought against their gradual dispossession through legal channels and, at times, with violence.

Because they resisted an economic project of modernization that turned these free villagers into disenfranchised workers, the militarized *serranos*, writes Ana María Alonso, once viewed as the agents of "civilization," were now redefined by the Mexican state as the "new barbarians." The state now made every effort to ensure their acquiescence and obedience to the policies of the central government.[50] The *serranos'* struggles against their new enemy, the Liberal dictatorship of Porfirio Díaz, would continue intermittently through the turn of the century. Not surprisingly, when the 1910 revolution erupted, the inhabitants of the former military colonies were among the first to join the armed struggle.

The violent tradition of frontier culture was fully reactivated during the revolutionary war, and Villismo was to be the insurgent movement that best embodied the bellicose and territorial mentality of the military colonists.[51] Forces alien to the region were by definition enemies, or, at the very least, viewed with suspicion. According to one historian, the Carrancista troops from central and southern Mexico that controlled the major cities in the state of Chihuahua after 1915 were widely perceived as an occupying army.[52] General Villa himself, who is known to have labeled revolutionaries from other regions of Mexico as "*extranjeros*" (foreigners), clearly articulated this mentality,[53] the warlike state of mind latent in the everyday life of the people, the permanent state of alert against outside forces. Villa even envisioned the establishment of military colonies throughout the nation for veterans of the revolution after the war.[54]

In *Cartucho*, the ideology of regionalism, emphasizing territorial identity and anticentralist politics, frames the viewpoint from which the stories are told. "Ismael Máynez and Martín López," the final story in the book, anecdotally and structurally provides an ideological closure that illustrates the author's intended message. The anecdote celebrates Villista violence in the context of a struggle to defend and preserve a territory under siege and renders conflict in spatial terms: an inside that wages war against an outside. In this story, Villa's troops ambush and rout Carranza's forces. Ismael Máynez, a Villista soldier who participated in the battle of Rosario, south of Parral, near the border with Durango, recalls: "What a pretty picture that was! In the entire five years of our campaign against Carranza, we never saw so many dead *changos* at one time. Two thousand eight hundred Carrancistas died. For Murguía, that ambush was one of his biggest failures. Even more so, if you take into account that at that time they considered us already defeated" (89). The narrator comments at the end: "Mama said that the town of Parral had celebrated that victory . . . The people of our land had beaten the savages. Horses' hooves would be heard again. Our street would be joyful once more, and Mama would take me by the hand to church, where the Virgin was waiting for her" (89).

For Máynez as well as the narrator, the massacre of Carrancistas restores regional dignity and internal order. The Carrancistas are labeled "savages," a term formerly reserved in the lexicon of the frontier for the seminomadic Indians from the north. The book concludes with a resounding Villista victory over the outside invaders that reaffirms and preserves the territory's integrity.

Historically, however, the regional war did not end with this military victory, which took place in 1917,[55] but with Villa's surrender in 1920, which fell short of being a definitive defeat. The ending of *Cartucho* belies historical reality, but it does reflect a nostalgic desire for epic greatness and regional autonomy. The use of the conditional tense poignantly renders that longing: "Horses' hooves *would be heard* again. Our street *would be joyful* once more, and Mama *would take me* by the hand to church, where the Virgin was waiting for her"(89). In fact, in the late 1930s, when Campobello was working on this ending for the second edition, the entire region was well along in the process of succumbing to the policies of Mexico's central government.

THE RECONSTRUCTION OF SUBALTERN PERSPECTIVES

As mentioned earlier, *Cartucho* is a book about memory and identity, about memory and survival. To understand how Campobello articulates the idea of individual and collective survival, and the question of memory, I propose an approach centered around three interrelated perspectives: the child's, the mother's, and the region's. The last is the most relevant in terms of articulating a weltanschauung from "below" and therefore will be treated more extensively.

The Child's Perspective: Violence and Fantasy

"More than three hundred men shot all at once, inside a barracks, is really extraordinary," the people said, but our young eyes found it quite natural.

NELLIE CAMPOBELLO, *Cartucho*

One aspect of *Cartucho* that has captured the attention of the critics is the apparent indifference of the child narrator to the violence and death surrounding her. Gamboa remarks on the innocence of those childish eyes, which observe tragic occurrences with the same curiosity with which other children watch the circus or a puppet show.[56] Dennis J. Parle is struck by the contrast between this conduct and the emotionality of the mother and talks about the pathos that the juxtaposition of these responses produces.[57] Manuel Pedro González, on the other hand, reacts with irritation toward the child's behavior when confronted with death. He is repulsed by what he sees as the writer's inhumanity: "The normal child does not react in this manner to blood and death, especially girls—as in this case—who are generally more given to reactions of pity, or at the very least, of fear and horror."[58] Unfortunately, González's critical assessment is more telling of his own moral and gender biases than of his analytical skills. A closer scrutiny of the text reveals precisely the opposite, that these stories depict a profoundly human reaction to the palpable presence of death and vividly display the mechanisms by which the human psyche tries to protect itself in the face of danger.

Exposed to scenes of gruesome and at times unbearable violence threatened the mental health of the population of Parral in *Cartucho*. In order to withstand the psychological impact of the war and preserve a sense of sanity, characters resort to various defense mechanisms. This is especially true in the case of the child narrator, who, because of her age, is particularly vulnerable to the daunting spectacle of death. In the stories in which the child is also the protagonist, the basic defense mechanism she uses to protect her mental health is to disassociate, or try to disassociate, her feelings from the horror of what she sees. "The Guts of General Sobarzo" and "Grime," among others, illustrate the narrator's apparent emotional numbness as she searches for ways to confront the overwhelming presence of death.

"The Guts of General Sobarzo," for example, reproduces one of those unusual incidents of the war: the gross image of a dead general's guts being carried away on a tray to the cemetery by two soldiers. The ferocity of the fighting and the horror of the outcome—blood, suffering, a dismembered body—are concentrated in those guts. Yet the child's apparently casual curiosity ("Guts, how nice!" [35]) denotes her will to integrate the absurd scene into her everyday life, to incorporate the horrific consequences of the violence into the normal experience of a girl who is growing up in the middle of a war.[59]

In the most personal stories, the child's mechanism of disconnecting her feelings in the face of the disturbing realities of war is expressed through the assimilation of tragic events into the world of childhood fantasy. In some, the childhood perspective is manifested in the way the narrator appropriates the adult characters and views them as toys or objects of entertainment ("Zafiro and Zequiel," "From a Window," "The Dead").[60] In others, it comes from the realm of fairy tales, as when she remarks of a beautiful woman who is visiting from out of town: "One day a queen arrived at Anita's house; she looked like a peacock" (10). In another story we read: "Babis must have been wearing green trousers and soldier's buttons. How eager I was to see him. He probably looked like a prince" (27). The element of fairy tale fantasy and its psychological importance is fully developed in "Grime," where the reader is told the terrible fate of José Díaz, a handsome and elegant man. The story is also an example of Campobello's technique of combining two narrative levels:

one articulates the innocent fantasy world of the child's imagination while the other records and comments on the devastation and brutal reality of war. The shifts between these narrative levels and the striking contrast between them produces the ironic edge of the story.

In the first five paragraphs of "Grime," the girl's innocent imagination predominates. In her childlike reverie, she transforms José Díaz, a delicate character (a dandy who always wears a suit, drives a red car, and hates the sun), into a princely character. Díaz "wore a glittering sword and gold and silver buttons," she says. She then adds, tellingly: "or so they seemed to my child's eyes" (30). In fact, the original text does not use the verb *parecer* (to seem) but the more suggestive *empañar* (to cloud or to blur) to qualify the girl's perspective. A translation closer to the sense of the original would be "or this is what my eyes, blurred by the mist of childhood, told me." It is more than just "seemed": the narrator emphasizes the inability to see clearly (and, therefore, to fully understand) that is distinctive of childhood. This is a relevant detail in the analysis of the story's contrasting perspectives. Díaz, she imagines, is the perfect match for Pitaflorida, her princess doll. The narrator assumes a child's view and tone of voice to convey the girl's fantasy world: "I used to sit Pitaflorida in the window so she could see him, and when I dressed her I'd tell her the things he said. My doll was very moved" (30).Within this fairy-tale setting the child projects the ethnic bias of the adult world represented by Díaz: "I would never dream of marrying my princess to a swarthy type" (30), she says, after learning that her conceited "prince" hates the sun.

Halfway through the story, the child's imaginative game comes to a halt when the need to recount the true fate of José Díaz produces a sudden change in perspective and narrative tone: "There was a seven-hour battle, with the Villistas surrounded. The fighting was fierce" (30). Significantly, this abrupt shift also mimics the matter-of-fact approach and rhythmic narrative style of the corrido ("Hubo un combate de siete horas, los villistas dentro. El combate era zumbido").[61] At this point the narration loses its subjective, childlike quality; an external, adult perspective of events that is conveyed in a direct, realistic style not uncommon in popular testimonial chronicles takes over.

Hereafter the second narrative level, without erasing the first, dominates the story almost until the end. Following the battle between the Villistas and the Carrancistas in the streets of Parral, the girl and her mother go out in search of El Siete, the narrator's thirteen-year-old brother, who fought with the Villistas and is presumed dead. The scene in town is Dantesque. They walk down streets littered with corpses lying in the most improbable positions; at times, they dispassionately turn the heads of dead soldiers to see if one of them is El Siete. They do not find him, but in a narrow street reeking with the smell of urine they discover the body of José Díaz, "smothered in grime" (32).

The last two paragraphs provide the story with two endings, one for each narrative level; both are charged with irony and indifference toward Díaz's tragic fate. In the first, the narration reverts to the infantile, fairy-tale imagination. The dead body of José Díaz, found under sullying circumstances, destroys the girl's ideal image of him. Unable to mentally assimilate an event of this magnitude, the child narrator copes with the shock of death by deflecting it and constructing a narrative in which José Díaz is unworthy of her doll: "No, no! He was never the beau of Pita-florida, my doll, who broke her head when she fell out the window. She never laughed with him" (30).

In this ending the girl takes refuge in her fantasy world to avoid confronting the trauma of the violent death of someone she knows. She resorts to denial (distancing herself from a violent event) because she wants nothing whatsoever to do with such a tragic and disagreeable character. Even in her fantasy world, however, violence and death cannot be totally suppressed; they reappear, albeit in a displaced fashion: "My doll . . . broke her head."

In the final paragraph, the child's blurred yet imaginative view is replaced by a realistic social perspective that is close in spirit to that of the popular revolution: "Young, handsome José Díaz died devoured by grime. He was shot so he would no longer hate the sun" (30).These words of social contempt (he died "so he would no longer hate the sun") suggest that the immaculate, soft-skinned José Díaz deservedly lost his life because he was a vain, delicate, and well-to-do dandy. Popular revolutionary justice based on the legitimacy of class and ethnic resentment is hinted at in these ironic remarks about the demise of the ostentatious Díaz. In contrast with the girl's distancing mechanism, this paragraph signals a moment of recognition (identification with violence) and vengeful approval of José Díaz's horrible death.

It follows that the perception of beauty and cleanliness has opposing values in the story, depending on which narrative perspective is at work. Díaz's elegant attire and clean-cut appearance are attractive qualities that trigger the child's fantasy and social markers of privilege that the revolution seeks to destroy and is scornful of (from the popular, collective point of view). The conflicting built-in perceptions of José Díaz that are evident in the two endings of "Grime" illustrate Campobello's tendency to use a dual-perspective technique in stories where the child narrator is also a central character.

The reactions to death in "Grime" and in other stories in the book reveal a combination of social influences that reflect the adult world's values and the child's personal strategies for confronting the tribulations of the revolution. The girl attempts to put the horror of war behind her by mixing facts with childish fantasy, that is, by altering reality, thus diminishing the impact they might have on her. This mechanism makes life in a world full of death more bearable. In "Grime," moreover, popular social values like contempt for the well-to-do are also made explicit. To better understand these social values, we must move beyond the limited perspective of the child.

The Domestic/Maternal Perspective: Rebellion and Social Memory

Stories saved for me, and never forgot. Mama carried them in her heart.

NELLIE CAMPOBELLO, *Cartucho*

Memory implies a certain act of redemption. What is remembered has been saved from nothingness.

JOHN BERGER, *Selected Essays*

Dennis J. Parle has noted that the female character of the mother embodies the tragic awareness of life that the girl has not yet developed, because she is so young.[62] The mother, in fact, although not a female soldier, or *soldadera* (like the protagonist of the story "Nacha Ceniceros" or the female character La Pintada in Mariano Azuela's *Los de abajo*), is a strong and dramatic figure. A compassionate person ("Mama was very sympathetic towards those who suffered" [59]), she deplores war and mourns the many lives that are lost. Yet the mother is also an active Villista backer, not merely an "observer of the struggle but rather a participant on the domestic front, a 'collaborator' who loves peace."[63] In "Pancho Villa's Wounded Men," she cures Villa's wounded soldiers and takes personal risks in her desperate effort to try to save their lives. Her Villismo, however, does not blind her to the realities of war and gender abuse. Aware of the perils experienced by young women during the war, with a shrewd display of female solidarity, she reacts swiftly to protect a niece from a Villista general in "Agustín García."[64] She passionately intervenes to save her son, nicknamed "El Siete," from being executed by the Villistas in "My Brother and His Deck of Cards." She accepts the frightening vicissitudes of life in Villista territory as part of the uncertainty brought about by war, but she regrets the excesses and calamities and endures them with stoicism.

Besides compassion, strength, and female solidarity, the mother embodies the epic faculty of memory,[65] a quality vividly brought to life when General Rueda (in "General Rueda") and his soldiers burst into her home in search of arms and money. Their hostile presence transforms that domestic space into another revolutionary battlefront. General Rueda insults the mother and orders his soldiers to destroy all the furniture during the search in retaliation for her Villista sympathies. The soldiers fail to turn up any arms and leave, but not before having "carried off what they wanted" (33). Because it is virtually impossible for the unarmed woman to fight the soldiers' intrusion into her home, she endures the situation in silence and without losing her composure. The mother's outrage and strength are concentrated in the look in her eyes: "Mama's eyes, grown large with revolution, did not cry; they had hardened, resting on the rifle barrel of her remembrance" (33).

For the mother, the revolutionary struggle against abuse and injustice represents a profound learning experience: it is the beginning of consciousness; her eyes have been opened. It follows that she will not allow herself to be provoked by the soldiers' affronts. Her defiance is concentrated in her gaze; her eyes, "hardened" by the experience of war, acquire the metallic quality of a rifle, the symbol of the popular revolutionary struggle. The figurative permutation of the mother's eyes into an instrument of war is the key to the story; it reveals that the arms General Rueda's soldiers seek in vain are located, in this case, in the mother's subjectivity and desire. The soldiers have raided the house and humiliated its dwellers, but they cannot find and confiscate that which keeps the rebellious spirit of the Villistas alive and intact: the weapon of memory. From her mother, then, the child learns the subversive function of memory.[66]

What does the mother remember? Mostly, though not exclusively, stories of personal integrity and resistance. By telling these stories, she upholds pride in a regional identity under siege. She represents the domestic, maternal world of oral culture, the world of women, of children, and of the people, with all their beliefs and prejudices, as opposed to the world of written culture, laws, public life, and virile pursuits. This kind of popular and gendered knowledge produces exemplary tales, crucial to the daughter's upbringing, since it is through them that the mother passes on to her the values and the vision of her people.

The importance of the maternal figure as a source of knowledge and social identity is expounded clearly in the last two paragraphs of "Urbina's Men," which were added in the second edition. In this final section, the mother takes her daughter to visit her godmother. On the way, the mother instructs her daughter on the norms of traditional society that she ought to know: "You must kiss my *comadre*'s hand. She is your godmother, your second mother" (40). The high point of this pedagogical encounter occurs shortly before arriving, however, when the mother suddenly decides to veer off the road. She says, as if talking to herself, "I'm going to show my daughter something" (40), and she leads her by the hand to an abandoned spot:

> "Here it was," she said, stopping by a blue stone. "Look here," she said to me. "This was the spot where a man died. He was our countryman. José Beltrán. He kept firing on them until the last moment. They riddled him with bullets. Here's where it happened. Even down on his knees, as God taught him, he fired at them and reloaded his rifle. He took on a lot of them. He had been tracked down and followed to this spot. He was eighteen years old." She couldn't go on. We left the stone, and Mama didn't say another word. (40)

The pilgrimage to the spot where José Beltrán died enacts an entire sentimental and political education. The mother's brief but passionate speech; her references to Beltrán's stoicism (he never surrendered, he fought to the end), to his youth and his territorial identity ("He was eighteen years old," "he was our countryman"); the use of anaphora to deepen the evocative effect ("Here it was . . . Here's where it happened"); the contrast with the silence that follows her words ("and Mama didn't say another word") to convey a latent and contained emotionality, all of these elements are meant to have an edifying effect. By reminding her daughter of José Beltrán's bravery, by paying respect to a local hero, the mother performs the cultural task of assuring that certain of her people's traditions of struggle will not be lost or forgotten.[67] In this passage, as in many others, the mother assumes the responsibility for keeping the memory of the dead alive. In short, she embodies the epic faculty of memory.[68]

The mother's stories extend the geographical consciousness and identity of the narrator, moving her out from the domestic world to the larger world of her fellow countrymen. When she tell stories that touch on deaths caused by the split within the Villista movement between the followers of Villa and the followers of Tomás Urbina, the mother is particularly overtaken by grief. In such cases, her heart goes out to the Urbinistas, men from northern Durango, her home region, the place toward which her most intense memories are directed. For her, the emotional and social bonds of *paisanaje*, of identification with the people from her own region, rule and precede any other kind of loyalty. And because many of her acquaintances were killed, "[t]elling about the end of her people was all she had left" (40).

Memory, storytelling, and epic grief combine in her accounts. A case in point is the story of Santos Ortiz in "Urbina's Men." When Ortiz's chief, General Urbina, is put to death for betraying Villa, his troops are obliged to sign papers declaring themselves Villistas or face execution. Santos refuses to sign: "Santos had told them he didn't want to be a Villista. No one wanted to shoot him, even the staunchest Villistas pleaded for his life and had hopes of convincing him" (38). Ortiz's sister pressures him to change his mind and save himself; however, clinging to an inflexible military code of honor, he chooses to die rather than to be disloyal to General Urbina. Ortiz's stubbornness sets the stage for his inevitable execution, which is experienced not as an individual event, but as an event of collective sorrow, as a shared disgrace brought on by the unforgiving, merciless nature of war.

Ortiz's dignified behavior in the face of death contrasts with the mother's inconsolable account. How she is described telling the story of the tragic ending of Santos Ortiz is as moving as the story itself. With "her voice sad and eyes filled with pain" (38), the mother begins to remember Urbina's soldiers, and when she mentions Ortiz, her "voice tremble[s]" (38). As her account of his death unfolds, she becomes animated, "very anxious to tell the tragedy of that brave man" (39). Signs of her suffering are visible when the story approaches its climax: "'Poor Santos Ortiz,' exclaimed Mama with tears in her eyes. 'May God preserve him in heaven'" (39–40).

By describing the mother's "performance," the narrator enacts the ritualistic and therapeutic elements involved in the narrative act of resurrecting the memory of the dead for the bereaved survivors. Storytelling assuages her grief because it satisfies an emotionally desirable need; it is a survival mechanism for the individual (the mother) and for the culture she represents.

For the adult narrator recalling her childhood, the mother is the vital link between domestic space and the outside world, between family life and social responsibilities. All the vital information about what it means to belong to a specific region, or a *patria chica*, comes from her. And in *Cartucho* this identity has a decidedly anticentralist political character.

The narrator learns through her mother to associate local identity with notions of pride and military honor. This cultural code reaches its full development in the stories that deal with regional issues and in which the mother is also a participant.

The Regional Perspective: Constructing the Villista Mythology

What would happen to the people if their champions were irrevocably dead?

ERIC J. HOBSBAWM, *Primitive Rebels*

The twenty-four new stories included in the second edition of *Cartucho* are not directly related to the narrator's childhood experience. They are stories told to her by others, sometimes many years after the events took place. Transmitted to Campobello with a mix of admiration, astonishment, humor, or tenderness, these stories are part of the region's social memory. As mentioned before, Campobello gathered many of them in the mid-1930s, when she was doing field research in northern Mexico for her historical book on Villa (*Apuntes*). Intended to praise and redeem Villismo, the stories are largely responsible for the mythological construction of the movement's regional heroes in *Cartucho*. Campobello even resorts to the folk wisdom of the corrido ("The Poor Man's Song," "Abelardo Prieto," "The Tragedy of Martín") to reinforce the regional and subaltern class outlook of the stories. The ballads celebrate the deeds of fallen heroes, some of them anonymous, while denouncing political and social injustice and confirming the degree to which the author's aesthetics and politics are integrated. The new stories that were added to and superimposed on the original collection imbue the text with an anti-Carrancista, anticentralist political orientation not easily discernible in the first edition.

In these stories, Campobello follows the "political poetic of oral history."[69] The recurrent theme is resistance to outside domination and the collective reaction to the death of local Villista combatants. Word of mouth spreads the news, and the repetition and recollection of any event simplifies and abstracts the story, molding it into a conventionalized narrative plot, where the process of selecting certain elements and forgetting others establishes paradigmatic relationships (a teaching, a moral truth, a parable) with the present.[70] These images, in turn, concentrate the social values that give meaning to the life experiences of the collectivity.

"Pablo López's Crutch" recounts the execution of one of the generals who led the attack on Columbus, New Mexico, "a deed that made him a folk hero among the Villistas of the North."[71] He is wounded in both legs in the assault and captured shortly thereafter in Chihuahua and executed in the public plaza as a warning to the townspeople. A collective perspective is articulated in this story, one conveying feelings of warmth and affection for the tragic Pablo López: "Everyone had something to say about the execution. Mama said they even cried for Pablito. She didn't actually see it because she was in Parral. Martín told her all about it" (44).

Word of mouth tells the story of Pablito, as the mother affectionately calls him. The narrator re-creates this collective effort and adds her own impressions, embellishing the facts. A fundamental antagonism is established from the start between the people and the two enemies of the people: the Americans, "who hated him [Pablo López], and wanted to see him hanged from a tree" (44), and the Carrancistas, the military force from outside the region whose version of the capture of the hero is rejected by the masses. "To all appearances, Colonel del Arco had gone looking for Pablo, despite the risks involved. Not everyone believes that. They say the colonel was a dandy" (44).

Popular lore discredits the notion of the colonel's valor by calling attention to his genteelness ("[he] was a dandy"), a not-so-veiled expression of popular contempt for well-to-do fatuousness. Pablo López, by contrast, is remembered for his calm demeanor on the day of his death. He eats breakfast, drinks coffee, smokes a cigar, and smiles, as if his impending death has no bearing on his state of mind. Throughout the ordeal he maintains a dignified silence, for selfless stoicism is beyond words: "He didn't complain, said no last words, sent no letters" (44). He breaks his silence only when he spots an American among the crowd gathered to witness the execution: "I don't want to die in front of that guy," he says angrily (45).

In spite of his wounded legs, which prevent him from standing up, the hero never appears lying down or fallen. A crutch—emblematic of the dignity that sustains the character to the very last minute of his life— helps him stand up straight. Only after his execution is there a "fall," but at this point another device—the poetization of death—is ready to replace the symbolic role of the crutch: "The bullets took him down from his crutch, and laid him out on the ground. The wounds from Columbus no longer bothered him" (45). Death comes not as a disgrace but as a relief, a rest that will free him from his suffering.[72]

In the final paragraph, the narrator explicitly merges her point of view with that of the people: "I think Colonel del Arco was the type who probably perfumed his mustache and enjoyed his triumph, right down to the heels of his elegant military boots" (45). Thus, in "Pablo López's Crutch" the derisive description of the enemy contrasts with the hero's traits (courage, insouciance, pride) that confer on him an image of strength and honor. The crutch functions as a symbol of the hero's integrity, and the narrator also poeticizes his fall in order to lessen the impact of his death.[73]

In other stories, death is recounted in the seriocomic, ambivalent fashion typical of popular culture. One of several recurring images in this ironic modality is that of laughter. In the medieval tradition, carnivalesque laughter was associated with the denial of death (mockery) and the affirmation of life (resurrection).[74] Traces of this primary function of laughter in the human psyche are evident throughout *Cartucho*, but this idea is most completely developed in "José's Smile."

The story begins by describing how the narrator heard about the death of Gen. José Rodríguez.[75] Salvador, a neighbor from Segunda del Rayo who served under Rodríguez, obsessively returns to the memory of his general whenever he talks about the revolution. The narrator begins by repeating Salvador's words, but gradually she takes over the story, and in her retelling of what happened her own ironic folk perspective emerges.

Victim of a betrayal, José Rodríguez dies not far from the Mexico-U.S. border. "Everybody in Parral wept for José Rodríguez," comments the narrator (47). The same cannot be said, however, of the people of Ciudad Juárez, where the bodies of Rodríguez and another man are laid out on boards under a merciless sun and exposed to public curiosity. Nobody knows who they are. The Carrancistas, who have taken control of the town, are convinced that they are bandits. They are unaware that one of them, the "strong tall one," is José Rodríguez, the renowned Villista general. Their ignorance prompts the following observation from the narrator: "Laughing to himself, José Rodríguez was probably saying to them in a friendly voice, 'Anyway, fellows, let me rest a bit in the sun, lying here in front of the people' (but he didn't say it, because José was actually mocking them)"(47).

From the standpoint of the people of Parral, the exhibition of Rodríguez's inert body in the public plaza, as if he were a common criminal, denigrates the memory of this brave Villista. Therefore, the objective of the narrator's imaginative, if not festive, interpretation of the hero's grotesque death grin is to ward off and, ultimately, to deflect the listener's (the reader's) attention from the reality of shame and dishonor. She does so by introducing a causal logic that not only hides but also inverts the original meaning of the scene. Having failed to identify their victim, the narrator's rationale goes, the incompetent Carrancistas are unable to recognize the real and symbolic importance of their own action. Hence she can playfully suggest that even in death Rodríguez continues to evade and to mock his enemies. His posthumous laughter, a final bit of roguishness attributed to him by the narrator, ambiguously transforms José Rodríguez's tragic death into the symbolic triumph of the hero over his enemies.

Although resistance to outside domination, specifically Carrancismo, is a dominant theme in the 1940 edition, some of the stories touch on internal schisms, personal revenge, or the betrayals of Villa. "The enemies were their cousins, their brothers, and friends," the narrator observes in one of the new stories (68). The treatment of these internal splits varies greatly, reflecting the delicate complexity of the subject matter. One narrative approach is to vindicate the protagonist in spite of his offenses, because the storyteller esteems his personal attributes. This is the case in "Tomás Urbina."

Historically, the most serious conflict within the Villista movement occurred when General Urbina, the pride of the Northern Division and Villa's right hand, abandoned his attack on El Ébano, the oil-rich center he had been ordered to take by storm, and inexplicably withdrew to his hacienda in Nieves, Durango. Shortly thereafter, accused of insubordination, he died at the hands of the Villistas. Urbina's military retreat and his refusal to be held accountable for his actions led to his demise. Some historical testimony and popular lore have it that he had made a deal with the Carrancistas.[76]

General Urbina was a native son of northern Durango, Campobello's *patria chica*, and his tragedy had a special impact on people from that region who had known him. The "Lion of Durango," as he was called, had been one of their own who had achieved great military prestige.[77] Traditional bonds and ties of friendship that went back to their years as bandits united Villa and Urbina. Urbina was known to be one of Villa's closest allies and his compadre (the godfather of his daughter). In a world ruled by traditional loyalties and based on primary networks of sociability (kinship, vicinity, territoriality), Urbina's disloyalty to Villa, his commander in chief as well as his intimate friend, subjected him to a heavy burden of censure and disgrace. Yet for the people of Urbina's home region, this general's courage would always be more significant than his weaknesses. "Tomás Urbina" shows how Campobello, at the narrative level through plot displacement, negotiates and resolves the dilemma of remembering a local hero who betrayed Villa.

A number of people (the narrator's great-uncle, el Kirilí, Martínez Espinosa) tell the story of Tomás Urbina. The narrator brings together these complementary voices and adds her own observations. Once again, she begins by revealing how she came to know the details of the events surrounding the death of Urbina (known as El Chapo): "My great-uncle knew him well. 'What they say about El Chapo is all lies,' he said. 'El Chapo was a real man of the revolution.' These *curros* [city boys] who now try to make a saint of him never even met him! And he narrates, as if it were a story" (48).

The story is conceived as a popular counterdiscourse: to set the record straight by giving the local, testimonial version of the life and death of the celebrated Villista, a version that differs substantially from the stories generated in urban settings by the *curros*. As befits oral memory, Campobello's "true" version conforms to the conventionalized (tragic, sentimental) plot typical of traditional narrative. The violent *serrano* way of life that tempered the ruthless character of Urbina and instilled in him the qualities needed to excel in the art of war are celebrated: "He knew how to break in ponies, lasso animals and men" (48). Because he was able to force men and beasts to submit to his will, and because of his skill with firearms, his disposition, and his boldness, he rose to the rank of general in the revolution. As events unfold, the crucial need to explain this formidable soldier's betrayal of Villa in a story that aims to exalt his memory leads the narrator to transport the reader abruptly from the epic world of the revolution to the realm of love, death, and popular mythology. A one-sentence paragraph marks the transition: "Urbina, the general, succumbed to Urbina the man" (48).

The conflict between civilian and military identity surfaces in this passage, and the civilian wins: Urbina's personal passions are stronger than his military obligations. This twist allows the narrator to suggest that it was the hero's passions rather than his military irresponsibility that caused him to stumble. According to this version, Urbina is in El Ébano when he is notified of his wife's infidelity back at his Nieves ranch; it is never mentioned that he is assaulting a military objective. The interloper who has defamed his honor is inevitably ordered killed by Urbina. Yet the episode does not end there. The news that his wife is holding a wake for her dead lover, honoring him in the bedroom of his own house, proves too much for the general, who loses control of himself: "Urbina learned of this, and it undid him completely. His emotions exploded" (49).

The following scenes place Urbina at the Nieves ranch, and henceforth Campobello incorporates the accounts of two new informants (el Kirilí and Martínez Espinosa). The narrative logic leads the reader to infer that the general has left El Ébano and returned to Nieves, driven by the impulse to confront his wife. In fact, with the change of scene and the introduction of two new testimonies, the dramatic tension has been unexpectedly displaced to a different reality: the confrontation between Villa and Urbina. Now the wife completely disappears from the story. The subject of marital betrayal has been skillfully used to veil and therefore to justify the real motive for his return to Nieves: his military betrayal, which is referred to only in passing, as if it were no more than a rumor. In Nieves, Villista soldiers ambush Urbina, wounding him and taking him prisoner. Villa talks for a good while with his compadre and apparently has a change of heart and is ready to let him go. But General Fierro, Villa's most famously murderous lieutenant, refuses to countenance a pardon and presses Villa to give Urbina what he deserves. In the end, Fierro (backed by the presence of troops loyal to him rather than Villa) prevails over Villa's objections, and Urbina is taken away and executed.

"Oral tradition," writes Américo Paredes, "often forgets the faults of its heroes, while extolling their virtues."[78] Such is the case with Urbina's story. The upshot is that Urbina's tragedy is obscured by a confusing web of passion that, in accordance with a pattern common to patriarchal folk narrative, claims adulterous treachery as the cause of the hero's downfall. In this case, the commonplace of female betrayal serves to conceal a military betrayal, which is the real motive behind the actions that lead to the death of the main character. Furthermore, the sentimental explanation of the protagonist's behavior helps humanize Urbina and hence mitigate his culpability. Villa, who defends Urbina but to no avail, is absolved from having condemned his intimate friend to death—he is simply outgunned and unable to impose his will. With Urbina's betrayal understated and Villa ultimately not guilty of ordering his compadre's death, the severely tested traditional ties and values ruling this world remain unbroken.

Hence Campobello re-creates the selective process characteristic of oral memory, whereby people elaborate stories that serve to hide, validate, or deny certain aspects of historical reality at the level of collective consciousness. In "Tomás Urbina," a crisis within the Villista movement is dealt with and resolved satisfactorily based on the testimonials of the people of northern Durango by weaving a collective story that justifies and preserves the integrity of the favored historical actors.

A common thread that unites "Tomás Urbina," "José's Smile," and "Pablo López's Crutch" is the presence of a discourse of desire whereby history is transformed into myth. The function of myth in *Cartucho* is to erase, figuratively speaking, the fatal line dividing the dead from the world of the living and the present. The symbols, poeticized images, ironic inversions, plots from folk tales, and other literary devices in these stories all serve the same ideological and sentimental objective: to rescue the historical figure from the tragic circumstances of his death in an effort to ensure that his heroic status remains intact.[79] Just as the emotional coping mechanisms of the child who witnesses violence and death are motivated by a basic instinct of self-preservation, the psychological value of myths—the class myths of the Villista movement—is to safeguard the rebel identity of those who did not prevail. The survival of the oppressed requires that the local Villistas be shaped into memorable, exemplary figures, for they are called to represent the collective ethos that is central to the cultural functioning of the community that produces them.

The regional, the maternal/domestic, and the child's perspectives combine to construct popular subjectivities in which the protection of the mental health and cultural identity of the collectivity is paramount. Yet at the same time, these perspectives offer a contradictory, multiple, and dispersed image of the war in Villista territory. Certain stories reinforce each other in order to extol and to justify the actions of the Villista fighters. In other stories, the description of the internal tensions and conflicts within the movement reveal these same fighters as profoundly human, at fault, antiheroic.[80] By not suppressing contradictions, Campobello's own mythological construction of Villismo becomes a problematic site, where power struggles and human nature forestall any essentialized or uncomplicated idealized image of subaltern rebellion.

As mentioned previously, the act of telling and retelling popular anecdotes, structuring them into conventional and evocative images— that is, the mythification of history—implies a metaphorical connection between the storied past and the writing of the present. The question then arises: what is this present for which it is so vitally important to preserve the memory of the fallen soldiers? The present is the discursive and ideological battles of the reconstruction era to determine the place of Villismo and what it represents—regional sovereignty, anticentralist ideology—in the social imaginary of the nation. In this political and cultural milieu, Campobello's self-appointed mission was to ensure for herself and for the vanquished a voice in the production of discourses about the revolutionary past. By retrieving and rewriting regional oral histories, she hoped to articulate an alternative, noncentralist, historical memory that would validate and, ultimately, redeem for the nation the revolutionary identity of the local Villista soldiers who died in the war.

Articulating a regional, popular, alternative memory of the war in Villista territory was important for Campobello because, as Adolfo Gilly has written, the oppressed "more that anybody else, need the memory of their own past which power wants to erase." As the story of "Tomás Urbina" suggests, however, this memory "also needs forgetfulness, just as shadow when it accompanies light makes bodies visible."[81] The stories in *Cartucho* record, from the perspective of the vanquished, this double movement of light and shadow, of memory and forgetfulness.

Martín Luis Guzmán's *Iconografía*, a book of photographs published in
1987, reveals a certain attachment to Mexico's presidents, perhaps like no
other intellectual of his generation, or since.[1] To be sure, his journalistic
work and political career, his literary prestige, and the fact that he lived
a long life may reasonably explain the inordinate number of photographs
in which Guzmán appears with the country's leaders. Nevertheless, it is
difficult not to see in these images a man drawn almost instinctively to the
higher echelons of power. Guzmán's presence in the photographs suggests a tacit endorsement of the nation's successive authoritarian regimes,
even though a careful review of his biography indicates that the doors of
the powerful were not always open to him. There were times, in the early
stages of his life as a public intellectual, when his political loyalty raised
suspicion and led on several occasions to a falling out with the nation's
strongmen and to self-exile in 1915, and forced exile in 1923. It was during these periods that he wrote some of his most memorable works, as
if he had to regain (or compensate for) his loss of presence and influence in the political and cultural arenas through the power of the pen. *El
águila y la serpiente* (The Eagle and the Serpent),[2] an extensive testimony
of Guzmán's participation in the revolutionary war, was written during
his second exile.[3]

The events leading to Guzmán's expulsion from Mexico and eventually to the writing of *El águila* tell a cautionary tale, not untypical of the
time, of an ambitious revolutionary intellectual abruptly ostracized from
the nation's top political circles. In 1919, Martín Luis Guzmán, a lawyer
by profession and a writer and journalist by calling, returned from exile
in New York to a country precariously pacified after the ravages of war.
What prompted his return was an offer to head the editorial section of
the daily *El Heraldo de México*. At the time, Guzmán was already a well-
respected and established writer. A collection of sociological essays on
Mexican politics, culture, and history, *La querella de México* (The Quarrel
in Mexico, in *Obras completas*, 1915), published during his years abroad,

had earned him a name in intellectual circles. This was soon followed by a second collection of essays, *A orillas del Hudson* (By the Banks of the Hudson, 1920).

On arrival in Mexico City, he immediately became a political insider, well connected in government circles and quite visible in the sphere of public opinion. In 1921, he was appointed personal secretary to Alberto J. Pani, minister of foreign affairs. A year later, he was elected to the Chamber of Deputies (1922–1923) and founded the evening newspaper *El Mundo*, which he owned and directed. By all appearances, his return to Mexico was a political and financial success, and a promising future seemed to lie ahead of him.

His good fortune, however, was to be short-lived. During the 1923 presidential campaign, Guzmán and his newspaper declined to support the candidacy of Gen. Plutarco Elías Calles, Pres. Álvaro Obregón's handpicked successor, backing instead the opposing ticket of Gen. Adolfo de la Huerta. In the face of growing government repression against his campaign, de la Huerta issued a call to arms against Obregón.

The precipitous turn of events placed Guzmán in the perilous position of having publicly endorsed a candidate who was now the leader of a seditious military movement against the legitimate government. His fall from grace was swift and dramatic. Warned that an order to have him killed was imminent, the writer had to relinquish control of his newspaper and hastily negotiate his departure from the country in December 1923.[4] Like other intellectuals who had found a place in the Obregón regime (notably, José Vasconcelos), Guzmán fell victim to the volatile world of power struggles between the military caudillos. He would never make the same mistake—challenge the powers to be—again.

After a short stay in the United States, the author worked his way to Europe, where he made a living writing for newspapers and magazines. Although he settled in Spain and apparently became a Spanish citizen, *El águila y la serpiente* was written "for the most part in Paris between August 1926 and October 1927," according to Juan Bruce-Novoa, and published in periodicals in the United States and Mexico.[5] The collection appeared in book form in Madrid in 1928 and was a literary success, enthusiastically received first in intellectual circles in Spain, where the first edition sold out in one month, and later in Mexico City.[6]

El águila offers the reader an exceptionally rich and varied canvas of revolutionary Mexico. The narrative moves smoothly from Guzmán's travels over half the nation and abroad to the internal struggles within the constitutionalist leadership, in which he was a minor participant, to occasional run-ins with the rank and file. Memorably, *El águila* includes incisive physical and moral portraits of key historical actors, most prominently Francisco Villa, who is a formidable presence in the book.

Several factors motivated Guzmán to write about his own past in the revolution. Among them was the need to support himself and his family while living in Europe. Readership in Spain, the United States, and Mexico could be guaranteed at the time by writing accounts of the Mexican Revolution based on the authority of the "I" who sees, that is, on the belief in the narrator's privileged access to facts as an eyewitness. Credible "real life" stories about the war sold well, a fact that did not escape the exiled writer's attention. His subject matter, it follows, was partly motivated by economic considerations.

Personal vindication was also a factor. At the height of the 1923–1924 electoral dispute, General Calles declared that the de la Huerta revolt had had the social benefit of categorically separating "the false and the genuine revolutionaries."[7] In *El águila* Guzmán counters the charge of being a "false" revolutionary and clears his name by chronicling his travails as the young lawyer in the Constitutionalist and Villista movements, and in the ephemeral *convencionista* government of Eulalio Gutiérrez, whose collapse is recorded in the closing chapters of the book. By placing himself, as much as possible, in the middle of the conflict, the author records, justifies, and perhaps magnifies the role he played in the war.

Sly references to his political enemies in Mexico were also in order. In the chapter entitled "The Piety of General Iturbe," for example, Guzmán celebrates the revolutionary general's public demonstration of religious faith, thereby attacking, however obliquely, the moral and political legitimacy of President Calles, who at the time was waging war against the Catholic Church.[8] Gen. Álvaro Obregón is labeled "a comedian" (70) and ridiculed for concocting absurd historical metaphors in his speeches (67). Furthermore, Guzmán's frequent indictment of militarism and calls for urban citizenship point toward the urgent necessity of civilian rule in Mexico, and for a moral and political role for the intellectual class, to which the author belonged, in bringing about this transformation.

Finally, writing *El águila* was the author's mode of participating in and contributing to the intellectual and political debates taking place among the educated classes in Mexico City over the aesthetic dimension of "Mexicanness." The nationalist endeavor of locating the "soul of Mexico" in the common people and the landscape is manifested in the vignettes of popular characters and parade of unusual encounters, the portraits of revolutionary leaders, and the vivid descriptions of the nation's geography (the cities and the countryside). Thus the collection belongs to a larger trend in Mexican literature that reflects the cultural propositions and search for national identity typical of the period.[9] In sum, writing and publishing *El águila* reinserted Guzmán in absentia in the fray over the meaning of the past and the direction of the country's politics and culture and served to rationalize his own role in the revolutionary struggle.

This chapter examines, first, the politics of Guzmán's aesthetic approach to the revolution in *El águila*, which is based on the elitist ideology of Arielismo. A dominant influence in the intellectual life of Latin America in the first three decades of the twentieth century,[10] the Arielista school of thought advanced the belief that culture and the life of the spirit should be the guiding principles in the social development of modern life; hence it is important to study this ideology in its relationship to Guzmán's ideas on social reconstruction and to issues of spirituality and cultural identity in *El águila*.

I discuss the paradoxical role played by Gen. Francisco Villa in the author's ideological scheme in the second and third sections of the chapter. Villa's prominence in *El águila* is such that Guzmán's original title for the book was *A la hora de Pancho Villa* (Pancho Villa's Time).[11] Unpredictable, violent, ruthless, the unruly Villa is a permanent source of uneasiness for the narrator, who is highly critical—and slightly patronizing—in his depiction of the popular leader. Yet Villa also concentrates enormous social energies and acts as intensifier of the material forces moving the popular rebellion. Like no other character in the book, he radically divides the revolutionary world along lines of class and culture and comes across as the popular embodiment of Mexico's "manhood." I shall discuss how Guzmán's representation of this radical version of Otherness can serve the dual purpose of allocating popular subjects a distinguished space in the nationalist imaginary *and* of advocating the resubalternization of the masses in postrevolutionary Mexico.

ARIELISMO AND THE AESTHETICS
AND MORAL CONSTRUCTION OF OTHERNESS

El águila y la serpiente is divided into two parts. The first, "Revolutionary Hopes," begins shortly after the assassination of President Madero in February 1913, when Guzmán leaves the country and joins the Constitutionalist movement at the U.S.-Mexico border. Personal adventures, encounters with notable military leaders, and gripping stories about the war—Venustiano Carranza, Francisco Villa, Álvaro Obregón, Felipe

Ángeles—ensue. The second, "The Hour of Triumph," covers his return to Mexico City, where most of the action takes place, as well as the Convention of Aguascalientes and the creation and downfall of the *convencionista* government. It concludes when Guzmán deserts General Villa and heads north, to the U.S. border, in early 1915.

Artistically, an essential feature in both books is the writer's desire to make of his contact with the revolution, however unsavory, a positive aesthetic experience. Hence real life occurrences are systematically submitted to, and transformed by, the conventions of fiction writing. His overwhelming concern for producing satisfactory literary effects takes precedence over historical accuracy, as Guzmán himself acknowledged years later.[12]

Plots, Characterization, and the Art of Composition

Each chapter in *El águila*, some more than others, constitutes a well-wrought retelling of real or legendary episodes lived or heard of by Guzmán in the course of the war. These incidents are placed in a narrative framework of adventure and suspense, typical elements of a novel. In some chapters, the plotting of events can be readily traced to pre-established narrative molds. The opening chapter, "The Beautiful Spy," and the events that follow are a playful and slightly parodic imitation of period spy novels or romance and intrigue on the high seas. "Murder in the Dark" is plotted in the tradition of the classic whodunit. The deductive logic of General Hay, an improvised "investigator," holds the key to solving the mysterious case of a serial killer in the city of Culiacán. In another story, "Pancho Villa of the Cross," General Villa hastily issues a countermand, in a race against time, to stop the execution order of 166 prisoners. Guzmán heightens the suspense by juxtaposing the inexorable ticking of the clock, the passage of objective time, with the subjective angst of the restless general.

Life as art or dramatic spectacle rules Guzmán's construction of characters. In representing Francisco Villa, Álvaro Obregón, Venustiano Carranza, and other prominent generals, what matters most to Guzmán is not their ideas or political programs, to which he pays little attention, but their "personalities and their respective outlooks and behaviour."[13] Performance replaces "hard" politics, Christopher Domínguez has noted, because the writer chooses to see life as representation and his mission as communicating how well or how poorly each revolutionary leader represents his role on the great stage of history.[14] The leader of the Constitutionalist movement, Venustiano Carranza, is not judged a great politician or a hero, "but at least he doesn't fake his title: he knows how to be [play the role of] the First Chief" (48). The opposite is said of Gen. Álvaro Obregón. He "did not live in the world of matter-of-fact sincerity, but on the boards; he was not a man of action, but an actor" (70). The good-natured but politically naïve Gen. Roque González Garza is depicted as an unwilling buffoon during the Convention of Aguascalientes (268–270). Fiery speaker Antonio Díaz Soto y Gama, on the other hand, who dresses down to display himself more effectively as a "man of the people" (266) and desecrates the Mexican flag in front of his rowdy audience, plays—in a masterly manner, according to Guzmán—the political role of the *provocateur* (267–273).

It follows that in writing *El águila* Guzmán consistently erred on the side of art and readability. Events and historical figures gravitate toward literary types, narrative models, and plots from the Western tradition, an undertaking for which he was well prepared and, by all accounts, uncommonly gifted. As a result, chapters have, for the most part, a pleasurable and entertaining appeal, though, in many instances, they are artistically overdetermined.

Guzmán's composition technique relies heavily on the careful re-creation of human perception and sensations, or sensorial experience. In this he follows the artistic sensibility of the *modernista* writers, particularly Juan Ramón Jiménez, a Spanish poet of whom he admiringly writes: "Sensoriality seems to be at the base of his intelligence of things. His spiritual yearning is translated into relations or contrast of color, sound, smell."[15] Likewise, data and impressions—auditory and olfactory references, matters of taste and consistency—are filtered through the realm of the senses in *El águila*. Of Adolfo de la Huerta Guzmán recalls "the extraordinary timbre of his voice, beautiful and rich in sonorities"; of General Diéguez, his perennial smell of coffee, "not roasting or ground coffee, but of coffee per se, the essence of itself, eternal" (100). Guzmán is delighted when, from the ship that is taking him to New Orleans, he unexpectedly sees in the reflection of the sun on the sea the natural phenomenon known as "green ray," one "of the most amazing sights I have ever seen" (31).[16] In San Antonio, Texas, he takes pleasure in the "aesthetic quality" of a breakfast where "[w]hite, or at most, cream, was the predominant color. Butter melted on the steaming, fluffy pancakes" (35). Consistency, color, smell, texture—all are sensorial stimuli, a feast of the senses.

True to his personal inclination, however, detailed attention to the effects of light, line, color, and contrast are the primary tools of his composition technique. "Unless I can see a thing, a character, a scene, I cannot describe it," he once declared.[17] It would indeed seem that for Guzmán the aesthetic dimension of the revolution only became a reality when he was able to transform it into a visual experience. An uneventful night scene, soldiers silently smoking as they wait for the train in Maytorena station, is a case in point. The feeble little lights of cigarettes enable visualization and, in this particular case, what amounts to a quiet revelation: "Sometimes the fireflies of the soldiers' cigarettes carved out of the darkness with their illumination the wavering lines of dark faces, the gleam of buckles and rifle barrels, the shiny wood of gunstocks, the crisscrossing of cartridge belts over the folds of dirty shirts" (75).

The contrasts of shadow and light, the depiction of lines and color, underscore the vividness of the soldiers' presence and give the scene a pictorial quality. With a few quick strokes, as in the murals of José Clemente Orozco, Guzmán evokes with a routine scene a simple but transcendental reality: that of the ragged, dark-skinned, anonymous masses up in arms, dignified by the fleeting sight of their weapons. Tenuous cigarette tips—fireflies in the author's poetic imagination—have briefly brought out of the dark the popular face of the revolution.

Guzmán's composition technique, uses of plot, and characterization, inextricably combine and reinforce each other in *El águila*, elevating his narrative account of life in revolutionary Mexico to the category of aesthetic experience.

The Arielista Tradition in Mexico

The writing in *El águila* is heavily influenced by the ideas of Uruguayan social philosopher José Enrique Rodó. In his canonical essay *Ariel* (1900), Rodó rules that the highest state of perfection humankind can aspire to is to be found in beauty or aesthetic harmony.[18] His social doctrine called for the defense of "selfless spiritual idealism—art, science, morality, religious sincerity, a politics of ideas" over selfish interest and crass materialism.[19] Inspired by the classics, Rodó assigned the greatest importance to sensibility and beauty in the "education of the spirit" and opposed these values to the utilitarianism of Anglo-American culture, which, he wrote, equivocally preached success as the supreme goal in life.[20] For the Uruguayan thinker, material progress fulfilled its proper social function solely when subservient to the gospel of exquisiteness, intelligence, and disinterest. In his essay, this gospel was expounded by the magisterial figure of Ariel, whom Rodó identified with the region's Latin/Hispanic cultural tradition.[21]

The incorporation of the Arielista doctrine into Mexico's cultural and political life was carried out by an elite group of young intellectuals, who founded the Ateneo de la Juventud in Mexico City in 1908. Among them were future distinguished writers José Vasconcelos, Alfonso Reyes, and Martín Luis Guzmán. The *ateneístas*, or affiliates of the Ateneo, were critical of the Porfirian educational system, which was rooted in positivistic thinking and the scientific method. They welcomed and cultivated metaphysical speculation and called for a return to the study of philosophy and the humanities, areas of knowledge that had been banned from their academic training. In their gatherings they read the classics and discussed contemporary streams of thought, knowledge founded on intuition, inspired by European thinkers like Bergson and Boutroux. They also read *Ariel* and, echoing Rodó, believed intellectual labor should not be reduced to utilitarian purposes, but should be a "disinterested activity," founded on the act of contemplation and intellectual sympathy and guided by the ethics of harmony and beauty.[22] For this cognitive activity they coined the term "*atelesis*," a "spontaneous and spiritual energy," in the words of José Vasconcelos, unleashed from the chains of the material world.[23] Guzmán, for his part, wrote about the ideal of "*vida atélica*," or life illuminated by unencumbered intellectual curiosity, open to the plurality of form and aesthetic contemplation.[24]

Arielismo, in its Mexican version of *atelesis*, summed up the reformist ideology of a young generation eager to carve a niche for itself, with new ideas and sensibility, in a cultural and political world still dominated by the "*científicos*" of the Porfiriato.[25] In this struggle, the *ateneístas* opened a space for the emergence of a new kind of public intellectual, one whose authority would be grounded on spirituality, humanistic culture, and idealism. The influence and legitimacy of this authoritative position would peak in the 1920s, after the revolution had destroyed the ancien régime and the intellectual and political dominance of the *científicos*.

Arielismo and El águila

Two interconnected ideas of Arielismo had an enduring influence on Martín Luis Guzmán and other intellectuals of his generation. The first was Rodó's insistence on the intimate relationship and, in fact, interdependence between aesthetics and ethics, an idea profoundly ingrained in ancient classical culture: beauty as a way of communicating virtue.[26] The second was the notion of "spiritual selection," a criterion of social discrimination whereby Rodó envisioned aesthetic sensibility and intellectual culture producing "natural" hierarchical divisions within society that would be recognized and admitted by all.[27]

The first idea is critical to Guzmán's aesthetic approach to the revolution, for in his assessment of events he uses light to connote moral or spiritual knowledge and meaning, as critics have pointed out.[28] The absence of light eliminates visibility (the aesthetic experience), signals the depravation of spirituality, that is, an inferior stage of human existence—a world where moral turpitude or the lack of human virtue reigns. Stories in which blind impulse or violence prevail over reason take place in darkness ("The Race in the Shadows," "The Carnival of the Bullets"). Beauty, spirituality, and liberty, on the other hand, are associated with light, as in Guzmán's entrance to Mexico City in "The Return of a Rebel." Culture is defined as "luz y suavidad" (light and gentleness [360]); that is, it contains aesthetic and moral qualities. At times, the author's use of light alternates between chapters to emphasize, by contrast, his didactic message. The uplifting "The Piety of General Iturbe" thus follows the alcoholic debasement of soldiers in "A Night in Culiacán." The former takes place in broad daylight, and Iturbe, who has ordered the construction of a shrine at the top of a hill, is portrayed as a man of superior moral quality.

Guzmán's aesthetics and moral gaze are readily apparent in the treatment of national space, which he divides into rural and urban zones. Rural zones untouched by modern technology hold few redeeming qualities for the Arielista Guzmán. In the northern sierra, inhabited by Yaqui Indians, he breathes "a dense atmosphere of barbarism, incivility, of satisfaction with the crude, the formless, the primitive and ugly, which made the spirit shrink" (70–80). In contrast, well-kept urban settings are spatial metaphors of the moral beauty Guzmán associates with the presence of modernity. The small city of San Luis Potosí, he remembers, "seemed to me a species of urban paradise: such clean, well-paved thoroughfares; such intimate, inviting squares; such well-laid-out streets; such pleasant architecture! . . . There was something urbanized and domestic in the surrounding country, a certain refinement which seemed to radiate from the city to the countryside, from the city to the sky, and had a civilizing influence on all alike" (259–269).

San Luis Potosí is aesthetically appealing because the rational norm that precedes the exercise of modern citizenship—engineered, functional space; light; and public hygiene—has replaced the uncertainty of chaos. An orderly, harmonious society is to be found in locations where the domestication of space has been achieved.

Guzmán locates the geographic center of urban modernity in the Valley of Mexico. In 1915, *ateneísta* Alfonso Reyes labeled the valley, literally and metaphorically, the region "where the air is clear" and went on to explain its invigorating effect on the life of the soul and the intellect.[29] Likewise, Mexico City is the gravitational center of Guzmán's spiritual map of the nation inasmuch as it is the space most heavily endowed with qualities of *atelesis:* transparent atmosphere, visual clarity, majestic setting. It is a feast for the eyes that arouses the experience of the sublime: "a world of serene happiness whose essential quality resided in the invariable achievement of equilibrium: equilibrium between design and detail, line and color, surface and edge, mass and contour, the diaphanous and the opaque"(192). Perfect harmony reigns in Mexico City. In the author's hierarchical system it is the symbolic seat of national values and power, the inevitable locus of the country's civilization and culture.

Guzmán's aesthetic and moral geography presupposes the superiority of city life—the site of modernity, civility, and rationality—over rural existence, as well as the cultural and political hegemony of Mexico City over the rest of the country. Thus in passages where the representatives of the rural world overtake urban political space, Guzmán treats the transgression with open sarcasm and contempt. In "Zapata's Troops in the Palace," Gen. Eufemio Zapata is the custodian of the National Palace, in Mexico City. When Zapata walked up the elegant staircase of honor, writes Guzmán, he "looked like a stableboy who was trying to act like a president . . . Every time he moved his foot, his foot seemed surprised at not getting tangled in brush and undergrowth. Every time he stretched out his hand, it seemed to feel in vain for a tree trunk or boulder" (327). The narrator's ironic description stresses the incompatibility of the rustic man in control of the National Palace and the urban forms of polity required to occupy, in his view, the political seat of national government. The treatment of space in *El águila*, it follows, reveals the author's fear of the displacement of the urban code of life, refined and privileged, with the raw power of rural Mexico.

The concentration of "spiritual" qualities in Mexico City sanctions the dominance of city life and urban citizenship over the campesino tradition of sociability and culture, shared by the majority of the population.[30] The location is also significant in that it amounts to an implicit endorsement of the project of centralization, that is, of subordinating rural

Mexico to the political control of the capital city. Although the revolution is fought in the country by—mostly—agrarian armies, to view Mexico's provinces or states as strong political entities is not contemplated in *El águila*. On the contrary, Guzmán's spatial politics is at one with the centralist ideology of Venustiano Carranza and Plutarco Elías Calles, his bitter enemies.[31]

Along with space, Guzmán evaluates characters in accordance with the criterion of "spiritual selection," or moral Darwinism. At the apex of his aesthetic, moral, and social order, or spiritual pyramid, are the educators. Here Guzmán appears to closely follow Rodó's enthusiasm for the figure of the schoolteacher as a civic and moral leader whose function in society is to inspire and elevate the youth of Latin America through culture.[32] One pedagogue is Delfino Valenzuela, whom the narrator judges to be above generals and presidents because he dedicates himself to the transmission of knowledge and upholds the sacred principle of patriotism.

Another pedagogue is scientist Valentín Gama, a university professor who is asked to join the provisional government of Eulalio Gutiérrez. When the narrator visits his old professor he finds him "[b]arricaded behind piles of books and instruments" and so absorbed in his meditations that he appears "fleshless." "It was as though matter were turning into spirit, as though the physical were being burned away in the unquenchable flame of the soul" (332). Gama falls into the stereotype of the brilliant but absent-minded professor, whereas Valenzuela is more of a romantic figure. Both illustrate the desirable movement away from self-interest and material gratification; they are cast as role models of a moral order moved by civic duty and deeply seated patriotic feelings.

Valenzuela and Gama are, however, marginal figures in the turmoil of the war, more spectators than actors; they represent the exception to the norm in *El águila*. The characters that crowd Guzmán's recollection are generals, politicians, and soldiers who seldom rise above personal ambition or brute camaraderie. Few historical figures escape unharmed from the judgment of the author's moral reformism. Among them are Gen. Felipe Ángeles, an archetypal "atelic" figure, "alone and melancholy, his head lost in the stars" (50), and the sad and taciturn Rafael Buelna, who, unlike other generals, is aware of the "moral tragedy" of the revolution, the almost impossible mission of social regeneration; thus his depressive mood. The romantic aura and deep spirituality that surround both men are markers of their prominence in the author's moral configuration.

Other characters occupy an intermediate position. Guzmán's liking for the Villista general José Isabel Robles, for example, is explained by the fact that the author surprises him reading Plutarch's *Parallel Lives.* Robles may be a rude and, at times, violent soldier, but by reading one of the classics he redeems himself in the eyes of Guzmán, who sees in this personal inclination a sign of hope, a definite potential for moral improvement.

The unruly revolutionary masses occupy the bottom of the spiritual order. They are ignorant, violent, uncouth, and insensitive, the antithesis of the *vida atélica.* The inebriated soldiers in Culiacán seem to Guzmán "the soul of a huge reptile with hundreds of heads, thousands of feet, which [crawl], drunken and sluggish" (94). Rodolfo Fierro, Villa's brutal lieutenant, personally—and joyously—kills three hundred prisoners in "The Carnival of the Bullets" (163). When the ragged masses travel by train, a symbol of modern transportation and progress, orderly comfort and civility undergo a regressive transformation. The "distinction between freight and passenger cars," the narrator complains, "had disappeared; coaches and boxcars were used interchangeably for the same purposes. As a result the difference between people and bundles had disappeared." In the aisles and on the platforms of the coaches, he notices the rediscovery of a long-forgotten "pleasure": people "eating on the floor, amidst all the dirt and rubbish" (126). The revolutionary masses are a depressing spectacle, a repeated return to an earlier, undifferentiated state of chaos and amorality, of self-willed degradation. They are filthy and subhuman, their manners and mentality portrayed as a setback for the cause of civilization and what Guzmán calls the main objective of the revolution: the "moral regeneration" of the country.

Yet Guzmán is ambivalent about them. At times, the same ragged masses are portrayed as the intimate, almost secret, purveyors of the "spirit" of the nation. His poetic appraisal of revolutionary soldiers, "rifle on shoulder, and hip as though grown to the shape of the revolver, sure of their way, indifferent to their fate" (75), summons the presence of a purposeful, courageous, even suicidal collective soul. The "intimate essence of Mexico" (75), the narrator remarks, is located here. The emergence of a new cultural consciousness can be detected in this and similar passages. Mexicanness is not to be found in the manners of polite society (Guzmán's world), but in the resolute body movements of the Other the narrator alternately fears, despises, and, at times, admires. Paradoxically, this "essence" is marked by the fighters' distinctive "manliness," a quality (the willingness to fight against oppression) the author finds unsettlingly redeeming, especially when it comes to Villa.

Guzmán's assumption that the aesthetic is the essential precondition of the moral and his categorization of the revolution's historical actors, inspired by Rodó's criterion of "spiritual selection," reflect the influence of the tradition of Arielismo in *El águila*. This ideological framework condemns the masses to a social and political position of subalternity as long as they remain morally indifferent to the prerogatives and values of urban citizenship and culture. Yet, sporadically, the author sketches evocative images of the fighting masses that attest to the rise of "spiritual nationalism" among the Mexican cultural elite of the 1920s. It follows that Guzmán's aesthetic treatment of the rank and file in *El águila* entails negotiating a symbolic place for the still-belligerent masses in the social imaginary of the nation, an ambivalent enterprise that is most egregiously condensed in the literary treatment of Gen. Francisco Villa.

CONSTRUCTING CULTURAL SUBALTERNITY: VILLA AND THE CIVILIZING PROCESS

In Part 1 of *El águila y la serpiente* the narrator mentions how in late 1913 he caught his first "glimpse" of General Villa in Ciudad Juárez. The city had just fallen into the hands of the revolutionary forces, and Villa, then a rising star in the Constitutionalist movement, was being sought by political agents and sympathizers. Guzmán was one of them. Lodged in El Paso, Texas, Guzmán and friends Alberto J. Pani and Neftalí Amador, all Liberal Maderistas, cross the border and make their way to Villa headquarters, located on the outskirts of Ciudad Juárez. As they walk, the narrator observes, with a certain discomfort, the gradual disappearance of external signs of urban life—first, the absence of public lighting; a few blocks down, unpaved streets. At one point, sidewalks vanish altogether. Finally, they arrive at their destination "in the blackness of the night" (40), where the countryside begins. Figuratively, the spatial displacement from north to south of the border is a journey to the world of the formless, of what has not yet been subjected, as on the American side, to the civilizing principles of geometry and order. They have entered a more primitive world.

In the poorly lighted one-room house that serves as headquarters, the narrator finds Villa lying in the darkest corner. The visitors approach his bed. Two chairs are placed in a semicircle for Pani and Amador; Guzmán is invited to sit on the very edge of Villa's cot, where the "warmth of the bed penetrated through my clothes to my flesh" (42). More than the content of the dialogue, Guzmán remembers being overtaken by a feeling of estrangement:

> For over half an hour, a strange conversation went on. Two absolutely opposed categories of mind were revealed. Every question and every answer from one side or the other made it plain that here were two different, two irreconcilable worlds whose only point of contact was the chance fact that they had joined forces in the same struggles. We poor visionaries—for then we were only that—had come armed with the feeble experience of our books and our early ideals. We came fleeing from Victoriano Huerta, the traitor, the assassin, and this same vital impulse, with everything that was good and generous in it, flung us into the arms of Pancho Villa, who had more of a jaguar about him than a man. A jaguar tamed, for the moment, for our work, or for what we believed was our work; a jaguar whose back we stroked with trembling hand, fearful that at any moment a paw might strike out at us. (43–44)

The scene evokes with extraordinary accuracy a defining image of the times: the revolution as the fortuitous encounter of two very different worlds: one, the world of the subaltern classes, rural and illiterate; the other, that of middle-class Liberals, educated and idealistic. The scene suggests that the war has created a dramatic readjustment in the hierarchical relationship of the two worlds, one hardly imaginable three or four years earlier. Villa, a former cattle rustler and social bandit, occupies a position of authority and power in the revolutionary army; he is sought after, respected, and feared while the university-trained Guzmán, Pani, and Amador find themselves in the humble position of newcomers and subordinates.

Guzmán's endeavor throughout *El águila* will be to challenge what he perceives to be the anomaly of this hierarchical relationship and to "correct" it, if only at the level of discourse, by exposing this unusual reality to the normative standards of the "civilizing code." From "My First Glimpse of Pancho Villa" on, the general is framed into the extreme paradigm of the "low-Other," an antiatelic figure whose body language is that of a dangerous animal (the jaguar). In contrast, the narrator presents himself as a disinterested and idealistic young man who, in the struggle to restore the rule of law in Mexico, must contend with the primitivism of the world of the Other, on whose actions the triumph of the revolution depends. Villa, therefore, is constructed as the narrator's antithesis, the necessary Other on which Guzmán consolidates his own self-identity and status.

"My First Glimpse of Pancho Villa" sets the stage for a quiet battle, one in which force must be countered by intelligence and instinct carefully tempered by reason. Villa, Guzmán writes, must "submit to the fundamental principles of the Revolution" or condemn the revolution to defeat by following "nothing but his own blind impulses" (178). Their personal encounters henceforth will be construed by the narrator as a challenge to temper, control, even transform the unruly Other (and thus "save the revolution") by confronting, judging, and exposing Villa to the cultural rationale emanating from what Norbert Elias calls the "civilizing process."

According to Elias, the civilizing process entails, among other aspects, a slow but fundamental shift in individual conduct: from expressive forms of violence (emotional discharge) to constant self-control in the affairs of everyday life. The move from outward manifestation of feelings and passion to self-constraint, the softening of manners, urbanity, politeness, is a behavioral change that takes place in the West over a considerable historical span, from the medieval to the modern age.[33] The process involves the "transformation of the whole drive and affect economy in the direction of a more continuous, stable and even regulation of drives and affects in all areas of conduct, in all sectors of his [the European man's] life."[34] To civilize is to discipline the body, a learning tied to the social demand for harmonious (nonthreatening) human relations in increasingly complex societies. The civilizing process, in short, is predicated on the individual's internal control of aggressive impulses, a restraining activity that is justified in the modern age in the form of morality. Physical manners and regulations are thus connected to "the historical formation of the self" in Western societies.[35] It is a civilizing model that begins to take hold in Mexican society in the nineteenth century, particularly during the Porfiriato, when the implementation of the modernizing project begins in earnest.

Guzmán's personal encounters with Villa in *El águila* cover and enact a range of possible outcomes within the "affect economy" associated with the civilizing process.[36] In "Pancho Villa in the Cross," for example, Guzmán and lawyer Enrique Llorente visit Villa, who is terribly upset because his "boys" are fighting one another. One of his finest generals (Maclovio Herrera) has defected with his troops and is now waging war against him. Villa's anger is such, the narrator recalls, that it "made our

blood run cold to look at him," and he remembers feeling "the giddi-
ness of fear and horror" (292). Uncontrollable anger slowly gives way
to calmness after Villa receives a telegram informing him that his forces
have defeated the enemy. He replies by ordering the immediate execution of the 166 turncoats who have surrendered. At this point, Guzmán
and Llorente, fearful of Villa but also determined to prevent unnecessary
killings, intervene and play the part of urgently needed tutors for the uncouth leader. Through rational argument, they convince Villa to revoke
the execution order. The general even feels moral angst when he realizes
his countermand may arrive too late. In the end, the prisoners are not
killed, and Villa gracefully acknowledges the sound advice he received
from his civilian friends. Guzmán and Llorente's role turns a potentially
tragic event into an exemplary tale of moral redemption.

In this story, anxiety is aroused in Villa only when he internalizes the
meaning of the established international rules for the treatment of prisoners of war who have surrendered.[37] Before being exposed to Guzmán's
enlightened rationale, Villa is free of any guilty conscience; morally, he
remains in a state of indifference not unlike that of a child or an adolescent, according to the civilizing code.[38] The change in Villa's personality
structure, from visible emotional upheaval to intimate anguish, points
toward the desirable code switching the advocates of the civilizing process, like Guzmán, would like to see take place—permanently—in the
general. The broader message is that military subordination to civilian
counsel and the rule of law (or of strength to reason) ensures justice and
social reconciliation.

No such internalized change occurs in "The Death of the Gaucho
Mújica." On the contrary, Villa orders the immediate execution of Mújica,
an enemy agent and Argentinean national who has befriended the leader
with the intention of killing him. Because the culprit is a foreigner, the
general's advisers object, arguing that the law requires an international
trial before Mújica can be condemned to death. A special trial is hastily
arranged, and the American consul is brought in to hear the confession
and sign the statements. Only then is Mújica declared guilty and executed.
Here Villa follows the law pro forma. He orders "more seals and signa-
tures" put on the paperwork (278), believing they add weight to the legality of the case, but the content and spirit of the law—due process, fair
trial—elude him. His overriding concern is solely to ensure the proper
punishment—death—of a man who, under the guise of friendship, was
plotting to kill him. In this story, cultural code switching, from the vengeful and personal to the impersonal and legalistic, is a mere formality.[39]

A more dramatic and perilous encounter for Guzmán is recalled in "Pancho Villa's Pistol," in which the narrator faces the direct threat of being killed by the "illiterate guerrilla leader" (210). The episode begins auspiciously with an amiable exchange between both men. As they confer about who should be the interim president of Mexico, Villa speaks to him confidentially, in "the mysterious form of secret conclave" (211). Disagreements prevail, however, upsetting Villa. The situation is unexpectedly aggravated when, at the friendly request of the narrator, Villa willingly gives him his enormous pistol, only to realize that he is now unarmed and vulnerable.

Villa's figurative castration dramatically changes his mood. Feeling shamed and deceived by Guzmán, his visceral distrust for city lawyers and his vengeful spirit abruptly surface. Borrowing a pistol from one of his associates, he takes aim directly at Guzmán's head. Villa's quick temper, friendly and intimate one moment, brutally menacing the next, that is, his wildly fluctuating behavior, stands in contrast with Guzmán's, who, in spite of his tremendous fear, remains poised in the face of danger and is able to weather the storm. In the end, his controlled demeanor impresses and "disarms"—figuratively speaking—Villa. Against threatening rage and the law of the gun, Guzmán successfully wields the subtle power of emotion management.[40]

The narratives about the Guzmán and Villa meetings underscore the symbolic confrontation between civilian Arielismo and military might, reason, and brute force, between the civilized and the barbarian. The normative presence of the civilizing paradigm strategically places the powerless Guzmán in a position of moral authority in his relationship to General Villa, who is imposing, but lacks the cultural and legal attributes (self-control, urban manners, formal education, strict submission to the rule of law, etc.) of modern citizenship.[41] Villa's untamed, aggressive outbursts, the narrator implies, make him unfit to administer justice or to hold any responsible decision-making position in the revolution's leadership. Thus systematic references to his violent personal impulses are not innocently neutral, but integral to Guzmán's ideological agenda.[42]

The conflation of the civilizing code and *atelesis* in Guzmán's approach to Villa and the masses fulfills two complementary, though apparently contradictory, distancing purposes. The presence of the civilizing code brings to mind anthropology's "denial of coevalness,"[43] in this case, between the intellectual and the soldier (the latter belongs to an earlier period of human moral evolution); hence the intellectual's disidentification with *and* "natural" authority over his object. *Atelesis*, on the other hand, is aimed at creating a safe distance for making the aesthetic experience possible. Aesthetic detachment enables the transformation of what is perceived as a disagreeable (and, at times, repugnant) reality into a source of pleasure (that is, a qualified identification with the Other).[44]

TWO EPIC NARRATIVES:
VILLA AGAINST THE MEXICAN STATE

Two conflicting impulses shape Guzmán's discourse of populist nationalism: one leads toward modernity and the future; the other construes essentialist views of Mexico. The former is represented, among others, by the author himself, who extols and embodies the virtues of citizenship needed for the construction of modern Mexico. But nation building also requires the elaboration of images of collective identity. These images of *lo mexicano*, as we have seen, are located in the revolutionary fighters, in the Other Guzmán is wary about, at times despises, but also admires (he attaches spiritual value to them) and would like to identify with, if only figuratively.[45] The tense coexistence of these two impulses is most visible in the treatment of Villa.

Gen. Francisco Villa is a site of conflicting desires for Martín Luis Guzmán, a source of fear and rejection, but also of perennial fascination. Villa's Otherness (particularly his hypermasculinity, or excessive bravado) generates fear in Guzmán, who, next to him, feels personally insecure. The general's threatening personality represents nonurban backwardness, a serious inadequacy, and, in fact, an obstacle in the nation's path toward modern citizenship and the rule of law. Ideally, as articulated in "Pancho Villa on the Cross," this version of revolutionary manhood should subject itself voluntarily, in matters concerning justice, national politics, and leadership, to the guidance of enlightened citizens, that is, to people like Guzmán and his educated friends (Llorente, Pani, Domínguez, et al.).

On the other hand, ambiguity arises when Villa's extreme Otherness is effective in more ways than one, marking a division in the author's mind. Throughout *El águila*, the overbearing and unrestricted Villa generates fear in Guzmán, but he is also a magnetic presence. One can surmise that this is the fascination the sedentary intellectual often feels for the man of action, a sort of compensatory dependence and subliminal desire for the vitality of the "low-Other" he has in effect sought to repress in social life. The awe caused by Villa's personality and life of action is most discernible in stories that touch on the antagonism between him and the Mexican state. These are stories that attest, paradoxically, to modern civilization's longing and admiration for the life of adventure and danger it is intent on leaving behind.

In his reflections on the civilizing process, Norbert Elias sees a correlation between the phasing out of expressive violence in everyday life and state formation in the development of Western societies. In these societies, he argues, the state's gradual control of the monopoly over the means of violence secures—theoretically, at least—the peace and eliminates the necessity of, or tolerance for, expressive violence. Only when such control is assured can the modern state assert its hegemony over the population.[46] In *El águila*, Villa performs the type of expressive violence that must disappear if the Mexican state and modern civilization are to consolidate. Such is Guzmán's reiterative view. Anecdotal accounts of his reunions with the general invoke the civilizing paradigm to expose, denounce, at times even relish, but, ultimately, indict the latter's aggressiveness.

Two anecdotes included in *El águila*, however, explicitly re-create and enhance the mythology of Villa's resistance to the power of the Mexican state. These are stories others tell in conversations with Guzmán during the course of the revolution. Retrospective (an aura of myth surrounds them) and epic (individual struggle against adversity through daring actions) in content, the narratives of Villa's deeds stress his audacity and resourcefulness.

In "Pancho Villa's Escape," Carlitos Jáuregui, one of Villa's closest associates, relates to Guzmán how he met the general in Mexico City's Santiago Tlatelolco prison and eventually aided him to escape. The story is mostly made up of dialogues between the narrator and Villa, whereby the reader learns of the general's ability to earn the affection and complicity of a stranger, the details of Villa's ingenious escape plan, his self-assurance at the time of implementing it, and the shrewd actions he takes to mislead potential pursuers. Jáuregui's account displays Villa's practical intelligence, decisiveness, and subtle understanding of human nature. In short, Villa's legendary traits (charisma, cunning, and courage) are dutifully re-created in this story.

In "A Perilous Sleep," Villa, in an apparent act of courteous civility, decides to accompany Guzmán and other political associates to the railroad station after a working meeting. As they wait for the midnight train, Villa, "a vivid and entertaining talker" (299), remembers an incident that occurred in the mountains of Durango during his social banditry days, when the *rurales*, or rural police, were vigorously pursuing him and his compadre Tomás Urbina. The *rurales* tried to hunt down the bandits like wild animals (tellingly, Guzmán's description of Villa as a jaguar also plays into this dehumanizing view), but Villa's account of his plight provides a revealingly different perspective. On the run day and night and unable to stop for rest, both men were terribly worn down. Urbina's body finally succumbed to sleep, and he refused to wake up. With the *rurales* closing in, a desperate Villa threw his partner on his horse, tied him like a bundle to the animal, and resumed their flight. He headed toward the steepest area of the mountain, shielding his compadre's head with his own body from rocks and tree trunks. Hours later, with Urbina still sleeping, they reached a safe, sheltered place where, finally, he, too, could lie down to rest. Refusal to leave behind his sleeping compadre, a burden that puts his own safety at risk, foregrounds Villa's fraternal abnegation, generous solidarity, the kind of human qualities his enemy—the Mexican state— is unwilling to recognize in him.[47] The primitive, natural man appears transformed, observes one critic, into a spiritual man.[48]

It should be noted that in both stories the protagonist is a social outcast who escapes from two repressive institutions of the Mexican state: the penal system, and the army. The objective of these institutions is to take control of his body or to eliminate him altogether. Hence in his individual struggle for dignity and survival, he comes across as a victim of state power more than as a threat to society. The state imposes violence on him, rather than his being the instigator of violence. The actions the protagonist takes to liberate himself from the grip of his oppressors are therefore morally justifiable, and even distance Villa from the strictly menacing and amoral image of Guzmán's eyewitness descriptions of him.

"Pancho Villa's Escape" and "A Perilous Sleep" open a space in *El águila* for the articulation of a point of view that is empathetic to Villa's plight. He is not the brutal and revengeful man who is "too irresponsible and instinctive even to know how to be ambitious" (178), but the brave, plain-speaking outlaw whose long history of defiance of the state made him, during the revolution, a mythical hero, an assertive symbol of popular Mexican manhood. It is a point of view that is not unrelated to the popular tradition of the corridos. In the corridos, a willingness or capacity to refuse individual submission, typically by a bandit, is due to a wrong that has been unjustly committed against him. In addition, behind the folk hero's actions a more general cry for freedom and justice can be heard.[49] This narrative rationale underlies Guzmán's re-creation of both Jáuregui's and Villa's stories. Furthermore, the author deliberately exploits the vernacular element (Villa's colorful speech, boldness, charisma, etc.) in an effort to produce enticing literary versions of the oral accounts. He thereby contributes to the construction of the Villa myth in the culture of nationalism.

These legendary narratives, however, given the author's ultimate ideological stand, do not remain unchallenged. In the end, they must be submitted to the order of the civilizing code. In "Pancho Villa's Escape" and "A Perilous Sleep," the authorial "I" takes control of the stories at the moment of closure to neutralize these flattering images. Epic action gives way to the mundane; high must recede to low. The first story ends with Guzmán's reference to Villa's control of Ciudad Juárez's lucrative gambling houses and the nature of the reward Carlitos Jáuregui receives for having helped Villa escape: the monopoly over the lottery games. The second ends with the unexpected appearance at the train station, or so it seems to Guzmán, of the lover Villa has been lasciviously waiting for all along. The image of the spiritual man quickly dissipates.

In the conclusion of both stories, the dominant narrative code moves in to relocate the historical character in the overdetermined role he has been assigned in the book. The main narrator has the last word, and Villa, the symbol of low-Otherness, resurfaces. The oral anecdotes about the epic Villa, the icon of Mexican manhood, are framed in a way that ensures their subordination to the normative order of written discourse. By writing the epic Villa into the discursive order of his own world, Guzmán symbolically appropriates this identity, making it "instrumentally constitutive of the shared imaginary repertoire" of an emerging nationalist culture, urban and middle class.[50]

In *El águila*, the images of the epic and spiritual Villa and, more pervasively, of the uncivilized brute are integrated into an implicitly hierarchical discursive framework that enables Guzmán to praise and bond with the spirit of the popular Other while politically delegitimizing it.

Chapter 5

SOLDIERLY HONOR AND MEXICANNESS IN RAFAEL F. MUÑOZ'S *¡Vámonos con Pancho Villa!*

MARKETING VIOLENCE, SEARCHING FOR MEXICANNESS

In 1930, the literacy rate in Mexico was 34.4 percent, up from 23.1 percent in 1910.[1] The increase was largely due to the expansion of public education and the literacy campaigns launched in 1921 by José Vasconcelos, then head of the Ministry of Education. The benefits were concentrated in urban centers like Mexico City, which had the highest literacy rate in the country (77.1 percent), about twice the national average.[2]

The growth of the reading public increased the demand for reading material, not so much from classical authors, as Vasconcelos would have preferred, but from the more mundane genre of the literature of cheap thrills found in newspapers and magazines. Because the Mexican Revolution was very much alive in the collective memory and also because most readers were males (75 percent) drawn to the subjects of war and violence, the print media sought to capitalize on this interest by publishing preferably gruesome anecdotes of the revolutionary war.[3]

Predictably, Gen. Francisco Villa, the bandit-turned-revolutionary whose life and deeds thrilled and terrified the population, was a focal point of curiosity and entertainment. Tall tales about his primitivism, charismatic leadership, military campaigns, and criminal behavior proved irresistible for the newspaper industry. Ilene O'Malley, who has researched Mexican periodicals of the 1920s and the 1930s, summarizes this fascination with Villa: "Following the war years, many people migrated to Mexico City, where peace and an improved educational system expanded the market for periodical literature, particularly for that aimed at the new urban masses. Among the new tabloids and sensationalist magazines which specialized in blood, guts, sex, and romance, Pancho Villa was one of the favorite topics."[4]

Not only tabloids but well-established "respectable" publications like *El Universal,* the country's leading newspaper at the time, included stories about Villa in their Sunday magazines, for Villa was a source of continual interest among readers of all social origins. The Centaur of the North was the stock figure of the popular revolutionary, a folk hero depicted in a style that frequently embraced an uncertain combination of admiration, humor, and class contempt—an ambivalent approach, to be sure, but one that captured both the seduction and the fear his name conjured up in the imagination of the urban middle class.

Mexico's most accomplished writer along these lines was Rafael F. Muñoz. No writer during the 1920s and the 1930s would be more prolific or adept in supplying enticingly dramatic stories about Villa and his men. Muñoz's straightforward, dispassionate narrative style and his "packaging" of stories in accordance with the journalistic tendency to concentrate on spectacular, unusual, or strange occurrences, which were the basis of his literary production, were in tune with the reading public's craving for morbidly violent anecdotes.

Muñoz was well aware of this appeal. For example, in *¡Vámonos con Pancho Villa!* a book that began as a collection of stories originally published in the newspaper, he includes an opening note in which he declares his intention to offer the reader an exciting work that contains all the elements of a popular novel: "daring, heroism, loftiness, sacrifice, cruelty, and bloodshed, around the imposing figure of Francisco Villa" ([1989], 8). His sensationalist approach and deliberate mass marketing are manifestations of what Carlos Monsiváis has called "a literature of pre-consumerism" in Mexican postrevolutionary narrative.[5]

Rafael F. Muñoz's life experience made him uniquely qualified for writing such stories.[6] Unlike most writers of his generation, he had not witnessed the violence of Villismo from afar. He grew up virtually trapped in the middle of a war zone in his native Chihuahua. "From that period I remember hardly anything," he once said, "except acts of war: greatness and crime."[7] One thing he did remember was Villa storming in and out of the city and the terror, particularly among the upper classes, caused by his troops occupying the state capital from 1913 to 1915. Muñoz, himself a member of a well-to-do family (his father was a state magistrate), saw Villa as "a kind of Huitzilopochtli [the Aztec god of war]: horrifying but enormous," and treated him as such in his works.[8]

This view is not fundamentally at odds with that of Martín Luis Guzmán. Unlike the latter, however, Muñoz's literary treatment of Villa and his followers often expresses empathy for and pride (albeit ambivalent at times) in their violent actions, thanks to the author's grasp of the militarized regional culture that conditioned the Villista mentality, a knowledge he used productively in his fiction.

Muñoz completed his formal liberal education (probably not beyond secondary school) at the Instituto Científico y Literario in Chihuahua. In 1920, he moved to Mexico City and shortly thereafter began writing for *El Heraldo* and other newspapers. The daily *El Universal* commissioned him to travel to Hidalgo del Parral to cover the story of Villa's assassination in 1923. That same year, he completed the second part of a brief biography, *Memorias de Pancho Villa* (the first part was written by Dr. Ramón Puente years earlier). The work established his reputation as a promising writer and an expert on Villa.

In 1929, Muñoz became a founding member of the Partido Nacional Revolucionario (PNR), the official party of the revolution, for which he served as a press liaison. He also joined the Sindicato de Escritores Revolucionarios (Union of Revolutionary Writers), a writer's guild affiliated with the PNR. A few years later (1936), he was appointed editor of *El Nacional*, the PNR's official organ. Muñoz, it follows, was an ideologue of official revolutionary nationalism at a time when this concept was being defined in the culture of the Mexican state.

In 1927, Muñoz was contributing a weekly story on the revolution to *El Universal*. Three collections of short stories appeared between 1928 and 1934, his most productive years: *El feroz cabecilla* (The Ferocious Chieftain, 1928); *El hombre malo* (The Evil Man, 1930); and *Si me han de matar mañana . . .* (If They Must Kill Me Tomorrow . . . , 1934). These collections were largely based on material previously published in newspapers. These books and the publication of his first novel, *¡Vámonos con Pancho Villa!*, firmly established his place among the so-called novelists of the revolution (Mariano Azuela, Martín Luis Guzmán, Gregorio López y Fuentes, Francisco Urquizo, et al.). Berta Gamboa de Camino wrote in 1935 that Muñoz was considered, in the world of Mexican culture, "the best story-teller of the Revolution."[9]

Muñoz's key work of this period, *¡Vámonos con Pancho Villa!* is symptomatic of the role played by journalism in the evolution of Mexican literature. The novel is not the product of a preconceived narrative plan.[10] The first chapters were originally written in the form of short stories and appeared in the Sunday edition of *El Universal*. The weekly pressure to produce dramatic anecdotes for a readership with a taste for the unexpected and avid to experience strong emotions forced Muñoz to "push [my] memory and imagination to find material."[11] He came up with the idea of writing about the military deeds of six fictional characters— Tiburcio Maya, Máximo Perea, Rodrigo Perea, Melitón Botello, Martín Espinoza, and Miguel Ángel del Toro—all *serranos* from the state of

Chihuahua who together join the Villista army. "I had written 80 pages," Muñoz later recalled, "and only one character was left: Tiburcio Maya. The other five I had killed in as many Sundays," when his collaboration with the paper was abruptly ended.[12]

At this point, Muñoz decided to turn his published stories into the first half of a Villista novel. The rest of the work, not written under the pressure of meeting a newspaper deadline, would forgo the brief dramatic format of mostly self-contained anecdotes. The vicissitudes of the tense relationship between Villa and Tiburcio Maya, the last survivor of the original group, whose mental inquiries add an introspective, even psychological, dimension to Muñoz's work, are narrated in the cause-effect, sequential style found in conventional novels. Hence the production of the text itself exhibits overlapping styles and the transition from the sensationalism of journalistic literature to the subjective exploration of character typical of the modern novel.

¡Vámonos con Pancho Villa! was written at a time when the search for *lo mexicano*, a branch of cultural nationalism concerned with the representation and the meaning of the Mexican ethos, was being appraised in popular and academic circles.[13] Villa's famous ruthlessness, his followers' deeds and excesses, provided abundant material for this kind of cultural endeavor. The popular legend surrounding Villa's outlaw years, his reputation as a daring fighter (quick on the draw, a good horseman), his womanizing, and, above all, his cruelty facilitated his portrayal as the quintessential Mexican "macho." In a country where the tradition of the macho was closely associated in the collective mind with the insurrectional, charismatic, and patriarchal appeal of the military caudillos of the nineteenth century, Villa ratified popular traditions and historical images already rooted in Mexico's past.[14] Since the widespread connection of rebelliousness with manliness had been reinforced during the war, the search for Mexicanness in postrevolutionary culture inevitably touched on the issue of masculine violence, or machismo, for which Villa was a formidable prototype. Regardless of authorial intentions, stories about Villa were tacitly bound to the ongoing cultural construction of the so-called Mexican character.[15]

Against the background of the marketability of violence and the search for *lo mexicano*, which strongly intersect and complement each other in the single process of modern nation-building, I will examine how regional elements of popular subjectivity are re-created and mystified for commercial as well as cultural reasons in *¡Vámonos con Pancho Villa!* My analysis focuses on the military code of manly loyalty and its relation to the legend of Villa and the ideology of nationalism. The structural and signifying function of gender as well as "the destruction of the bridge motif," which is central to the novel, frame my discussion of the text and of its relevance to postrevolutionary culture.

DESTROYING THE BRIDGE (1)

The opening chapter, "El puente" (The Bridge), was originally published as a short story in the collection *El feroz cabecilla*. Skillfully deceptive, "El puente" sets the ironic tone, tropes, themes, motifs of the novel and functions as an allegory of events to come. The chapter intertwines two exemplary stories. The first sets a young rebel, the daring and vigorous Miguel Diablo, against Captain Medina of the federal army, the man in charge of protecting a vital train route (a lonely bridge strategically located in northern Mexico) from an assault by revolutionaries. Repeatedly, Medina comes across as an impostor with regard to the manly gestures expected of an army captain. He has an "artificially hoarse voice," a German-style mustache (in vogue among Mexican officers, who admired Germany's military power) "that was out of place on his Indian face,"[16] and his power stems not from confidence in his self-worth but from the backing he receives from the army.

The narrator's unsympathetic treatment of Medina is in striking contrast with the assertive depiction of his antagonist. Miguel Diablo's physical strength, marksmanship, and arrogant acts of defiance toward the captain come across as genuine personal qualities and are highlighted throughout the story (he is called Diablo, or Devil, because of his mischievous nature). The narrator's point of view closely identifies with Diablo's riotous spirit, anticipating the outcome of the confrontation.

Miguel has surreptitiously killed fourteen sentries. Medina suspects him of being the sniper and tries to arrest him so he can be court-martialed. The young rebel escapes to join forces with other revolutionary sympathizers. He later returns and successfully blows the bridge to pieces. The captain, having failed in his mission, faces the court-martial he had envisioned for Miguel and is condemned to death. Here the first story ends.

Two aspects of this story require attention. First, the ironic reversal of fortune (Medina, not Miguel Diablo, is court-martialed), a standard feature of the traditional short story genre, is used to surprise readers and satisfy their desire for the unexpected. This type of ending is systematically implemented in the first half of the novel. Second, the captain's faked virility contrasts with and enhances the authenticity of Miguel's revolutionary manliness, which is the salient attribute in the military behavior of the *leones* (lions) of San Pablo in the novel. The distinction in the story between "false," or weak, men and strong, or "real," men makes gender a structuring category in the production of meaning about the war and relations of dominance in the novel.

The second exemplary story simultaneously at work in "El puente" is a deceptively minor one; it deals with the changing relationship between Miguel Diablo and an elderly woman, the humble Tía Lola, who makes a living cooking for the people working at the train station. Tía Lola rears the orphan Miguel and loves him like a son. She passionately defends him when he is about to be detained and is the victim of revenge by proxy when he escapes: she receives the whipping Captain Medina intended for Miguel. This anecdotal information about Tía Lola is woven into the first story.

After Captain Medina's demise (ending the first story), the second story unfolds, but unbeknownst to the reader, the narrative logic has changed. In the closing section of the chapter (which is also the end of the second story), the revolutionary forces are triumphantly moving south. Several months of intense fighting have gone by, and Miguel returns on a military train to the station where Tía Lola lives. Success in battle, however, has transformed him. Inside a well-lighted passenger car, the now handsomely dressed rebel, wearing a cowboy hat, an expensive suit, and a red scarf, is drinking and talking to his friends in a self-important manner. He is completely oblivious of Tía Lola, his former protector and faithful ally, who by chance catches a glimpse of her "boy" from the railway platform.

Astonished to see him and disheartened by his inattention, Tía Lola readily comes to terms with the unanticipated changes brought about by the revolution and in the last scene renders him symbolically dead. When asked in her modest quarters about his whereabouts, she coldly replies: "Well . . . only God knows if he has died . . . without the slightest alteration in her tired voice" (18). Miguel's stunning indifference toward the woman who fed him and risked her life to save him provides an ironic twist, which is crucial for grasping the complete meaning of the first chapter. Miguel's ingratitude and the old woman's reaction indicate that a different and less-tangible kind of bridge, the "bridge of affection," which for years connected the woman to the young man, has also been blown to pieces. It is another casualty of the war.

The estrangement and loss of Tía Lola's putative son to the war is meaningful in that it foreshadows the Villista soldier's plight in the novel. All the emotional bridges that connect the fighter to domesticity and civilian life by way of kinship or friendship are destroyed, for the culture of warfare creates its own self-centered code of camaraderie, pride, and honor (which often, as with Miguel, verges on swaggering), which is indifferent to the outside world.

The spatial and social mobility of those who join the train of the revolution and are empowered by it creates a growing divide between them and the noncombatant population. It is significant that this division again makes gender a source of tropes for the "production and inscription of more general effects of power and meaning."[17] Clearly, revolutionary success and the masculine culture of warfare, which confer a low status on women, are what separate Miguel, the rebel, from Tía Lola (the "destruction of the bridge" motif). At a more abstract level, civilian life and the immobility associated with it is a "feminized" space insofar as it is the space occupied by the female character.

The two story lines in "El puente" have the same characters and take place in the same isolated train station, but follow distinct narrative paths. In story 1, Miguel challenges and defeats Captain Medina; Tía Lola is a passionate defender of Miguel. In story 2, the rebel triumphantly passes through the train station; he is not eager to see Tía Lola, as might be expected, and is oblivious to her. It follows that the role played by Tía Lola in story 1, as an ally of Miguel, has no bearing on the outcome of story 2. Therefore one must conclude that the system of causality is different for each story. The same anecdotal data serve the narrative logic of two contrasting stories.[18] Story 1, an epic narrative, extols daring actions and the struggle against oppression. Story 2 is an understated narrative about the culture of war and human nature. The narrator's gendered description of revolutionary struggle in story 1 foreshadows the hero's dismissal of Tía Lola in story 2. Both stories share two crucial elements—the treatment of gender and the "destruction of the bridge" motif—which bring together the divergent rationale behind these overlapping stories. The real and symbolic bridges destroyed in both narratives subtly bring to the fore the paradox of warfare skillfully exploited by Muñoz in the novel: its epic, liberating nature (story 1); and its alienating human consequences (story 2).

War, then, generates a life of its own, vigorous and self-fulfilling, divorced from society. "El puente" is an invitation to the reader to vicariously join the prime manifestation of this wartime reality in revolutionary Mexico: the Villista movement.

The Spectacle of Manly Honor

"El puente" is not organically integrated into the plot line of *¡Vámonos con Pancho Villa!* There is no explicit reference to Villa or to the Villista movement at all in this chapter, nor does it introduce the novel's main character or initiate the sequence of events. In fact, as noted above, it was originally published as a short story in the collection *El feroz cabecilla.*[19] The inclusion of "El puente" as the opening chapter of the novel serves the function of a prologue: to acquaint the reader with the literary prototype of the future Villista soldier; to set the ironic narrative tone; and to establish the dominant tropes for expressing relations of power. The material and symbolic destruction of the bridge, moreover, effectively prepares the stage for the reader to enter the epic, self-absorbing world of the revolutionary fighter in the following chapters.

The action proper begins in Chapter 2, when six ranchers from the town of San Pablo, Miguel among them, voluntarily join Villa's army and are baptized the *leones* of San Pablo by General Villa himself. Miguel Diablo is renamed Becerrillo (Little Calf), a new and diminished identity that separates him from his former role of isolated hero, as he is now part of a fighting group. The narrative shift from the individual to the six *leones* emphasizes the collective identity of the new protagonist. Becerrillo, we soon learn, is a minor character in the novel (he dies in this chapter).

The *leones* embody the expected code of honor in the military culture of Villismo: a masculine dedication to preserving reputation and pride through personal valor, fighting skills, and extreme loyalty. They belong to a world where the rules of war and patriarchal society promote the idea that men must be "real men" (i.e., fearless in the face of danger) and try to behave accordingly. "What kind of men are you?" Villa boldly asks the *leones* on meeting them for the first time (20). The gender category of "real men" (Villa's desired answer) is not a natural but a cultural one, forced on males who, in turn, assimilate it into their identity and use it as a measure of their own worth. To be real men is a key organizing principle in the constitution of the soldiers' subjectivity, of the fighters' sense of self-identity.

The cultural construct of "real men" took shape on Mexico's northern frontier during the war against the Apache dating back to the eighteenth century. In this protracted struggle, "personal honor and fighting skills became salient to the construction of male honor."[20] The ideology of male honor permeates the *leones'* actions. To achieve military status and soldierly respect, they must be good fighters. They are aware that their honor depends solely on how their "manly performance" in war is viewed by them and by Villa, hence their eagerness to be at the front in battle, to compete with others for soldierly recognition, prestige, and glory.

The passionate identification of the *leones* with the code of honor of real men is what makes them tragic heroes. Becerrillo's devotion to the struggle drives him to blindly and inadvertently face enemy fire, and he is fatally wounded (24–25). In the adrenaline-charged heat of the battle for Torreón, Rodrigo Perea wrests a bayonet from a federal soldier with such intensity that he ends up impaling himself on it. Rodrigo "fell on his shoulders, throwing a spout of blood and a gaze perpendicular to the stars" (34). The one-armed Martín Espinosa, wounded in the legs, faces certain death throwing grenades into the enemy camp from very close range. Hidden by darkness, the crippled Espinosa ferociously yells and throws grenades at the enemy until his position is spotted and he is torn apart by gunfire; the cigar he used to light the grenades slowly "extinguished itself in his forever tightened jaws" (36).

The warlike qualities of Becerrillo, Perea, and Espinosa are supreme values that encapsulate the ethos of the revolutionary soldier: courage and generous self-sacrifice. Through poetic images of death on the battlefield, Muñoz pays homage to the *leones'* heroism.[21] These images also highlight the unsettling nature of their code of honor.

Roughly reproducing the narrative technique established in "El puente," with different degrees of intensity, each story sets in motion an ironic play between the code of honor that powerfully binds the *leones* of San Pablo together and the pattern of destruction and self-destruction that this code ultimately leads them to. A shaken Tiburcio will mercifully put an end to the agonizing suffering of the mortally wounded Becerrillo by killing him (in "Becerrillo"). Melitón Botello shoots himself in the head to prove his manhood, which has been placed in doubt (in "El círculo de la muerte" [The Circle of Death]). Tiburcio, against his will, burns alive the ailing Máximo Perea, who has been overtaken by smallpox (in "Una hoguera" [A Bonfire]). The tragic irony of these endings is integral to the author's hyperbolic style of enhancing the "manly spectacle" of Villismo (the "push the imagination" syndrome) to garner readers' attention.

The ending of the first half of the novel reaffirms the soldierly ethics of the *leones*. Tiburcio, the last of them alive, grows disillusioned with the Villista leaders when, in his view, they break the code of honor that unites the fighters by ordering that Máximo Perea, who is dying agonizingly of smallpox, be burned alive. Feeling abandoned by his superiors and unauthorized to fight because he has been exposed to Perea's disease—even Villa moves hastily away from him—the dignified Tiburcio, who cannot bear the idea of being a noncombatant, finds a rationale to desert ("El vagón 7121" [Boxcar 7121]).

The notion of honor in this segment of *¡Vámonos con Pancho Villa!* relies exclusively on the redeeming qualities of machismo. Muñoz's ironic but unapologetic exaltation of Villista manliness constitutes an ideological break with the approach taken by Martín Luis Guzmán in *El águila y la serpiente.* The latter sees in Villismo's bravado a deplorable show of brute force and senseless violence, while Muñoz perceives a popular expression of revolutionary subjectivity. In this, he proves himself to have been a step ahead, ideologically speaking, of the illustrious *ateneísta.* Muñoz understood that, in spite of its limitations (which he criticizes), revolutionary manliness represented a step forward in relation to the social consciousness of the Porfiriato. In the caste hierarchy of the prerevolutionary period, Ilene O'Malley has observed, lower-class men were exploited and physically abused. The denial of sociopolitical equality with upper-class men deprived them of their manhood or personhood. The revolution's assault on the caste system became a vehicle of social empowerment whereby lower-class men recovered their manhood by destroying an oppressive order. Inasmuch as the violence of the fighting masses was motivated by the quest for social justice, it carried the imprimatur of a superior form of consciousness.[22]

Liberation from social oppression and rebel bravado came to be intimately connected in the public perception. The tendency to glorify revolutionary manliness in postrevolutionary culture would make this attribute an essential ingredient in the constitution of *lo mexicano.* A major problem with Muñoz's celebration of revolutionary manliness is that it requires the concrete and symbolic suppression of the female figure in the elaboration of this cultural identity, a point to be discussed later.

Self-Consuming Machismo

The stories about the *leones'* deeds are tall tales of honor and death, as befits narratives about war written for a mass audience. For realism and commercial reasons, Muñoz approaches the revolutionary conflict as the ultimate spectacle of masculinity, and nowhere in the novel is this truer than in the chapter entitled "El círculo de la muerte." The death of Melitón Botello in this chapter takes the soldierly culture of machismo a step farther. Botello does not fall on the battlefield like his companions; he dies by his own hand in a deadly game of chance. Conceived under the influence of alcohol and reinforced by superstition, the game—a kind of Russian roulette—has thirteen men seated at a round table. The lights are turned off and a loaded pistol is thrown into the air. When it hits the table and goes off, it wounds or kills one of the men, supposedly the most "cowardly." The death of one of the players, at the same time, eliminates the bad luck associated with the number thirteen. The game, called the "circle of death," is designed to test the participants' nerves, to show their contempt of danger.

Botello, Máximo Perea, and Maya, the three remaining *leones*, are challenged to play the game and demonstrate that they are not afraid. They do so out of pride, and the unfortunate victim is Botello, who is wounded in the stomach. To demonstrate that he is not the most cowardly in the group, he decides to end his life and shoots himself in the head; he prefers death to dishonor.[23]

The circle of death is a deadly ritual designed to reenact the intense emotions aroused by the fighting (the sense of danger and the need to overcome the fear associated with it) and to test the players' macho code. The arbitrary and perilous nature of the game suggests that the trauma of war lingers after battle, engendering curiously psychopathological conduct. The purpose of the episode is evidently to shock the reader by creating a dramatic situation in which Muñoz takes the self-destructive logic inherent in the characters' code of honor to the limit, with a spectacularly gruesome outcome.[24]

Ever more significant in the context of postrevolutionary cultural formation is the fact that the game is a tragic act of pure exhibitionism in which the performance of macho "virility" has taken on a life of its own. Unlike what happens in other chapters, where violence is embedded in the struggle against the federal army, here it has been stripped of the military context, which may give it a transcendent, altruistic meaning. Uprooted from the war setting, the soldier's willingness to die and prove his manhood becomes a depoliticized, gratuitous act. Veteran Tiburcio, the most conscientious of the *leones*, points this out when he says: "Killing each other for no reason, because we are drunk, is not what brave men do" (57). Yet Tiburcio, too, is drawn into the game because peer pressure (camaraderie, sense of honor) pushes men to become prisoners of a manly identity that, while necessary on the battlefield, can be foolish and self-defeating elsewhere.

The socialization of death during the Mexican Revolution made the idea of dying more acceptable, or inevitable, and the masses' willingness to die for a just cause became a reasonable expectation, writes Carlos Monsiváis. In this context, machismo is an "act of social obedience" and not an act of private bravado.[25] In "El círculo de la muerte," however, the display of manliness has been abstracted from its original source and transported to the domestic, private setting. This marks a decisive step in the direction of transforming revolutionary machismo from an act of social solidarity in time of war into a prideful but empty histrionic gesture deprived of any revolutionary content. Subjected to creative manipulation, the spectacle of manly honor would have great popular appeal (the film industry quickly learned to commercially exploit this visually viable spectacle) precisely because it retained traces of social rebelliousness.

Muñoz's description of the *leones'* spectacular deaths in the first half of the novel exploits the literary and sensationalist possibilities of performing the ideology of machismo. The "surprise" technique, the twist involved in each chapter's ending, enhances the ironic effect and confounds and startles the reader. Furthermore, the poetic images of death exalt the soldiers' generous and selfless sacrifice and celebrate their stoic manliness. Seen in the larger context of the cultural construction of Mexicanness, Muñoz's hyperbolic images of machismo participate in the discursive process of shaping and promoting the creation of a national myth.

DESTROYING THE BRIDGE (II)

Events in "El desertor" (The Deserter), the chapter that opens the second part of *¡Vámonos con Pancho Villa!* are separated from the first by a two-year hiatus. The chapter is in many ways a hyperbolic repetition of the beginning of the novel in that it radically magnifies the antagonism between epic warfare and loyalty to family and friends advanced in the closing part of "El puente." Tiburcio Maya, now a peaceful peasant, works the land and attends to his family's needs, but in his inner self he yearns for the military glory of yesteryear. The basic conflict in "El desertor" springs from Tiburcio's nostalgic desire to once again lead an adventurous life of danger and excitement with Villa's army rather than meet the family obligations that tie him to the land and a monotonous, uneventful life. When the Villistas appear on Tiburcio's ranch and Villa himself, who is like "a sun touching the horizon" (89), demands that the veteran soldier rejoin his forces, the stage is set for the most atrocious scene in the novel (and in the entire body of Villista literature). Villa brutally solves the veteran's dilemma (loyalty to Villa versus commitment to family) by killing Tiburcio's wife and daughter immediately after they have fed him, thereby compounding the dramatic effect. In the closing paragraph, a stunned Tiburcio demands a carbine and, along with his son, silently joins the rest of the Villista soldiers. After a brief hesitation, he moves with his "chest forward, shoulders thrown back, head raised to the wind, ready to give his life for Francisco Villa" (93). We must infer that he is shaken but ultimately freed from a life of domesticity. Tiburcio closes ranks with the Villistas and recovers his identity as a "real man," though the circumstances of his reincorporation remain traumatic.

With the slaying of Tiburcio's wife and daughter, Muñoz reintroduces the "bridge destruction" motif. Now it is Villa's call to arms that demands the destruction of the bridge of affection connecting the soldier to civilian life. Here, however, the rupture is horrifying and of an unprecedented magnitude, because the author's main objective is to thrust on the reader the full intensity of Villa's incorporation into the plot. Prior to this chapter, he is an ancillary character, a vital but mostly distant point of reference for the actions carried out by the *leones*. Now he moves to the forefront of the action. The author has a strategic interest in projecting a foundational image of him that is at once shocking and extreme. Villa's unspeakable cruelty surpasses all expectations, because he must be immediately cast as the *non plus ultra* of the violent masculinity already displayed by the *leones* of San Pablo in the first half of the novel, a sort of arch-macho. Villa the literary character is born full-blown with this episode. With "El desertor" Muñoz effectively prepares the reader to enter the tumultuous world of the legendary Villa.

While Villa's heinous act is intended to shock the reader, Tiburcio's reaction is equally disturbing. The murders of his wife and daughter call for revenge, not identification with Villa. Nevertheless, the old man joins the Villistas, an apparently incongruent act ("madness," says the American sergeant who later interviews Tiburcio), but it is one that is consistent, though taken to the extreme, with the cultural rationale already present in Miguel Diablo's indifference to the plight of Tía Lola in "El puente." In both cases, the fighters are irrepressibly drawn to popular rebellion and the excitement of war itself, a veritable test of manhood, while the female characters are left behind (forgotten, killed). Miguel Diablo's break with Tía Lola, no matter how insensitive, and Tiburcio's break with his wife and daughter, however traumatic, are facts of life in a world at war. Patriarchy reinforces the social belief that male-to-male relationships must take precedence over males' relationships with females. This truism undergoes a radical test when Villa kills the female members of the veteran soldier's family. Tiburcio quietly accepts Villa's criminal act, corroborating the idea that, in a male-centered world, women are ultimately expendable because they occupy a marginal position.

In "El puente" and "El desertor," the emotional bond between the soldiers and the female characters ends in alienation and death, whether symbolic or real. Tía Lola and Tiburcio's wife and daughter are tropes for a life of routine domesticity that is sedentary and more civilized; they must be left behind or sacrificed because they stand in the way of the more primitive but vital life of nomadic warfare. The key "bridge destruction" motif conveys this break and provides the conceptual framework that ensures continuity between the first and the second sections of the novel.

Tiburcio: The Tribulations of Manly Loyalty

A different, more trying, historical reality has transformed the Villista army in the second half of the novel. In the first half, the *leones* are caught up by the military fever that swept Chihuahua's countryside during the rise of Villismo in 1913 and 1914. The second half takes place during the twilight of the movement (the invasion of Columbus, New Mexico, in 1916; the American Punitive Expedition and its aftermath), when only a few of Villa's diehard followers remain faithful to him. Short of soldiers and lacking the social support he once enjoyed (many townspeople who had supported him are now organized in *defensas sociales*, a local militia formed to defend towns from Villista raids), General Villa must resort to forced conscription, intimidation, personal charisma, and paternalism to keep his movement alive. The increasingly ruthless leader treats everyone with suspicion, as there is a hefty reward for his capture, dead or alive. Gone are the days when volunteers lined up to join his forces.

For a devoted follower like Tiburcio, the long-awaited reincorporation into Villismo is further complicated, to say the least, by Villa's deadly actions against his family. Voluntary and involuntary attachments (free will and coercion) bind the old man to Villa. These conflictive feelings add a new tense, subjective, dimension to the relationship of male bonding between the last of the *leones* and his leader. Loyalty to Villa, a man who "divides the waves of passions: either you hate him or you give yourself to him" (19), becomes an intense personal dilemma, a drama of consciousness for Tiburcio after the killing of his wife and daughter.

The dilemma brings to the fore the inner workings of the old soldier's code of honor, for if this code values male bonding, it also carries a strong dose of exaltation of men's patriarchal "rights" over women. The question of whether Tiburcio will continue to be faithful to Villa or rebel and exact revenge against him is resolved in favor of the former in "El desertor." Ilene O'Malley has noted that Tiburcio's "profoundest attachment was to Villa; his wife and children were only impediments. Villa also saw them as impediments and so he killed them. But he killed only Tiburcio's girl child; he spared the boy because he too could become a villista."[26] However uneasily, the principle of male solidarity, which is predicated on the exclusion of women, prevails. Nevertheless, given the brutal circumstances of the veteran soldier's reincorporation, the previously unproblematic notion of loyalty can no longer be taken for granted by Villa. Hence the rest of the novel is structured around a series of tests Tiburcio must undergo to prove anew his unconditional support of his leader. In this world, that can be measured only by trials of manhood.

Tiburcio starts his second military journey in the lowly position of foot soldier, hardly a warrior in the grand Villista tradition, but he slowly rises through the ranks by repeated demonstrations of allegiance. Ironically, his increasing closeness to Villa is directly proportional to his growing disillusionment with the caudillo's actions. Tiburcio disagrees with the decision to attack Columbus, New Mexico, and complains that his leader "ignores the consequences of his acts. He doesn't reason, he doesn't deduce" (126), a point of view that the narrator reinforces in a more vociferous tone with allusions to Villa's "madly bellicose spirit" (128) and "incomparable insanity" (168). Yet Tiburcio never fails to support his leader (as he never let down Botello in "El círculo de la muerte"), because his male honor is at stake. During the invasion, the old soldier and his son save the general's life. The son dies in the effort, embracing a machine gun that serves as a symbol of the fighting spirit of the Villista soldier. Villa is so moved he dares not lay the corpse of Tiburcio's son down on the ground because that would have "diminished the beauty of his death" (140). Tiburcio's personal courage and the sacrifice of his son to the cause of Villismo in Columbus make the old *león* one of the general's most trusted men, even a sort of critical moral presence, and leads to his induction into the Dorados.

The tests of loyalty reach their climax when Tiburcio is hunted like a savage animal and taken prisoner during the Punitive Expedition. Freed from the spell of Villa's direct influence and under terrible duress, he is given a choice between life and liberty if he reveals his leader's hiding place, or certain death at the hands of his enemies if he does not. He has a moment of hesitation, but quickly recovers his moral fiber and chooses not to betray his Villista identity. He is tortured and hanged from a tree, from which the rope "began to give, the branch descended, and Tiburcio Maya's feet still bled when the sobbing water of the Papigochic River kissed them" (206). This tragic, poetic image of ultimate loyalty and personal sacrifice brings the plot to a close. Masculine solidarity and honor, the ethics of Villismo, prevail to the very end. Muñoz is paying tribute not to Villa but to the Villista soldiers of the revolution.

VILLISMO'S WAR MACHINE

A thematic pattern is discernible in the first half of *¡Vámonos con Pancho Villa!* It is evident in each chapter in the *leones'* adherence to the manly code of honor. Another and perhaps less visible pattern emerges in the second half of the novel, one only hinted at before. As effective as the first in terms of meeting readers' expectations with its lurid sensationalism, the pattern focuses on General Villa and the culture of militarism on Mexico's northern frontier.

An overriding concern guides Villa's actions in the novel: to eliminate all obstacles and dangers that interfere with the strengthening and military advance of the Villista forces. A series of gruesome chapters reveal this pattern, whereby the logic behind the inflexible law that rules Villa's camp is dramatically reiterated. The pattern is announced in "Una hoguera," a chapter at the end of the first half of the novel, when Gen. Tomás Urbina orders the incineration of Máximo Perea to protect the soldiers from smallpox. In "El desertor," the chapter that opens the second half, Villa kills Tiburcio's wife and daughter so that they do not stand in the way of his rejoining the troops. In "Consejos" (Advice), a soldier tells the story of how the distrustful general personally shot a young recruit who lagged behind during the exhausting trek through the sierra; the message is that he is unfit for war or that Villa is suspicious of him. In "Diálogos" (Dialogues), Villa orders the execution of all Carrancista prisoners who refuse to join the Villista movement; the reader gathers that they are an impediment to the guerrillas' mobility. All obstacles, be they contagious disease, family obligation, physical and moral weakness, or anti-Villista sentiment, are speedily eliminated because, from the military point of view, the survival of Villa's army is a moral imperative that overrides any other concern.[27] Consistent with the centuries-old law of frontier warfare, Villa's brutally pragmatic rationale immediately suppresses those who are not considered able bodies for the war: the sick, women, soldiers lacking the necessary physical resistance, and the uncommitted.

In this second pattern, Villa embodies the laws of frontier warfare—permanent mobility and unforgiving destruction of human obstacles—in all their dehumanizing nature. Perhaps more important, the pattern presents a raw and radical vision of life, whereby war is not the exception to the rule but a way of life: sublime, barbarous, yet ethically coherent. The Villista tradition of war and its attendant violence is a permanent—normal—state of being according to this pattern, an integral aspect of human reality that the cloak of civilization, the modern state, and humanistic culture try to negate or conceal.

Although he is ambivalent about it, Muñoz's articulation of this radical view signals a decisive cultural shift from his predecessors Mariano Azuela and Martín Luis Guzmán, particularly Guzmán, whose Villista works were still enmeshed in the mores of Porfirian values (civility, decor, refinement) and the class and ethnic biases of positivistic thought.

VILLA'S LEGEND

Friedrich Katz has stated that three legends surround and obfuscate our knowledge of the historical Villa. The official discourse of the revolution promoted the legend of the unscrupulous bandit; the legend forged by the corridos depicts him as a popular hero or a leader of limitless cruelty; and the Hollywood legend made him a Mexican Robin Hood, a Napoleon, or a Genghis Khan.[28] Muñoz's Villa comes closest to the version of the corridos, though Muñoz does not exclude elements of other legends (references to banditry, for example).

Several interconnected aspects of the Villa legend are cultivated in Muñoz's novel. Foremost (as we have seen) is the popular leader's reputation for cruelty, which falls within the popular and "deeply ingrained" tradition of the Mexican macho.[29] The narrator stresses the primitivistic aspects of Villa's macho behavior by describing him in bestial terms, referring to his "beastly mouth," "dreadful smile" (91) and his devouring "like a jaguar" (92). Then there is the image of Villa, the avenger of the dispossessed, "the only one who could have liberated them" (106). The corridos emphasize the image of the charismatic leader who, like all popular champions of the oppressed, is surrounded by a quasi-religious aura in the collective mind. This is the Messiah, or saviorlike figure, Tiburcio is waiting for in "El desertor." "Someday you will see him," he tells his son, "and like your father, you will go after him, and will never feel fear" (85). He is also the military leader the people of northern Mexico imagine riding West, "red and ardent like the ball of fire that illuminates the afternoon" (130). Whether the point of view is sympathetic or critical, it promotes the myth of Villa, the greater-than-life leader.

The greatest promoter of Villa's myth in *¡Vámonos con Pancho Villa!* is the general himself. Aware that his survival and that of his movement depends not only on military strength but also on the psychological impact he personally has on his enemies, on his followers, and on the population at large, Villa relies on oral culture and popular belief to manipulate and spread the myth of his own immortality. Wounded in the knee, the leader disbands his men and goes into hiding, but not before issuing a specific instruction: "In the villages where you go say that the *changos* [Carrancistas] killed me. That way there will be more fear when they see me back" (170). The religious notion of "resurrection" is another way of projecting a supernatural mystical aura.

Villa's association with the forces of nature is also a critical element of his legend and enhances his semidivine attributes. Threatened by the massive manhunt that has led to the Punitive Expedition, an intimate knowledge of the territory allows Villa to assume a clairvoyant pose when he tells Tiburcio: "Just as I know the countryside, the countryside knows me. The trees speak to me when I pass by to warn me if there is danger, the roads show me the tracks of animals or humans. . . . I know when it is going to rain and when there will be wind. I know the stars and at night I know where I am going" (147–148). By propagating the image of a man of destiny who cannot be caught or defeated, who will survive because he is guided and protected by the earthly and heavenly elements, Villa forges the self-serving myth of the "chosen one."

The collective perception advanced by Villa himself, and by others, of his symbiotic relation with nature, of his being part of nature (animal-like), an entity that, like nature, can die and resurrect, has the cumulative effect of "naturalizing" his personal behavior and military actions. It is as if they were part of a quasi-natural order. And just as nature gives and takes away life in sometimes unexpected and violent ways, so, too, does Villa. His symbolic role in the novel is to uphold the unmerciful laws of frontier warfare, which appear to be as self-perpetuating as the laws of nature.

A sacred and mundane figure, Muñoz's Villa exists only in the truth of his legend. Muñoz re-creates the awe of Villa's legend, carrying to the extreme (for commercial purposes) the internal logic of the historical elements on which it is based. At the same time, the author takes a critical and ironic distance from the legend by contriving scenes in which a shrewd and manipulative Villa deliberately fosters the construction of his own mythology.

GENDER AND NATIONALISM

Benedict Anderson has defined the nation as an "imagined community," and one of the features of that imagining is the feeling of a "deep, horizontal comradeship."[30] Feminist scholar Linda McDowell has noticed that this feeling, though "theoretically gender-neutral, brings with it connotations of masculine solidarity."[31] Because the rise of modern nations is linked to war, sacrifice, and death, war is tacitly (that is, unquestionably) understood to be a male enterprise, evidence to the contrary notwithstanding. The exclusion or invisibility of women in the cultural "imagining" of the nation is an extended practice that attests to the power of patriarchal normativity, which manifests itself with different degrees of intensity in modern societies.

The case of Mexico is particularly telling. During the Porfiriato, the exploitation and abuse of lower-class men by upper-class men deprived the former of their manhood. This kind of class-based deprivation, as Ilene O'Malley has noted, also had a patriarchal sexual expression. Poor men could not adequately provide for their family or "exercise their patriarchal privileges of exclusive sexual control over 'their' women" in the same way as wealthy men could.[32] During the revolution, the poor fought and defeated their class enemies, recovered their manhood, and this "included the prerogatives of the patriarch," the right to reassert their control over women.

Although women participated in the Mexican Revolution as fighters, couriers, nurses, cooks, writers, and spies, their massive contribution to the struggle is seldom acknowledged.[33] Because the revolution did not attempt to destroy the social institution of patriarchy, but, rather, reinforced it by reaffirming the "patriarchal privileges of lower-class men,"[34] women's contribution to the struggle remained largely ignored. This was compounded by the fact that real or symbolic sexual dominance became a positive expression of lower-class strength and liberation from oppression during the war. Revolutionary culture, writes Jean Franco, "constituted a discourse that associated virility with social transformation in a way that marginalized women at the very moment when they were, supposedly, liberated."[35] If, as mentioned earlier, the discourse on rebellious manliness expressed a superior form of class consciousness in relation to the prerevolutionary period, in terms of gender, it, in effect, sanctioned the oppressiveness of patriarchal society.[36]

Muñoz makes gender the prime site for signifying relations of domination and subjugation in *¡Vámonos con Pancho Villa!* Gender is integral to the plot, most visibly in the fate of the minor yet centrally symbolic female characters of Tía Lola and Tiburcio's wife and daughter. It is at work in the *leones'* displays of masculinity and the manner in which they and the narrator "feminize" the federal army (in the character of Captain Medina, for example).[37] Moreover, gender is critical to the definition of national identity in the novel.

Just as violence reaffirms the manhood of the *leones*, violence against the foreign enemy (the United States) serves to define the masculine identity of the Mexican nation. As Villa's troops move menacingly to the north, we learn that, beyond the American border, "like a woman who bends forward out her window, the city of Columbus offered herself; she seemed to come to them, loose and seductive" (127). The narrator's feminization of an American territory into something seductive, ready and willing to be assailed by a "virile" Mexico, prepares the reader for Muñoz's treatment of the Villista invasion of Columbus. The town is described in explicitly sexual terms: "When they crossed that imaginary line [the border] they experienced a sense of sexual satisfaction . . . blood completed the illusion of a violent hymeneal entry" (142). The "rape" of American territory symbolizes the reassertion of a Mexican masculinity that has been emasculated by the continuous abuse and mistreatment suffered by poor Mexicans who enter the United States and are treated as "beasts of burden at the service of capitalism" (131).

One last aspect of Villa's legend is reactivated in the representation of this historical incident and its aftermath. He is the "avenger of Mexico's humiliated honor—the man who attacked Columbus, New Mexico, and eluded Pershing's pursuit."[38] This feat made him a symbol of Mexican nationalism. The novel identifies the patriarchal ideology of machismo and its attendant sexual dominance with a vengeful popular nationalism containing anticapitalist overtones.

Villa's faithful follower, Tiburcio, who is captured by the Americans, is also a figure in this nationalist symbolism. At the anecdotal level, Tiburcio's solidarity with Villa marks the success of male bonding over the "disruptive" presence of women. At the nationalist level, his participation in the "rape" of American soil and his manly endurance and silence in the face of adversity represent the ultimate moral triumph of the

Mexican character in the face of a foreign oppressor. What ties together Tiburcio and Villa and, metonymically, the "masculinized" Mexican nation in *¡Vámonos con Pancho Villa!* is the ideology of machismo, associated with popular rebelliousness, male honor, and anti-Americanism. It is a sexist identity, however, that is built on the premise of, and requires for its very existence, the literal and symbolic oppression of women.

The Mexican Revolution opened a space for the participation of women in national affairs. Azuela acknowledges this reality in *Los de abajo* through the character of La Pintada, though he does not know exactly what to do with her and quickly eliminates her in the most melodramatic scene of his novel. The fate of the female characters in Muñoz's novel suggest, to the contrary, that women have no place in the culture of Villismo and thus are deprived of any historical agency in the process of nation building, which is viewed as an exclusively male enterprise.

Muñoz is the Villista writer who most forcefully articulates and, in fact, fosters the convergence of masculinity and nationalism. This convergence goes beyond literature and is part of a larger struggle in the contested field of cultural politics during the Maximato. A power struggle began to take shape in the late 1920s and broke open in 1934, when Muñoz and other revolutionary intellectuals made a successful request to the Committee of Public Health to purge counterrevolutionaries from the governmental bureaucracy.[39] The counterrevolutionaries in question were individuals of "dubious morality" whose "effeminate acts" had the harmful effect of corrupting the "virile virtues found in youth."[40] Among them were homosexual writers oriented toward European themes and styles and relatively unconcerned about the culture of nationalism. This homophobic attack exposed the growing link between patriarchal notions of moral integrity, Mexican identity, and "virility" in revolutionary nationalism, a connection Muñoz—a cultural ideologue—vigorously pursued in his work. *¡Vámonos con Pancho Villa!* is a prime example of the new "virile" literature that was being shaped and also contested by other groups in the nation's mainstream culture.

Through Villa, Rafael F. Muñoz exploits the premodern sublimity of frontier warfare, barbarous and unforgiving, and converts it into a consumer product of considerable literary quality. The novelist resorts to hyperbole to offer the urban reader a thrilling glimpse of the Other, the "uncivilized" world, of what is free and unrestrained, along with the morbid and the cruel. This is a terrific subject in term of entertainment.

On the other hand, Muñoz incorporates this world into the mythology of nationalism. As treated in *¡Vámonos con Pancho Villa!* Villista violence is part of the nation's experience of self-discovery. Men like Villa, the author says in the novel, for all their faults, were what made the country "different," non-European; they were what made Mexico unique and, as such, were a source of pride. "Self-discovery" was, of course, a cultural construct that was heavily indebted to the tradition of patriarchy and machismo, hence its gendered bias and shortcomings.

Muñoz's view of Villa and Villismo contrasts dramatically with that of Guzmán. The latter obscures and suppresses the subjectivity of subaltern characters by framing them from the perspective of the civilizing code, while the former resorts to the manly code of honor to construct and exploit the perpetually warlike mentality of the oppressed in northern Mexico for the sake of sensationalism. In doing so, Muñoz, though not unproblematically, opened a space in the nationalist culture of the period for a more radical and uncompromising view of the popular revolutionary struggle.

Chapter 6

THE BATTLE FOR PANCHO VILLA
DURING CARDENISMO, 1935–1940

The Cardenista period (1935–1940) brought new life into the debate over the uncertain status of revolutionary hero Pancho Villa and his movement in the nation's memory. The regime's reorientation in political matters created a space in public discourse for the reevaluation of Villa's role in the revolution and his historical legacy. It did not overturn the ambivalent or outright anti-Villista rhetoric well entrenched in urban culture, but new views and voices were heard that, generally speaking, cast him in a more favorable light. Four interrelated issues that were intended to solidify the social base of the regime shaped Cárdenas's populist agenda and influenced the debate over Villa: the unification and strengthening of the labor movement; the priority placed on agrarian reform; the expansion of education; and the quest for national integration.

The presidency of Lázaro Cárdenas signaled a departure from the antilabor and antiagrarian policies of the *jefe máximo*, Calles. By 1934, rural and urban workers' organizations had become, for the most part, estranged from the state because of the previous administration's failure to meet popular demands for social and economic justice. With Cárdenas in office, a decisive move was made to implement reform-oriented policies and reestablish state control over the highly fragmented labor movement. The new president, unlike his predecessor, recognized the validity of the class struggle inherent in the relations of production and sought to achieve a "balance" among the forces of production within the system of capitalist development. Peasants and workers were encouraged to organize in new unions and received state support to more effectively defend their rights and fight against the *latifundistas*, or large estate owners, and industrialists. Cárdenas personally intervened in settling many strikes, siding more often that not with the traditional underdogs, the workers.

The regime's policy of protecting labor rights eventually led to escalating confrontations with foreign capitalist interests, which had little intention of abiding by Mexican labor laws. In 1938, a critical point was reached during a protracted strike by oil-field workers against their foreign bosses (Standard Oil, British Royal). After months of failed negotiations with oil companies contemptuous of Mexican Supreme Court rulings in favor of the workers' demands, Cárdenas settled the conflict by issuing a decree nationalizing the oil industry. The unprecedented action aroused feelings of nationalist pride throughout the country, and the regime was blanketed by a cloak of popular support.[1] Nationalization enabled the president to strengthen and dominate organized labor by incorporating peasant and workers' organizations, albeit in a subordinate position, into the political system's power structure.[2]

The new regime closely resembled Callismo, however, in that both favored state intervention in the direction of the national economy. Where Cárdenas differed from his one-time mentor was in his deeper commitment to social reform. He acknowledged the gross inequities in landownership that had motivated the rural masses' rebellion and made agrarian reform the cornerstone of his nationalist policy. During his tenure, approximately eighteen million hectares of land were allotted to the peasants, "more than twice the amount distributed by all previous post-1917 regimes combined."[3] Equally noteworthy, Cárdenas's land distribution was modeled partly on the ejido system, a traditional Indian form of land tenure that vested ownership in the community, not the individual. It was hoped that this kind of cooperative agriculture would promote social solidarity while improving the lot of the peasantry.[4] Along with land distribution came the agrarian bank and the rural school, reflecting the president's genuine, if paternalistic, concern for the material and educational betterment of the peasants and the Indians. Cárdenas, it follows, was more concerned—at least up to 1938—with building popular consensus and fostering national integration as a precondition for consolidating state hegemony, and therefore governability, than in immediate economic development.

The regime's interest in the peasants' welfare led to a positive revalorization of rural culture. This reassessment was aided by the rise of professional anthropological research.[5] Studies of the life and culture of peasant and Indian communities generated new knowledge and awareness of Mexico's agrarian and ethnic groups. The founding of the National Institute of Anthropology and History (Instituto Nacional de Antropología e Historia, INAH) in 1939 formalized the state's permanent commitment to matters concerning ethnicity and national integration.[6] The regime's propeasant cultural policy and the growing awareness of rural life influenced literary production. Novels inspired by peasant themes, by the Indian way of life (the so-called *indigenista* literature, which was written by non-Indians), and by the social drama of modernization became fashionable and officially rewarded. Gregorio López y Fuentes's novel *El indio* (The Indian), for example, received the National Literary Prize in 1935.[7] Even Mariano Azuela went along with the vogue of writing novels with *indigenista* themes in *San Gabriel de Valdivias, comunidad indígena* (Saint Gabriel of Valdivias, Indian Community, 1938).

The visual arts witnessed a second wave of mural painting under Cárdenas, similar to the one sponsored by secretary of education José Vasconcelos in 1922. Although more geared toward "social realism," in this wave, as in the first, *indigenista* and nationalist themes were the dominant subjects.[8] Cultural production, in short, geared toward popular nationalist subjects, stressed the plight of agrarian culture and life in Indian communities.

The first grand production of the Mexican cinema, made with private monies and official support, was the 1935 film version of Rafael F. Muñoz's *¡Vámonos con Pancho Villa!* directed by Fernando de Fuentes. The Cárdenas regime provided "railroads, a regiment of troops, arms, artillery, uniforms, horses and military advisors." The film adaptation was written by Fernando de Fuentes and Xavier Villaurrutia and was based solely on the first half of the novel. The music was composed by Silvestre Revueltas; Rafael F. Muñoz himself played the part of Martín Espinosa. The film brought together some of the brightest architects of the cultural nationalist movement; it was not, however, a commercial success.[9]

The masses', particularly the Indian population's, access to basic education was another major objective of the regime. Between 1935 and 1939, approximately forty-one hundred rural schools were built, an increase of more than 50 percent.[10] The Cardenista so-called socialist school instructed students in reading, writing, and hygiene; moreover, the schools were intended to help promote national, economic, and social integration by instilling anti-individualistic ethics, group solidarity, and economic independence among the students. Cardenista socialist education flirted with the notion of anticapitalist social change, but more often than not, it was simply the equivalent of rational and secular knowledge in the state's war against Catholicism. In the international political climate of the 1930s, the term had a futuristic ring to it that was invoked in reference to social and economic development (modernization) and the creation of the welfare state or a mixed economy.[11] Ultimately, "socialism" stood for collectivism, a kind of societal alliance that blurred (but was not aimed at erasing) class distinctions in the interest of a common national identity and shared goals.

The quest for national integration underlies the central themes of the Cardenista political agenda. Agrarian reform, state-supported unionism, measures to achieve economic and social justice, incorporation of the indigenous population into modern life, and massive expansion of education were all ultimately aimed at fostering the population's allegiance to the Mexican state—the sole and legitimate political body representing the interests of the nation. Cárdenas's revolutionary nationalism, most scholars agree, was successful in institutionalizing and cementing the relationship between the state and the masses while consolidating the hegemony of the former.

Cardenismo set the stage for a new cycle of Villista literature that was polemical at times. The key political episode for understanding this cycle was the president's break with the *jefe máximo*. Early in his administration, Cárdenas's agrarian reform and sympathy toward striking workers quickly led to a confrontation with Calles, who was critical of the president's populist policies and even encouraged social and political unrest among his followers.[12] In response, Cárdenas exiled the former president in April 1936. The expulsion marked the end of the Maximato and of fifteen years of uninterrupted rule by the northern revolutionary dynasty of Álvaro Obregón and Plutarco Elías Calles.[13] This break carried the burden of creating new sources of ideological support from the revolutionary past that could legitimate the regime's populist orientation. The ideological juncture inevitably led to a revisionist trend that was bound to situate Gen. Francisco Villa under a new and more favorable light. The fierce Centaur of the North had fought against both Obregón and Calles and symbolized the vindication of popular causes. He therefore represented an alternative revolutionary tradition anchored in grassroots struggles that had not yet been officially recognized. In elaborating its own brand of revolutionary nationalism, the regime opened a space for the political rehabilitation of Pancho Villa, the most charismatic and controversial of all the military caudillos.[14]

Historical revisionism expanded the sources of the nation's revolutionary memory. Old, previously unheard, voices could now bear witness to the past. The president's eschewal of Calles's ingrained anti-Villa sentiments clearly indicated that the time was right, particularly for those politicians and generals who had been close to Villa, to remove the stigma of having served under the leadership of a "bandit." For the first time since the end of the revolutionary war, army generals who for years had remained silent about their Villista affiliation now counted with moral and political support to publicly and proudly acknowledge their Villista past.

The vivid memoirs of a Villista veteran, Gen. Juan Bautista Vargas Arreola, *A sangre y fuego con Pancho Villa* (Blood and Fire [My Life] with Pancho Villa], were serialized in 1938–1939 in a Mexico City magazine. Vargas, a member of the famous Dorados, sheds light on the fate of Villa's elite cadre. His memoirs provide invaluable inside information about the military qualities, character, and violent death (in most cases) of these faithful soldiers. They also serve to vindicate and exalt Vargas's own participation in the Villista movement. Silvestre Terrazas, Villa's secretary during his tenure as military governor in Chihuahua, began serializing *El verdadero Pancho Villa* (The True Pancho Villa) in 1936. Terrazas, a newspaper publisher and Catholic intellectual, was moved to write by the need to justify his association with the popular leader. He depicts Villa as an uneducated yet wise man of the people, loving and sentimental, although at times blinded by terrible outbursts of hatred and revenge. In short, former Villistas now felt that there was a space open for them in the discursive construction of the revolutionary past.

Dr. Ramón Puente, Villa's assiduous biographer and political agent, published for the first time in Mexico City a full account of the revolutionary leader's life, *Villa, en pie* (Villa, Standing, 1937). The title itself, intended to convey the idea that the book should be viewed as a statue or monument to the fallen hero, is suggestive of the new, more tolerant, ideological climate. The positive reappraisal of Villa also gave rise to passionate, and violent, rebuttals, such as the highly critical *Villa ante la historia* (History Judges Villa), penned by Celia Herrera in 1939.

The following year, Nellie Campobello published *Apuntes sobre la vida militar del general Francisco Villa* (Notes on the Military Life of General Francisco Villa), an imaginative and sympathetic historical account of the Centaur of the North's deeds. *Apuntes* was the culmination of a decade of research and writing on the subject of Villa. The second edition of Campobello's *Cartucho*, which poignantly re-creates the intimate connection between popular culture, rebel subjectivity, and regional identity in northern Mexico, also appeared in 1940. This edition, more so than the first, was an attempt to insert a carefully constructed regional pro-Villista memory into the larger context of national memory. With Cárdenas in power, her efforts to rehabilitate Villa now coincided with the official ideology of a centralizing state (to which, ironically, Villa was opposed).[15]

Yet Martín Luis Guzmán, with his *Memorias de Pancho Villa*, made the greatest and most lasting contribution to the historical rehabilitation of Villa. The monumental work comprises five volumes, four of which were published between 1938 and 1940.[16]

THE POLITICS OF REMEMBERING IN
Memorias de Pancho Villa AND *Villa ante la historia*

Martín Luis Guzmán's political travails in the 1920s and the 1930s are intimately connected to the rise and fall of Plutarco Elías Calles. The novelist, former congressman (*diputado*), and publisher had been an old political enemy of the *jefe máximo*. He opposed Calles's candidacy in the 1924 presidential election, a costly mistake that led to the closing of *El Mundo*, the newspaper he founded, directed, and owned, and to his exile to Madrid.[17] There he wrote *La sombra del caudillo* (The Shadow of the Caudillo, 1929), a political novel in which a chillingly cold and aloof character named Gen. Hilario Jiménez is transparently modeled after the *jefe máximo*.[18] For Guzmán, a return to Mexico was out of the question as long as the seemingly unmovable Calles remained the key power broker in national politics. By early 1936, however, President Cárdenas was in the process of effectively breaking up his predecessor's power base, and Guzmán, whose prestige as a journalist and writer was well established in Mexico, was again welcomed in his native land.

The novelist's repatriation was prompted by an invitation from Cárdenas himself, who, in all probability, was in need of intellectual allies in his crusade against Callismo.[19] One may surmise that the prospect of a Spanish civil war lurking on the horizon also influenced the writer's decision to return to Mexico. It is unclear how close Guzmán's ties to the president and his regime were, but it is known that he mingled with the upper echelons of the ruling circle and even engaged in joint business ventures with several of them. In 1939, in partnership with two prominent Cardenista politicians,[20] he cofounded Edición y Distribución Ibero-Americana de Publicaciones, S.A. (EDIAPSA), an umbrella group that in the following years would establish publishing houses, book distributors, and bookstores.

As for his writing, official documents dating from 1937 to 1940 reveal that Guzmán was engaged in a project to write a history of the revolution, apparently with the president's consent.[21] The history never materialized, for reasons that have yet to be determined. Instead, Guzmán wrote *Memorias de Pancho Villa*, an ambitious, sympathetic, and voluminous work in which he attempted to reconstruct Villa's memoirs as if the revolutionary himself had dictated them. It was to be the greatest work of populist literature of the period.

Two fortuitous circumstances directly contributed to the writing of *Memorias*, according to Guzmán. First, his friend Nellie Campobello, a staunch Villa defender, convinced one of Villa's widows, Austreberta Rentería, to lend or donate documents from the general's archive to Guzmán.[22] These documents contained autobiographical information dictated by Villa to his secretary, Manuel Bauche Alcalde, in 1914, and other data on his military career. Another source was the informal conversations Guzmán had with Villa in 1913–1914, which, he assures us, he immediately and faithfully wrote down.[23]

His return to Mexico and access to the general's papers shortly after he arrived seem to have energized Guzmán, who had not produced a book-length work since 1933 and had not written about Mexican affairs since 1929. The novelist was now in a position to return to the revolution and Villa, subjects close to his life experience and his literary and political interests.

The Martín Luis Guzmán of *Memorias* appears to have experienced a rather dramatic change of heart about Villa since the publication of *El águila y la serpiente* in 1928. In that book, he describes the guerrilla leader as a jaguar, a dangerously primitive man driven by blind impulses, who needed to be controlled and guided by more enlightened minds if the revolution were to succeed. Guzmán, one of Villa's political agents but one who distrusted and was fearful of the caudillo, eventually conspired against him and succeeded in cleverly escaping from his "clutches."[24]

It was not uncommon among revolutionary intellectuals to try to distance themselves from Villa in the 1920s. In defeat, Villa had become the epitome of the rowdy fighter, and in educated circles he was perceived as more of a bandit than a revolutionary, an image promoted by Carrancista propaganda since 1915. Members of the urban intelligentsia who had been with Villa in the Division of the North's heyday did not want to be too closely associated with so discredited a figure. The Guzmán who wrote *El águila* was not indifferent to this cultural milieu.

By the 1930s, the intellectual atmosphere had changed. The Cárdenas regime directed its attention to alleviating the poverty, injustices, and abuses suffered by the people in the countryside. This political shift entailed official recognition that the revolution had yet to fulfill its mission of social redemption in rural Mexico, which produced the bulk of the soldiers who fought in the revolution. The regime's agrarianism carried an implicit condemnation of urban culture and favored the vindication of the campesinos, the Indians, and the social outcasts. All of this helped Villa's historical recuperation. Often uncomfortable in urban settings, in words and deeds, President Cárdenas himself repeatedly expressed his preference for the simple ways of peasant life, which, he believed, was the source of the Mexican nation's most enduring virtues.[25]

Cárdenas's agenda involved a shift from urban to rural settings, "from middle class to poor families . . . from the highly restricted notion of privatized, individual citizenship to an inclusive notion of public, group citizenship."[26] His nationalistic program, in short, was based on the political and cultural recognition of the rural poor, and Villa, the champion of the poor par excellence, symbolized the kind of popular historical subject that the regime preferred. Friedrich Katz has summarized the change that took place in the attitude toward Villa after Cárdenas came to power and its influence on Guzmán: "I believe that under Cardenismo there was a change: Calles and Obregón had fought against Villa, they were responsible for his death and obviously did not want him vindicated. Cárdenas wanted to achieve the unity of all the revolutionary groups and vindicate Villa's image, and I believe he probably had a lot to do with, at the very least he encouraged, Martín Luis Guzmán, writing those *Memorias*."[27]

Whether the president actually urged Guzmán to write about Villa, *Memorias* certainly was a cultural undertaking that captured the spirit of Cardenismo. Politically, the book was intended to exalt Villa's memory as eloquently as possible in order to offset the guerrilla leader's defamation by Callista counterrevolutionary elements. This time around, Guzmán's Villa would not be a savage, jaguarlike rebel, but a highly humanized individual, socially redeemed by an armed struggle of national liberation.

The book was also didactic or exemplary in that it set out to demonstrate how a poor, uneducated man, the victim of a dictatorial government, could rise above his life of banditry to become the greatest symbol of popular triumph over a well-entrenched, socially unjust system. The first volume of *Memorias* sets the moral tone for the entire work and is steeped in the romantic literary tradition about outlaws: the honest man of humble origins who is wronged by society and rebels. Honor and survival, revenge and a quest for social justice are the driving forces behind the hero's actions. Although sometimes gullible or ill-influenced, Villa the hero is never evil-minded; he is brave and cunning, a keen observer, considerably reasonable and fair-minded, ever patriotic and concerned about the plight of the poor.[28]

Guzmán sought an oral narrative style that would convincingly reproduce Villa's tone of voice and popular speech. Villa's spoken words had been transcribed in the documents Guzmán received in a manner that attempted to "improve" the general's verbal expressiveness. Bauche

Alcalde, Guzmán notes, "dedicated himself to translating into the language of a man coming from Mexico City what Villa had said or ordered to be written."[29] To correct the effect of estrangement and lack of authenticity produced by these urban prejudices concerning linguistic propriety, Guzmán decided to write *Memorias* to mimic Villa's colloquial and uncultured yet richly textured rural language, "Castilian from the mountains of Durango and Chihuahua, excellent Castilian, popular, not vulgar, archaic."[30] The challenge for the author, which made *Memorias* his most daring literary project, was to restore the voice of the Other in a convincing manner without transgressing the boundaries of literary art.[31] Not surprisingly, all three objectives—the political, the didactic, the artistic—were wholeheartedly in line with Cardenismo's populist cultural ideology.

Memorias is divided into five books. The first four—*El hombre y las armas* (The Man and His Weapons, 1938); *Campos de Batalla* (Battlefields); *Panoramas políticos* (Political Panoramas, 1939); and *La causa del pobre* (The Poor People's Cause, 1940)—were published by the prestigious Editorial Botas. *Memorias* begins with Villa's adolescent initiation as a reluctant outlaw and ends shortly after the 1914 Convention of Aguascalientes. A fifth book, *Adversidades del bien* (Adversities of the Good), added in 1951 to *Memorias*, which was now consolidated into a single volume, records Villa's military defeat by the forces of Álvaro Obregón in 1915.[32]

Roughly one third of *Memorias* is based on Bauche Alcalde's texts. Guzmán gathered information for the rest of the project through questionnaires sent to former Villistas and conversations with intellectuals like Luis Aguirre Benavides, one of Villa's personal secretaries.[33] With the considerable documentation at his disposal and his penchant for historical accuracy, the writer proceeded to weave together an impressive amount of information on Villa's military biography. Accounts of persecutions, incarcerations and escapes, skirmishes, robberies and killings from Villa's social banditry days are followed by the recounting of his revolutionary exploits, innumerable battles, big and small, strategic mobilizations, quarrels among the revolutionary factions, alliances, and betrayals. To increase the verisimilitude of his work, the former *ateneísta* skillfully inserted and rewrote historical documents and other material into the narrative, drawing on military communiqués, telegrams, political speeches, dialogues with key generals and advisers drawn from written and oral sources and his personal recollection.

The factual content of the narrative makes the book a standard reference for historians. Guzmán added to these facts a series of personal reflections purportedly made by the general on a variety of issues and incidents. Among these are Villa's thoughts on President Madero and why he remained loyal to him, his views on the expulsion of Spanish citizens from Chihuahua, the patriotic meaning of his soldiers' deaths, Carranza's divide-and-conquer tactics, and Villa's own lack of education.

These expressions of Villa the narrator's inner thoughts and feelings play a crucial role in the configuration of the "new" Villa, for they provide a plausible and morally responsible rationale for personal acts of violence and critical military decisions. Villa's thought process is conveyed through the logical unfolding of plain statements, causally connected by explicative markers ("but," "it so happens," "because," "that is"). A limited and somewhat melodramatic vocabulary befitting Villa's notorious sentimentality adds credibility to the soliloquies. A case in point is Villa's meditation on the corruptive force of money:

> The rich men who hold power exercise injustice and cruelty over the people. But these rich men are not men different from the men whom they persecute and exploit. The rich, before being rich, are the same as the poor in regard to the inclinations of their spirit. But what happens is that when men are blessed with wealth, almost all of them are blinded by the desire to have more and . . . they no longer remember the suffering of the poor, nor do they think about what it is like to suffer under the tyranny of another. (315)

Another example is Villa's moral justification for the widespread revolutionary practice of forced loans: "The money they [the rich] had given me did not really belong to them, but to the people, who are the true owners of all the money there is in a country, because it is the people who produce it with the labor of their hands" (284).

Villa's class consciousness, articulated in rudimentary, commonsense language, is more telling of the populist rhetoric adopted by Guzmán than of Villa's otherwise undeniable social awareness. The notion that the poor are the true producers of wealth and therefore the rightful owners of the riches amassed by the affluent is not too far removed from the collectivist economic ethics of Cardenismo. The evocative reference to the hands of working people brings to mind the poetic imagery of socialist realism. By having Villa's subjectivity gravitate toward the regime's populist socialism, Guzmán was positioning himself as an intellectual ally of the president he had embraced on his return to Mexico.

Guzmán's introspective asides and his profuse recording of belligerent actions had a deleterious effect on the overall literary construction of the protagonist. Villa the narrator was gradually reduced to the role of the author's mouthpiece; Guzmán was primarily interested in the description of military events and political incidents, in the utterance of opportunistic ideological postures, and in communicating his own well-meant, if slightly condescending, ideas about the popular leader. The problem is evident in Guzmán's brilliant effort to reproduce a believable narrative voice. Using rural grammatical constructions such as parallel structures and pleonastic phrases as well as word repetition and popular idioms,[34] Guzmán ably re-creates Villa the raconteur; however, after hundreds of pages, these recurring stylistic devices become conventional and predictable, testing the reader's endurance. In the end, *Memorias de Pancho Villa* seems too controlled by the author's awareness of the kind of narrative voice he is trying to reproduce. As a result of Guzmán's ventriloquist act, Villa the man of flesh and blood remains a curiously remote, evanescent figure throughout the book.

These problems notwithstanding, Guzmán's considerable accomplishment should not be underestimated. He was able to piece together the most comprehensive account ever written of Villa's life to 1915, disclosing in the process a wealth of historical information about the general's military career that was little known in the late 1930s. By assuming a point of view that purportedly gives Villa's exculpatory account of his own life, Guzmán portrays him not as a cold-blooded murderer but as a fighting man who insists on the moral dimension of his actions and is philosophical about war and social issues. Guzmán presents a Villa whose violent conduct appears less threatening, more socially acceptable to the values of Mexico's urban middle-class, the key social group in the formation of national public opinion. This revisionist portrayal of the caudillo invites the reader to come to terms with and acknowledge Villa's emancipatory role in the revolutionary struggle. For political as much as personal reasons, Guzmán's literary effort to rehabilitate the Centaur of the North coincided with the official stance of creating a space for him among the official heroes of the revolution.

The publication of *Memorias* also had a positive, albeit limited, influence on the evolution of Mexican literature. Using a popular, conversational style to reproduce Villa's speech, Guzmán departed from a long-standing tradition of literary authority sustained by erudite culture and the presence of an educated narrator,[35] a tradition upheld by his fellow *ateneístas* (José Vasconcelos, Alfonso Reyes, Julio Torri, Pedro Henríquez Ureña). This was a noteworthy change for a writer of his intellectual stature. His work implicitly fostered a new kind of authority based on the writer's ability to convincingly reproduce the voice of the people. This kind of literary effort, already at work at least partially in Azuela, Muñoz, and Campobello, required a life experience of social and physical proximity to the masses, or a certain amount of fieldwork. Many elite writers rejected this contact, for they thought it unbecoming of their social status and even distasteful. To Guzmán's credit, and in spite the narrative and ideological limitations of *Memorias de Pancho Villa*, the path he followed unquestionably helped support the cultural legitimacy of this kind of literary authority. Guzmán's apologia, however, would not go unchallenged.

Shortly after the appearance of the first volume of *Memorias de Pancho Villa*, Celia Herrera published *Villa ante la historia (a propósito de un monumento que quieren levantarle)* (History Judges Villa [Regarding a Monument They Want to Erect to Him], 1939), the most virulent diatribe ever written against Villa. The author belonged to the Herrera clan from the vicinity of Hidalgo del Parral, Chihuahua, and had good personal reasons to oppose any official or civic attempt to rehabilitate Villa. Her uncle was Gen. Maclovio Herrera, a prominent revolutionary who defected from the caudillo's forces to join Carranza in the fall of 1914. He even wrote a proclamation labeling his former military boss a "bandit."[36] Villa's feeling of betrayal ran all the deeper and his hatred for the Herreras was all the more unrelenting because the family came from the very heart of Villista territory. Their defection was a personal affront.

Within the boundaries of regional life, the Villa-Herrera conflict was to be a feud of tragic, even epic, proportions. The brave Maclovio Herrera was killed in 1915, although not in battle fighting his former commander, as he probably would have preferred, but by friendly fire during a reconnaissance mission on the outskirts of Nuevo Laredo, Tamaulipas.[37] His brother Gen. Luis Herrera met a less-ironic but more-terrifying death. Captured as he lay sick in his hotel bed after the battle of Torreón in 1916, he was thrown from the hotel window, shot, and then hanged by Villista soldiers in front of the train station, where he was left for two days with Carrancista currency stuffed in his hands. Three other members of the Herrera family were killed in 1919 when the Villistas took a number of prisoners from the *defensas sociales* that had unsuccessfully resisted an attack on Parral. Villa unexpectedly pardoned them all except Maclovio's father, José de la Luz, and two brothers, Zeferino and Melchor, who were among those captured; they were sentenced to death. Such was the caudillo's hatred for the Herrera family that he made it a point to be present when the sentence was carried out the following morning. The Herreras died a "manly death," in the words of one witness, shouting insults at Villa as they were about to be hanged in the city's cemetery.[38]

The Herrera clan had its revenge a few years later, when Jesús Herrera, the sole surviving brother, participated in an elaborate and successful conspiracy to ambush and assassinate Villa. Villa and his companions all died in a hail of bullets as they were leaving Parral one morning in the general's car. Villa, at the wheel, never had a chance to draw his gun. He was hit by nine bullets and died instantly.[39]

Celia Herrera was a schoolteacher, not a professional writer. What compelled her to take up her pen was a plan to erect a monument to the revolutionary leader, which she vehemently opposed.[40] She wrote *Villa ante la historia* to make her case against the project and to counteract the governmental campaign to redeem the history of her family's executioner. As such, her work stands at odds with and, in many ways, is a response to the publication of the first volume of Guzmán's *Memorias de Pancho Villa* and to the influence the latter was bound to have on public opinion. In a veiled attack on Guzmán and other intellectuals who were rewriting the historical importance of Villa and the Villista movement, Herrera confesses her indignation: "It surprises me that the truth, concealed by passions, would flee the mind of historians and cultured writers, to the extreme of glorifying the bestial man."[41]

Written in a melodramatic style, Celia Herrera's brief book is organized into two sections. Her animosity toward Villa is open and direct in both. She accords him no honorability or redeeming traits, as an individual or as a revolutionary leader. Her message is plain and direct: you do not build a monument to a ruthless provincial bandit, a criminal who found in the revolution the perfect excuse to exercise his predatory nature at will and on a grand scale.

The first section is an inventory of atrocities allegedly committed mostly by Villa himself between 1890 and 1919. Cattle rustling and random killings, kidnappings and rapes, hordes of Villistas terrorizing the towns and cities of northern Mexico, and executions of Chinese are among the iniquities she records, at times, in horrifying detail. She presents extorting money from wealthy people by abducting family members as Villa's preferred modus operandi. She claims that another common practice was tormenting and burning his victims alive, particularly women. Her inclusion of the names of victims, the towns or cities and the year in which the assaults and killings allegedly took place add credibility to the stories. These historical facts, the reader is told, come directly from the families of the victims, though it is clear that some references are petty fabrications or are impossible to prove. Although no reliable information exists on Villa's childhood and adolescence, Herrera states that his criminal tendencies manifested themselves before the age of twelve in a propensity to steal chickens. She writes how, after personally murdering several men, Villa wallowed in the blood of his victims. This story, among others, suggests that Herrera was harping on her claims of the general's monstrosity. In any case, whatever truth there may be in her book—and there is probably a great deal of it in many of her anecdotes—it is clear that it is enmeshed in and magnified by the aura of Villa's dark legend, which she actively cultivated.[42]

The second section, more personal and moving than the first, draws extensively from the author's traumatic childhood experiences. Her vivid testimonial centers on the Herrera family's nightmarish life of hiding during the Villista raids on Hidalgo del Parral between 1916 and 1919. Their very survival was subject to the battles for control of the city between Villistas, from whom they sought protection, and Carrancistas, with whom they sided. During guerrilla attacks, the family always feared being informed on, caught, and shot by the guerrilla leader, so they were constantly on the run. The men fled to the mountains and fought while the women and children surreptitiously moved among the houses of friendly families and, when possible, escaped from the city. In one such raid, Herrera's father was killed in the fray.

Herrera's account of life in hiding, of the anguish and suffering of her family, has biblical undertones. The moral righteousness of the anti-Villa families, their relentless persecution, call to mind the travails of the first Christians. The climax is reached when she describes the desperate battle by the *defensas sociales* to repel the enemy and the subsequent capture and execution of her grandfather and uncles during Holy Week, 1919. With the crucifixion of Jesus Christ lurking symbolically in the background, Herrera enshrouds the local anti-Villa fighters in the cloak of martyrdom.

Besides vindicating the members of the Herrera family who died fighting the Villistas, the author's testimonial unintentionally hints at the underlying class-based nature of the local resistance (the *defensas sociales*) to Villa's forces. Herrera's testimony calls attention to the members of the educated, professional class (doctors, schoolteachers) and merchants who repudiated Villa because of their respectability, social standing, and the fact that the popular leader allowed large-scale looting of stores.[43] In Hidalgo del Parral, the Herreras were aided by people from all walks of life, most of them respectable, sometimes even well-to-do, and their lower-class servants. It was a fairly privileged group, upholding the moral torch of order, work, and decency, that had to protect its property and interests from the encroachment of the unruly masses. The writer's father made a living as a merchant, we learn in passing, a significant piece of information, for, in *Villa ante la historia*, it is precisely the merchant community, as well as any person of wealth, that is alleged to be the primary target of Villa's actions.[44] Occasionally, we also learn, the guerrillas were aided by members of the lower classes, who joined in the plunder of stores and houses.

Other episodes bring to the fore Herrera's own class values. At one point, she recalls the story of a decent *señorita* hiding on a ranch who, the author was told, had to kneel behind a metate and pretend for several days that she was doing housework ("pasó los días 'disfrazada' de mujer del rancho . . . hincándose detrás del metate" [75]), so that she would not raise suspicions when visitors arrived. The anecdote vividly illustrates the agonizing fear of many women in those turbulent years. In telling the story, however, the narrator also communicates her shock at the fact that the *señorita* had to degrade herself by pretending to be kitchen help—inappropriate for a woman of her social status—in order to conceal her true identity. The book thus offers a gripping account of the violence and instability that overtook Hidalgo del Parral from the perspective of a local petit bourgeois living under intermittent siege.

If Villa's "white" legend, apparent in Ramón Puentes's books, reaches a culminating stage in Guzmán's *Memorias*, Celia Herrera's book is the most important source of his "black" legend from 1939 on.[45] Herrera's book aroused the sympathetic interest of two members of the intellectual elite. José Vasconcelos, a long-standing anti-Villista, praised Herrera's moral zeal and her commitment to practicing "the fertile heroism found in truth" and took the opportunity to rail against those literati "who suffer from the moral complicity complex of siding with the criminal."[46] Vasconcelos had become an increasingly conservative and bitter thinker. He loathed the revolution and its outcome, had returned to the teachings of the Catholic Church, and was a devoted enemy of Cardenismo.[47] Consequently, his review, abetted most likely by the underlying religiosity of the book, expresses genuine empathy with Herrera's moral outrage. It was also his way of criticizing "the Freemason" Guzmán's overtures toward the Mexican government.

A younger cultural and political commentator, Salvador Novo, commended Herrera's work for very different reasons. Novo, the son of a

Spanish merchant, lived in the northern city of Torreón as a child and, along with his family, endured the hostility of the Villistas. He fully agreed with Herrera's account of Villa's "reign of terror" and scorned Villa's panegyrists, the "Martín Luis Guzmáns and Ramón Puenteses."[48] An irreverent and caustic writer who had been expelled from the government bureaucracy by "the flood of leftists hauled in by Cárdenas,"[49] Novo published his review anonymously, mindful, perhaps, of not openly antagonizing Cardenistas (in contrast with Vasconcelos, who always did) from the intellectual and political world with which he was frequently in contact.[50]

Herrera's *Villa ante la historia* represents a significant effort to counteract the output of pro-Villista literature. The book suffered from editorial limitations, however. It was not printed by a commercial publishing house in Mexico City, but perhaps in northern Mexico, a culturally and politically marginal center where the writer was then residing. The edition was most likely paid for by the Herrera family as part of its crusade to prevent Villa's posthumous glorification. The number of copies printed and the distribution had to be limited.[51] In contrast, Guzmán's volumes on Villa were published by Editorial Botas, the premier publishing house for the literature of the revolution at the time.

The four volumes of *Memorias* produced between 1938 and 1940 represent the greatest contribution to the attempt during the Cárdenas presidency to include Pancho Villa in the pantheon of official heroes of the revolution. Endorsing this ideological endeavor were the leftist intellectuals organized around *Ruta*, the culture magazine of the Liga de Escritores y Artistas Revolucionarios (League of Revolutionary Writers and Artists), which supported the Cárdenas regime.[52] Reviews praised the respectful treatment of Villa and defended Guzmán's re-creation of popular language. Voices in the opposition, such as Herrera and her commentators, were also heard, but they were more isolated or marginal, reflecting the minority position they occupied in those years in relation to the government's policy of promoting national reconciliation.

Herrera's acrimonious testimony is significant not only as a personal or family vendetta; it was an expression of the grievances and animosity against Villa that were very much alive at the time. President Cárdenas had called on Mexicans to put behind them the mistakes committed by all the revolutionary leaders of the past and, instead, to remember their positive contributions to the nation. However, too many people had died and left hundreds of resentful widows and orphans, countless brutalities had been committed, and scars were still open. The revolutionary war had divided the nation, and Villa's participation was still too close in time and controversial. Many of his military and political enemies where still active and working for the Mexican government. Thus Villa's official rehabilitation remained an unfinished task during the Cárdenas presidency.

Guzmán's and Herrera's books participate actively in the politics of remembering at a time when Villa's historical role was being reassessed for ideological and political reasons in the nation's official culture.[53] It is possible that neither book would have been written had not the state's policy toward Villa changed after 1934. *Memorias de Pancho Villa* is in accordance with and, in many ways, a product of Cárdenas's conciliatory policy and cultural populism, whereas *Villa ante la historia* is a bitter reaction to that same policy, a work symptomatic of the difficulty of creating a national memory that wished to overlook the painful memories of grief-stricken survivors.

By the end of the Cárdenas presidency, in late 1940, Gen. Francisco Villa had yet to be included in the pantheon of official heroes of the Mexican Revolution, despite the president's reconciliation and inclusion policy. Villa's political and military enemies who were active in the revolutionary government, particularly in northern Mexico, apparently obstructed his historical rehabilitation. Cárdenas did succeed, however, through agrarian reform, economic nationalism, and revolutionary discourse, in building the social consensus necessary to unify the country. His consolidation of the Mexican state's hegemony brought to a close the reconstruction era. Thereafter, Mexico's presidents favored accelerated industrialization and adopted conservative policies on issues of social justice, thereby distancing themselves from Villa's revolutionary legacy.

During the 1950s and the 1960s, the Centaur of the North remained an unspoken subject in official revolutionary memory and politics. It was only after memories had faded and most veterans of the revolution had passed away that Villa's status in the nation's official memory was revisited. In 1965, Pres. Gustavo Díaz Ordaz, in need of popular legitimation, decided to identify himself and his regime with the revolutionary "spirit" of General Villa and officially recognized his status as a national hero.[1] In 1976, the Mexican government unearthed Villa's remains, buried in Hidalgo del Parral, and solemnly transferred them to the Monument of the Revolution in Mexico City.[2] A half century after his death, the unruly Villa had finally been co-opted by the Mexican state.

Literature also moved away from the subject of Villa and Villismo after Cárdenas left the presidency. Not only did the state's cultural policy abandon the emphasis on social literature, but the emergence of an urban society and mass culture beginning in the 1940s introduced new themes that gradually displaced the revolutionary past as the preferred topic of the nation's novelists. After Cárdenas, few literary works on Villa appeared.

The Villismo literature written during reconstruction, however, endured. Villista writers were among the first to construct, using a variety of innovative narrative techniques, powerful images of a people in arms, of the revolutionary masses who, until then, had been left out of the national project. In this sense, these writers contributed to outlining the physiognomy and the attributes of a popular national identity, which had not previously existed. In the cultural imagining of Mexicanness, the emphasis on Villa's machismo communicated lower-class strength and resistance to oppression, hence its appeal; but it also reinforced the values of traditional patriarchy in postrevolutionary Mexico and the continued marginalization of women in the affairs of the nation.

References to manly behavior during the revolution were also used to illustrate soldiers' limitations and thereby suggest the place they should occupy in the reconstruction process. In the works of Guzmán and Azuela, for example, Villa and the rural masses are portrayed—the authors' sympathies notwithstanding—as frightfully violent, backward, and antimodern, lacking the intellectual and moral attributes necessary to lead the nation into the future. By cultivating this kind of image, which was sustained on the tenets of urban citizenship (social discipline, literacy, individualistic bourgeois morality, and the subordination of the countryside to the city), these writers—regardless of their personal views on presidential politics—became unofficial advocates of the modernizing, middle-class project of nationhood promoted by the postrevolutionary regimes.[3] This national project was fueled by two contradictory impulses, which Azuela and Guzmán skillfully amalgamated: the nation's cultural need to rescue and represent nonurban, popular subjects, people from the "hinterland," the proud source of Mexican "values" and identity; and the social urgency to leave behind the rural world and culture this same project was intent on transforming.

Campobello and Muñoz did not follow this ideological scheme. They did not write to overcome or leave behind, but to preserve and remember and to mythologize the revolution in the hinterland. Their works mark the appearance in Mexican literature of an authorial consciousness that was less permeated by the moral standards of the hegemonic class project and its contradictions. By emphasizing different aspects of Mexico's northern frontier culture, Campobello and Muñoz introduced an ethics of violence, associated with subaltern struggles, that was removed from the realm of abstract meaning and liberal conceptualization found in the works of Azuela and Guzmán. The latter always distanced themselves in their work from popular violence, because they saw it as a defining trait of the Other. In contrast, Campobello and Muñoz portrayed violence as a fact of life in times of war. It was something to be identified with, celebrated, deplored, or condemned, to be amazed at or indifferent to, or even to be laughed at, depending on how and on whom it was exerted, who wielded it, and why. The meaning assigned to violent actions in *¡Vámonos con Pancho Villa!* and *Cartucho* is inseparable from the struggle for social liberation and inextricably woven into the contradictory dynamics of constantly evolving military and personal antagonisms; it is always contextualized. Violence is therefore a concept that never operates above the lives and travails of the characters, because it is seen as integral to human reality, never something external, distant, a social behavior that belongs only to Others.

The writings of Campobello and Muñoz were instrumental in incorporating the border region's memory of Villismo into the consciousness of the nation and in articulating a radical view of the war that had never been voiced in Mexican literature. Campobello did so by recalling her childhood memories and by re-creating oral forms of cultural politics that intellectuals usually looked down on and dismissed. Her regional knowledge and perspective of the war also made visible the irreducible heterogeneity of the Villista world and the decentralizing ideology behind the movement.

Muñoz, in *¡Vámonos con Pancho Villa!* written with a more commercial purpose in mind, preferred to work with the regional mythology surrounding the militaristic travails of Villa and his diehard soldiers. Using—hyperbolically—the soldier's perspective and rationale for fighting, Muñoz displayed a less judgmental (and thus more tolerant) attitude toward popular violence than did Azuela and Guzmán. Campobello and Muñoz, in short, reproduced, through different means, cultural codes in which subaltern alterity was the norm, thereby opening a critical space in mainstream postrevolutionary culture for the evaluation of popular rebellions on their own terms.

Villismo's legacy is critical in the development of Mexican literature and culture. Villa's charismatic leadership and the northern frontier culture of violence associated with him provided abundant material for writers, who introduced new techniques and narrative strategies that drew from popular (and elite) cultural sources. Their success—in the era of postrevolutionary nationalism—was contingent on their ability to represent, convincingly, subaltern subjectivities.

My subalternist-regionalist approach suggests that two distinct narrative genealogies emerged from this endeavor. The works of Azuela and Guzmán became the "master narratives" for a literary tradition in which cultural Otherness is celebrated and endorsed as well as, paradoxically, discredited and suppressed. The *indigenista* social novels of Gregorio López y Fuentes, Francisco Rojas González, and even Rosario Castellanos respond to this tradition. The representation of Otherness in this tradition carries implications beyond the realm of literature in that it has helped naturalize cultural and class biases regarding subaltern politics. At a time when political centralism and integrative nationalism have been weakened or are being redefined, the region-based forms of political identity and community of the historically disenfranchised become an important source in the collective democratic task of reconceptualizing and reinterpreting Mexico as a multicultural nation.

The works of Campobello and, to a lesser degree, Muñoz make the case for taking the subaltern seriously as a subject of knowledge, without previously disqualifying or patronizing him or her, as has been the case historically. These authors represent an alternative narrative tradition in which writers acknowledge and artistically explore the richness and human complexity of popular characters' subjective processes. Juan Rulfo, Antonio Estrada Muñoz, and some works by Elena Garro and Jesús Morales Bermúdez cannot be explained properly without an understanding of this genealogy.

Finally, in the broader context of the production of discourses about the past, my discussion of Villista literature points to the need for identifying and recuperating discourses of emancipation imbedded in the dominant culture, as well as recovering the works of regional and local intellectuals that, for cultural and political reasons, have been silenced or forgotten in the making of modern Mexico.

NOTES

INTRODUCTION

1. Friedrich Katz, *The Life and Times of Pancho Villa*, 206.

2. Social bandits are "outlaws whom the lord and the state regard as criminal, but who remain within peasant society, and are considered by their people as heroes, as champions, avenger, fighter for justice, perhaps even leaders of liberation, and in any case men to be admired, helped and supported" (Eric J. Hobsbawm, *Bandits*, 13). According to Hobsbawm, Francisco Villa falls into this category.

3. Friedrich Katz, the foremost specialist on Villismo, declared in an interview: "Of all the revolutionary movements, Villismo is the most difficult to classify.... In March of 1913 Villa could only count on eight supporters.... At the end of that year [1913], without forced conscription, 5,000 armed men followed him [Villa], most of them on horses. What happened in those nine months? This is just one example of the mystery of Francisco Villa" (Juan José Doñán, "Entrevista con Friedrich Katz," 11). For the making of the Villista movement in 1913, see Katz, *The Life and Times*, 203–228.

4. Héctor Aguilar Camín and Lorenzo Meyer, *In the Shadow of the Mexican Revolution*, 42. See also Adolfo Gilly, *La revolución interrumpida*, 87–105.

5. Jorge Vera Estañol, *Historia de la revolución mexicana*, 393–405.

6. Jesús Silva Herzog, *Breve historia de la revolución mexicana*, vol. 1, 47. All translations are my own unless otherwise noted.

7. Arturo Warman in Enrique Florescano, *El nuevo pasado mexicano*, 105.

8. Katz, *The Life and Times*, 566.

9. Ilene O'Malley, *The Myth of the Revolution*, 93.

10. "I do not believe that anyone has the support that Francisco Villa has," Villa bragged in a 1922 interview. "For this reason the politicians are afraid of me.... I am a real soldier ... I can mobilize 40,000 men in 40 minutes" (Katz, *The Life and Times*, 756). Villa probably exaggerated his capacity to mobilize his followers; however, he did represent a permanent threat to the Mexican government, and this is one of the reasons he was assassinated.

11. Ibid., 761–768, 771–782.

12. O'Malley, *The Myth of the Revolution*, 98.

13. Ibid.

14. Ibid.

15. Ibid.

16. Ibid., 95.

17. This procedure is unique to postrevolutionary narratives.

18. Florescano, *El nuevo pasado mexicano*, 104.

19. Popular consciousness can be defined as "politicized forms of knowledge and identity, that are consensually recognized by subaltern groups during particular historical conjunctures" (Gilbert M. Joseph and Daniel Nugent, "Popular Culture and State Formation in Revolutionary Mexico," in *Everyday Forms of State Formation: Revolution and the Negotiation of Rule in Modern Mexico*, 11).

20. The school of subaltern studies originated in India in the 1980s among historians who began questioning and revising elite nationalist versions (guided by the Western tradition of the Enlightenment) of the country's colonial history. The original objective was to recover the subaltern's perspective, the Other's consciousness of historical events the dominant versions of which tended to suppress or distort those events. The school has evolved and, consequently, the emphasis and critical perspectives have shifted and may vary greatly among subalternist scholars. For a summary, see Gyan Prakash, "Subaltern Studies as Postcolonial Criticism." See also Ranajit Guha and Gayatri Chakravorty Spivak, eds., *Selected Subaltern Studies*; Spivak, "Can the Subaltern Speak?" Subaltern studies have been productively applied to Mexican history; see Florencia E. Mallon, *Peasant and Nation*; and Daniel Nugent, "Rural Revolt in Mexico, Mexican Nationalism and the State, and Forms of U.S. Intervention." For subaltern studies and the humanities, see Latin American Subaltern Group, "Founding Statement." For a debate between U.S. historians and literary critics regarding the applicability of subaltern studies to Latin America, see Florencia E. Mallon, "The Promise and Dilemma of Subaltern Studies: Perspectives from Latin American History"; and John Beverley, *Subalternity and Representation*.

21. Prakash, "Subaltern Studies as Postcolonial Criticism," 1480.

22. Nugent ("Rural Revolt in Mexico," 17–20) agrees that Guha's ideas are relevant to the study of Mexican history.

23. Eric Van Young, *Mexico's Regions: Comparative History and Development*, 1.

24. The volume edited by Joseph and Nugent, *Everyday Forms of State Formation*, stresses the importance of popular politics and culture in the process of state formation in Mexico. See also Nugent, *Rural Revolt in Mexico and U.S. Intervention*.

25. Luis González et al. *Historia regional y archivos*; Thomas Benjamin and Mark Wasserman, eds., *Provinces of the Revolution: Essays on Regional Mexican History 1910–1929*.

26. Ranajit Guha, *Elementary Aspects of Peasant Insurgency in Colonial India*. His articles, "On Some Aspects of the Historiography of Colonial India," 33–44, and "The Prose of Counterinsurgency," 45–84, appear in Guha and Spivak, *Selected Subaltern Studies*.

27. The word *cartucho* was not translated in the English edition.

28. Carlos Pacheco, *La comarca oral*, 114.

CHAPTER I

1. The Cristero War was an agrarian conflict enmeshed with the century-old confrontation between the Catholic Church and Mexico's Liberal state.

2. The ejido is a form of land tenure, pre-Hispanic in origin, where ownership "is vested in the community, but the land may be farmed individually or collectively; in the former it is distributed as individual or family plots among members of the community" (Nora Hamilton, *The Limits of State Autonomy: Post-Revolutionary Mexico*, 68).

3. Plutarco Elías Calles, *Plutarco Elías Calles: Pensamiento social y político. Antología (1913–1936)*, 104–105.

4. Hamilton, *The Limits of State Autonomy*, 100.

5. Calles, *Plutarco Elías Calles*, 78, 102–103.

6. Álvaro Matute, "La revolución recordada, inventada, rescatada," 442.

7. Guillermo Palacios, "Calles y la idea oficial de la Revolución," 261–278.

8. Ibid., 261–263.

9. Ángel Rama, *La ciudad letrada*, 121.

10. Matute, "La revolución recordada," 442–443.

11. Enrique Montalvo, *El nacionalismo contra la nación*, 16.

12. John Rutherford, *Mexican Society during the Revolution*, 37–38.

13. Jean Franco, in Carlos Monsiváis, "Notas sobre la cultura mexicana en el siglo XX," 1447.

14. See Víctor Díaz Arciniega, *Querella por la cultura "revolucionaria," (1925)*, 54–99.

15. Guillermo Sheridan, *Los contemporáneos ayer*, 97.

16. See, for example, Antonio Castellanos, *Francisco Villa, su vida y su muerte: Sensacionales revelaciones y consideraciones sobre su vida y su asesinato;* Teodoro Torres Jr., *Pancho Villa: Una vida de romance y tragedia.* See also Dennis J. Parle, "The Novels of the Mexican Revolution Published by the Casa Editorial Lozano." The Spanish-language press flourished in the U.S. Southwest during and after the revolution; however, the economic depression of 1929 and the subsequent repatriation of thousands of Mexicans diminished the readership.

17. Hamilton, *The Limits of State Autonomy*, 76–77.

18. There was only one military rebellion in 1929, by General Escobar, which was promptly defeated (Jean Meyer, "Revolution and Reconstruction in the 1920s," 215).

19. O'Malley, *The Myth of the Revolution*, 97–98.

20. J. Meyer, "Revolution and Reconstruction," 216.

21. Hamilton, *The Limits of State Autonomy*, 97–100.

22. Arturo Anguiano, *El estado y la política obrera del cardenismo*, 40.

23. Hamilton, *The Limits of State Autonomy*, 100.

24. Ibid., 90–100.

25. Ibid., 120.

26. Mary Kay Vaughan, "Cambio ideológico en la política educativa de la SEP: Programas y libros de texto, 1921–1940," 85–91.

27. O'Malley, *The Myth of the Revolution*, 99.

28. José Vasconcelos, *El desastre*, 28.

29. Martín Luis Guzmán, *The Eagle and the Serpent*, 178.

30. The interpretation of the revolutionary war that gradually came to dominate Mexican historiography in subsequent decades, though not as hostile to these popular leaders as were Vasconcelos and Guzmán, continued to be consistent with the vision and aspirations of the middle class, the social sector that ultimately reaped the greatest benefits from the conflict. Arnaldo Córdoba aptly expresses this hegemonic perspective in his analysis of Mexican society during the revolution: "Positioned at an equal distance from all the other social classes, the middle sectors and their intellectuals were also in the best circumstances to explain *coherently* the causes of the ills that afflicted the country" (Arnaldo Córdoba, *La ideología de la revolución mexicana*, 89; emphasis added)—"coherently" from the standpoint of the interests of the middle class, that is. The idea that the middle class is situated equidistant from the other social strata and, consequently, is in a privileged position to understand the country's reality is part of the myth that it has created about itself. The myth suggests that the upper and lower classes, because of their positions at the "extremes" of society, are at an intrinsic structural disadvantage in their ability to evaluate the nation's problems. As a result, their interpretation of the issues, according to this rationale, is, by definition, tendentious, inadequate, and wanting in coherence; thus the self-serving myth of the middle class providing the only truly judicious norm.

31. Katz, *The Life and Times*, 391.

32. Alan Knight, "Peasant and Caudillo in Revolutionary Mexico 1910–17," 19.

33. Friedrich Katz, "El pensamiento social de Pancho Villa," 293–296.

34. For the idea of the nation as an "imagined political community," see Benedict Anderson, *Imagined Communities: Reflections on the Origin and Spread of Nationalism*, 14–16.

35. Alan Knight, "Peasants into Patriots: Thoughts on the Making of the Mexican Nation."

CHAPTER 2

1. Mariano Azuela, "Cómo escribí *Los de abajo*," 1268. For more on Azuela's petit bourgeois ideology, see Jorge Ruffinelli, *Literatura e ideología: El primer Mariano Azuela (1896–1918)*.

2. The novel appeared as a daily serial in the newspaper *El Paso del Norte* from

October 27 to November 21, 1915. The newspaper published the novel in book form that same year or early in 1916. See Stanley Robe, *Azuela and the Mexican Underdogs*, 93, 121. Robe's book contains a reproduction of the original serialized version accompanied by a detailed historical reconstruction of Azuela's actions throughout the revolution and the real situations that influenced the elaboration of the novel.

3. One notable exception is *Tomóchic* (1893), by Heriberto Frías, a novelized account of an episode during the wars of extermination against the indigenous populations of the northern frontier state of Chihuahua.

4. The change of focus in and of itself constituted an implicit acknowledgment that the revolutionary middle classes had been displaced from the vanguard of the revolutionary war. "The failure of the middle sectors to destroy the upper classes opens the way for the action of the lower classes, campesinos and, occasionally, the proletariat. It is they who, since 1913, have occupied the historical stage" (Ángel Rama, "Mariano Azuela: Ambición y frustración de las clases medias," 181).

5. Two critics have used the phrase "novel of the masses" to define *Los de abajo*. See Joseph Sommers, "Novela de la revolución: Criterios contemporáneos," 739–740; and Jean Franco, *The Modern Culture of Latin America*, 94. For a more extended discussion of the novel, see José Joaquín Blanco, "Lecturas de *Los de abajo*."

6. "Most of the events narrated," writes Azuela, "were composed with the material that I gathered in conversations with revolutionaries of different classes and conditions, above all, the exchanges among themselves" (Azuela, *Obras completas*, 1087).

7. Jean Franco, *Critical Passions*, 453.

8. In his inaugural address of December 1, 1924, José Manuel Puig Casauranc, Calles's new minister of culture, was explicit about the vigorous social criticism that ought to characterize the new literature, which he declared he was committed to "publishing" and "circulating." See John Rutherford, *Mexican Society during the Revolution*, 57–58.

9. See Adalbert Dessau, *La novela de la revolución mexicana*, 261–268; John Engelkirk, "The Discovery of *Los de abajo*"; and Luis Mario Schneider, *Ruptura y continuidad*, 159–193. For a review of the critical reception of the novel in the four decades after its appearance, see Jorge Ruffinelli, "La recepción crítica de *Los de abajo*."

10. Díaz Arciniega, *Querella por la cultura "revolucionaria," (1925)*, 14.

11. Díaz Arciniega's book provides an extensive review of the cultural and political debate and its results.

12. Robe, *Azuela and the Mexican Underdogs*, 1–71.

13. Mónica Mansour, "Cúspides inaccesibles," 269.

14. See, for example, Guha's *Elementary Aspects* and the articles compiled by Guha and Spivak in *Selected Subaltern Studies*. For a summary review of the uses

of subaltern studies by Latin Americanists in the U.S. academy, see Mallon, "The Promise and Dilemma of Subaltern Studies."

15. For the concept of "subjectivity," see Aralia López González, *Sin imágenes falsas, sin falsos espejos: Narradoras mexicanas del siglo XX*. López González defines subjectivity as "the structures of consciousness and the person's desiring activity, shaped by the norms, codes, and the discourse of society and culture, as well as by the position that [the individual] occupies in them. . . . Subjectivity has as much to do with conscious and unconscious desires as with sex, the body itself, perceptions, sensitivity, intelligence, imagination, health, etc." (14).

16. Mariano Azuela, *The Underdogs*, 61. All quotations cited in the text and the notes are from this edition.

17. I am using the Spanish names of the characters here because the English version slightly modifies the spelling of names. For example, Montañés becomes "Montáñez." I use the English spelling only when quoting from the English translation cited in note 16 above.

18. Monsiváis, "La aparición del subsuelo (sobre la cultura de la revolución mexicana)," 36.

19. After looting the house of a wealthy cacique, Cervantes informs Macías: "If this mess doesn't blow over . . . if the revolution keeps on, there's enough here already for us to live on abroad quite comfortably" (105).

20. Rama, "Mariano Azuela: Ambición y frustración," 147.

21. Positivistic criminology, in vogue in Mexico at the beginning of the twentieth century, shaped Azuela's ideas about social violence. His ideas are not unlike those of positivist sociologist Julio Guerrero, who in 1903 published *La génesis del crimen en México* (Genesis of Crime in Mexico). Guerrero explains rural rebellions and social unrest in terms of atavistic behavior, that is, discontinuous, savage ancestral traits, genetic in origin, that reappear in modern society. In *Los de abajo*, atavistic behaviors are linked to the indigenous race.

22. A group of revolutionaries exchange murderous anecdotes in a cantina: "When I was up at Torreón I killed an old lady who refused to sell me some enchiladas . . . I killed a storekeeper at Parral . . . I killed a man because I always saw him sitting at the table whenever I went to eat . . . Hmmm! I killed . . . " (88). On a crowded train, the conversation turns to theft: "God's own truth is this: I have stolen . . . Hell, I stole a lot of them sewing machines in Mexico . . . I stole some horses in Zacatecas . . . the damned thing about it was that General Limón took a fancy to the horses too, and he stole them from me!" (127).

23. Rama, "Mariano Azuela: Ambición y frustración."

24. Robe, *Azuela and the Mexican Underdogs*, 31.

25. One critic has observed that the protagonist had already appeared in other novels by Azuela. Macías "first came to life in the person of Gertrudis, the stableman in the novel *Mala yerba*. He reappears in *Andrés Pérez, maderista*, as Vicente, another stableman"(Luis Leal, *Mariano Azuela*, 58). It follows that Macías is fundamentally a social stereotype with added features that Azuela took from his ex-

periences in the revolution. My observations are not meant to express disapproval of Azuela's depiction of the character, but, rather, to underline the artistic and ideological factors that entered into his elaboration.

26. Sommers, "Novela de la revolución," 739.

27. Franco, *Critical Passions*, 453–454.

28. On the conceptual and social base of these naturalistic images, Ranajit Guha, a member of the Subaltern Studies Group, writes: "In conditions governed by the norms of unquestioning obedience to authority, a revolt of the subaltern shocks by its relative entropy. Hence the suddenness so often attributed to peasant uprisings and the verbal imageries of eruption, explosion and conflagration used to describe it. What is intended by such usage in many languages and many cultures is to communicate the sense of an unforeseen break, a sharp discontinuity" (*Elementary Aspects*, 36).

29. Franco, "Trends and Priorities for Research on Latin American Literature," 112–113.

30. Frank Tannenbaum, *Peace by Revolution*, 115, 116, 118.

31. Ibid., 187.

32. Alfonso Reyes, "Pasado inmediato," 185.

33. Octavio Paz, *The Labyrinth of Solitude*, 145.

34. Ibid.

35. Eric J. Hobsbawm, *Primitive Rebels: Studies in Archaic Forms of Social Movements in the 19th and 20th Centuries*, 1–12; see also chaps. 1–6.

36. Antonio Gramsci, "Espontaneidad y dirección consciente."

37. Guha, *Elementary Aspects*, 5.

38. Alan Knight, "Los intelectuales en la revolución mexicana," 41, 43.

39. Guha, *Elementary Aspects*, 15.

40. Mallon, "The Promise and Dilemma of Subaltern Studies," 1497.

41. Latin American Subaltern Group, "Founding Statement," 111.

42. Regarding the institutionalization of *Los de abajo*, see Ruffinelli, "La recepción crítica de *Los de abajo*."

43. On this point, I follow Danny Anderson's position on "cultural perspective" and the interaction of literary technique, ideology, reading, and subjectivity ("Subjetividad y lectura: Ideología de la técnica en *El luto humano* y el cambio narrativo a medio siglo," 114).

44. Mallon, *Peasant and Nation*, 5.

45. Roland Barthes, "Introduction to the Structural Analysis of Narratives," 93–97.

46. Ibid., 94.

47. Blanco, "Lecturas de *Los de abajo*," 211, 216.

48. Ruffinelli, *Literatura e ideología*, 80.

49. Class resentment motivates many of the excesses committed by the revolutionaries, but in the case of *güero* Margarito violence is indiscriminate.

50. Jorge Aguilar Mora, *Una muerte sencilla, justa, eterna*, 146.

51. Scraps of real events feed these legends, however. A grateful Villa, at the height of his power, gave the hacienda Las Delicias in Chihuahua to Cipriano Vargas, one of his faithful soldiers. Vargas had shown extreme loyalty to Villa during the latter's imprisonment in Mexico City. Vargas hid funds belonging to Villa from the *federales* when his boss was taken prisoner. He later traveled to the country's capital and surreptitiously turned over the funds to Villa (Juan Bautista Vargas Arreola, *A sangre y fuego con Pancho Villa*, 85).

52. Blanco, "Lecturas de *Los de abajo*," 223.

53. Ibid., 213.

54. Ibid.

55. Some critical comments, however, were not favorable. Victoriano Salado Álvarez, from the elitist literary position of the old, prerevolutionary intellectual class, complained of the author's "useless repetitions, tremendous flaws in style" ("inútiles repeticiones, faltas garrafales de estilo") (in Schneider, *Ruptura y continuidad,* 184). In an interview, Nellie Campobello, from the standpoint of her own regional experience of the war, decried the lack of historical truth in Azuela: "He told pure lies in his novels. Like a bad actor, he overacted what he said about the Revolution, about the revolutionaries" (Emmanuel Carballo, *Diecinueve protagonistas de la literatura mexicana del siglo XX,* 335).

56. Rutherford notes that the novelists of the revolution "had a universally recognized master—Azuela—whose lead to follow in questions of style, form, content, even attitude. And so the novel of this period tends to fall into well-proved moulds of plot and character; just like the western or the detective or the sentimental novel, the Novel of the Revolution, on acquiring popular appeal, tended to become stereotyped and standardized; and certain commonplace characters were evolved and appeared repeatedly" (*Mexican Society during the Revolution*, 68).

CHAPTER 3

1. Francisco R. Almada, *Diccionario de historia, geografía y biografía chihuahuense,* (1997) 252.

2. Doris Meyer, "Translator's note," in Nellie Campobello, *Cartucho; My Mother's Hands,* 2.

3. Dennis Parle, "Narrative Style and Technique in Nellie Campobello's *Cartucho*," 202.

4. It was not Campobello but the editor of the first edition, Germán List Arzubide, who organized the book thematically (Blanca Rodríguez, *nellie campobello: eros y violencia,* 157).

5. In an interview with literary critic Emmanuel Carballo, the writer stated that she was born in 1909 (Carballo, *Diecinueve protagonistas,* 328). Documentation unearthed by historians shows the correct date to be 1900. It follows that her memories of the revolution actually included not only her childhood, as she

always claimed, but her adolescence and the first years of her young adulthood. See José Ramón González León, *"La dama de las lilas": Apuntes biográficos de Nellie Campobello*, 33.

6. Carballo, *Diecinueve protagonistas*, 335.

7. Patricia Aulestia, "Entrevista con Nellie Campobello," Archivo Nellie Campobello, January 4, 1972; see also Rodríguez, *nellie campobello*, 74.

8. Francisca, *¡Yo!* (Mexico City: LIDAN, 1929). I was unable to consult the original edition. A facsimile can be found in Jesús Vargas Valdés and Flor García Rufino, *Francisca ¡Yo! El libro desconocido de Nellie Campobello* (107–142). The facsimile shows that Campobello's first book consists of fifty-four poems, far more than the fifteen she includes in *Mis libros*, her collected works published in 1960.

9. Her family called her Nellie, after her mother's pet dog (Carballo, *Diecinueve protagonistas*, 328).

10. Matthews mentions that the sisters were "disillusioned" with Spain's professional theater; Rodríguez talks about "deception" (Irene Matthews, *Nellie Campobello: La centaura del norte*, 62; Rodríguez, *nellie campobello*, 78).

11. With Fernández de Castro's encouragement, Nellie published a few articles and poems in the *Revista de La Habana* (Campobello, *Mis libros*, 20. See also Rodríguez, *nellie campobello*, 78.

12. The poems appear in Dudley Fitts, *Anthology of Contemporary Latin American Poetry*, 213–218.

13. Campobello, *Mis libros*, 15–16; Matthews, *Nellie Campobello*, 62–68.

14. Langston Hughes arrived in Havana in February of 1930, Federico García Lorca, in March. See Arnold Rampersad, *The Life of Langston Hughes, vol. 1: 1902–1941*, 178; and Ian Gibson, *Federico García Lorca: A Life*, 282. From this and other information provided by Campobello in her autobiographical "Prólogo" (*Mis libros*, 17), we can gather that the sisters were in Havana in late 1929 and the first months of 1930.

15. Campobello, *Mis libros*, 16–17.

16. There is no doubt that knowledge of Campobello's illegitimate child would have tarnished her reputation as she tried to make a living and work her way through Mexico City's male-dominated cultural and intellectual circles, hence the importance, in terms of social respect and survival, of being called "Señorita Campobello." Campobello's case poses an interesting contrast and alternative, worth exploring, with that of Antonieta Rivas Mercado, the divorced mother and writer who became, in 1929, the lover of then–presidential candidate José Vasconcelos, a married man. Rivas Mercado did not survive her well-known affair with Vasconcelos; she killed herself in 1931. For a solid account of Rivas Mercado's intellectual and personal plight, see Jean Franco, *Plotting Women: Gender and Representation in Mexico*, 112–122.

17. Campobello, *Mis libros*, 14.

18. Ibid., 13.

19. Ibid., 14.

20. Nellie Campobello, "Inicial," *Cartucho* (1931), iii–iv.

21. For the *estridentista* movement, see Luis Mario Schneider, *El estridentismo: O, una literatura de la estrategia.*

22. Campobello, *Mis libros,* 17.

23. See Rodríguez, *nellie campobello,* 158. In his presentation, List Arzubide mentions the "exhausted intellectualist groups" that write about the revolution to "adorn their names with bullets." He was most likely referring to the Contemporáneos group and other writers associated at the time with the Mexican state's cultural bureaucracy.

24. Germán List Arzubide, "Integrales," in Campobello, *Cartucho* (1931), n.p.

25. Campobello, *Mis libros,* 26; Carballo, *Diecinueve protagonistas,* 336.

26. Campobello, *Mis libros,* 26–27.

27. Berta Gamboa de Camino, "The Novel of the Mexican Revolution," 268.

28. Nellie Campobello, "Perfiles de Villa." Campobello mentions Calles's re-action to this article in an interview with Emmanuel Carballo in 1958. Perhaps because almost three decades had elapsed, she confused the date of publication; see Carballo, *Diecinueve protagonistas,* 337. The article assails what she perceived to be the false stories surrounding Villa and goes on to praise the Centaur of the North's complex personality, the irresistible magnet of his military leadership, and his love for the people. The most striking aspect of the article is Campobello's unapologetic defense of Villa's patriarchal violence: "The man . . . had been born to be at the service of the people," she writes, "whether by governing them, whether by forcing them to be good, whether by killing them" ("Perfiles de Villa," 15).

29. In one of these articles, Campobello reproduces two of Villa's love letters in order to reveal a facet of his personality that, she believed, would refute the frequent accusation that he was a senseless rapist ("El Pancho Villa que no conoce el mundo: Dos cartas de amor del guerrillero").

30. Nellie Campobello, "Los hijos del general Villa necesitan que se acuerde de una vez la pensión solicitada"; and Vito Alessio Robles, "Las memorias dictadas por el general Francisco Villa." The memoirs constitute the original inspiration for Martín Luis Guzmán's *Memorias de Pancho Villa.*

31. *Apuntes sobre la vida militar de Pancho Villa* (Notes on the Military Life of Pancho Villa) was published in 1940.

32. Dennis Parle notes that Campobello "was somewhat of an authority" on corridos and points to folklore specialist Vicente T. Mendoza's citation of her opinion on the corrido in his 1939 study *El romance español y el corrido mexicano* (Parle, "Narrative Style and Technique," 211). A few corridos recorded by Campobello in Durango and Chihuahua are included in Mendoza's book. Luz Corral, another of Villa's widows, scornfully recalled that when Campobello traveled to Chihuahua, she passed herself off as Villa's daughter; see Rubén Osorio, *Pancho Villa, ese desconocido: Entrevistas en Chihuahua a favor y en contra,* 132.

33. In the preliminary note to *Apuntes sobre la vida militar de Francisco Villa*, 9–10, Villa's widow Austreberta Rentería and Villista veteran Ismael Máynez are mentioned as informants. Stories told by Máynez ("Ismael Máynez and Martín López") and by Rentería ("Samuel's Cigarette") are included in the new version of *Cartucho*. Regional corridos appear in "The Officers of Segunda del Rayo," "Abelardo Prieto," and "The Tragedy of Martín."

34. Valeska Strickland Nájera, "La obra de Nellie Campobello," 55. Nájera also discusses the evolution of the narrative point of view (53–71).

35. For a study of the changes between the first and the second editions, see Rodríguez, *nellie campobello*, 155–229. Campobello's radical reaffirmation of Villismo in the 1940 edition stands in stark contrast to Azuela, who weakened any show of enthusiasm for Villa in the second edition of *Los de abajo* and, instead, accentuated the general's political nihilism (Aguilar Mora, *Una muerte sencilla, justa, eterna*, 49).

36. I use the 1940 edition with one exception: the story "Villa," which was dropped from the second edition. I use the translation by Doris Meyer and Irene Matthews (*Cartucho; My Mother's Hands*). Meyer translated the third edition (1960) of *Cartucho*, in which Campobello introduced only a minor addition: four paragraphs at the end of "Nacha Ceniceros," which do not enter into my discussion of the text. For the sake of consistency and precision, in my discussion I have, whenever necessary, altered Meyer's anglicized spelling of some words and modified those parts of the translation that slightly alter the meaning, and with it the connotative field, of the Spanish text.

37. "They told Mama everything that had happened. She never forgot it" (Campobello, *Cartucho; My Mother's Hands*, 38); "'El Peet' said that everything was very strange that night" (41); "'They're bringing Felipe Ángeles with some other prisoners. They aren't killing,' the people were saying" (42); "'The way his companions tell it, Julio said to them'" (68); "Pepita Chacón, laughing amiably, recounted the time General Villa himself turned up at her house" (73); "Isaías Álvarez says: 'One time . . .'" (75), etc.

38. Walter Benjamin, "The Storyteller," 86–98.

39. Parle, "Narrative Style and Technique," 208–210.

40. Pacheco, *La comarca oral*, 40.

41. The grotesque is an effective survival mechanism. Mikhail Bakhtin elaborates on the relationship between fear, laughter, and freedom in *Rabelais and His World*, chaps. 1, 3, and 5.

42. Pacheco, *La comarca oral*, 114–117.

43. T. Benjamin and Wasserman, *Provinces of the Revolution*.

44. Knight, "Peasant and Caudillo in Revolutionary Mexico," 43, 44.

45. A second, and larger, geographical area would include Santa Rosalía, Camargo, the city of Chihuahua, and as far as the city of Juárez and beyond the border with the United States to El Paso, Texas. Campobello once stated: "I am from the North—and the north of Mexico and the south of the United States are

for me one and the same." And she specified what she meant by northern Mexico: "the mountain region of Durango, Chihuahua, and the plains of the south of the United States: Texas, for me, continues to be part of Mexico, Arizona, and New Mexico" (Carballo, *Diecinueve protagonistas*, 331, 332–333).

46. Pedro Pérez Herrero, "Regional Conformation in Mexico, 1700–1850: Models and Hypotheses," 128–131.

47. Friedrich Katz, "Pancho Villa, Peasant Movements and Agrarian Reform in Northern Mexico," 60.

48. Barry Carr, "Las peculiaridades del norte mexicano, 1880–1927: Ensayo de interpretación," 323.

49. "The nuclear family and patriarchal values assumed particularly compelling dimensions in northern New Spain. Frontier Indian conflicts rekindled medieval attitudes emphasizing the valor of fighting men" (Cheryl English Martin, *Governance and Society in Colonial Mexico: Chihuahua in the Eighteenth Century*, 150; see also Ana María Alonso, *Thread of Blood: Colonialism, Revolution, and Gender in Mexico's Northern Frontier*, 98–99).

50. Alonso, *Thread of Blood*, 15.

51. Friedrich Katz, *The Secret War in Mexico: Europe, the United States, and the Mexican Revolution*, 143–144.

52. Osorio, *Pancho Villa, ese desconocido*, 12; Katz, *The Life and Times*, 646.

53. Daniel Cazés, *Los revolucionarios*, 146; John Reed, *Insurgent Mexico*, 144–145.

54. See "The Dream of Pancho Villa" in Reed, *Insurgent Mexico*, 144–145.

55. For a detailed description of this battle, see José María Jaurrieta, *Con Villa (1916–1920), memorias de campaña*, 87–95.

56. Gamboa de Camino, "The Novel of the Mexican Revolution," 268.

57. Parle, "Narrative Style and Technique," 202–203.

58. Manuel Pedro González, *Trayectoria de la novela en México*, 289.

59. Sophie Bidault de la Calle's *Nellie Campobello: Una escritura salida del cuerpo* also makes this point (47–48). This book studies the relationship between writing and body movements (dancing) in Campobello's work.

60. The preface to the 1931 edition of *Cartucho*, which was left out of subsequent editions, ends with the following words: "My executed soldiers, asleep in the green notebook. My dead men. My childhood toys" (iv).

61. Clementina Díaz y de Ovando, "Literatura popular contemporánea," 39.

62. Parle, "Narrative Style and Technique," 203.

63. Irene Matthews, "Daughtering in War: Two 'Case Studies' from Mexico and Guatemala," 152.

64. Female characters face the real danger of abduction and rape in *Cartucho*; however, they do not always occupy the most precarious position in Campobello's work. In the few stories in which Indian characters appear, they are mistreated by the women (by the narrator child, in an innocent display of childhood cruelty in

"Zafiro y Zequiel," and by the aunt in "For a Kiss") and are executed without a second thought.

65. "Memory is the epic faculty par excellence" (W. Benjamin, "The Storyteller," 97).

66. And, as the production of the text itself bears out, Campobello will assume the task of keeping alive this subversive function by shaping it into a literary form.

67. José Beltrán, Francisco Villa, and Tomás Urbina used to run raids together during their years as social bandits (Guillermo Ramírez, *Melitón Lozoya: Único director intelectual en la muerte de Villa*, 57–65).

68. W. Benjamin, "The Storyteller," 97.

69. Matthews, "Daughtering in War," 149.

70. Walter J. Ong, *The Presence of the Word*, 31.

71. Nájera, "La obra de Nellie Campobello," 58.

72. On the poetization of death, see Parle, "Narrative Style and Technique," 206–207.

73. Ibid., 207.

74. On the popular sources for this type of narrative and the ritualistic origins of the smile as associated with the notions death and resurrection, see Mikhail Bakhtin, *Problemas de la poética de Dostoievski*, 151–193.

75. This narrative procedure is typical of storytelling. "Storytellers tend to begin their story with a presentation of the circumstances in which they themselves have learned what is to follow, unless they simply pass it off as their own experience" (W. Benjamin, "The Storyteller," 92).

76. Katz, *The Life and Times*, 522–523; Federico Cervantes, *Francisco Villa y la historia*, 511–512; Vargas Arreola, *A sangre y fuego con Pancho Villa*, 278–285.

77. For an eyewitness account of "Urbina's country" and of the general himself, see Part I ("Desert War") of Reed's *Insurgent Mexico*.

78. Américo Paredes, *Culture and Folklore on the Texas-Mexican Border*, 148.

79. This brief list is far from exhaustive and does not fully represent the many variables offered by the text. Legends, corridos, and other popular narrative forms also have their place in these stories.

80. Kemy Oyarzún, "Identidad femenina, genealogía mítica, historia: *Las manos de mamá*," 71.

81. Adolfo Gilly, "Memoria y olvido, razón y esperanza," 7.

CHAPTER 4

1. Martín Luis Guzmán is pictured at least once in this book with seven presidents: Álvaro Obregón, Manuel Ávila Camacho, Miguel Alemán Valdez, Adolfo Ruiz Cortinez, Adolfo López Mateos, Gustavo Díaz Ordaz, and Luis Echeverría Álvarez. In a photograph from his days in exile, Guzmán is seen ac-

companying his political friend Manuel Azaña, the prime minister of Spain's Second Republic.

2. Martín Luis Guzmán, *The Eagle and the Serpent;* this is the edition I will cite in the text and the notes.

3. The novel *La sombra del caudillo* (The Shadow of the Caudillo), a scathing indictment of political scheming and repression under the Obregón-Calles regimes (1921–1928), was also written during this period.

4. Fernando Curiel, "Introducción," in Martín Luis Guzmán, *Caudillos y otros extremos,* xxi–xxv.

5. Juan Bruce-Novoa, "Introducción," in Guzmán, *La sombra del caudillo,* xx–xxi.

6. Ibid., xix. See also Curiel, *La querella de Martín Luis Guzmán,* 64. The English version, unfortunately, abridged, appeared in 1930. About the English translations, see Juan Bruce-Novoa, "*El águila y la serpiente* en las versiones estadounidenses."

7. Calles, *Plutarco Elías Calles,* 86.

8. President Calles introduced anticlerical provisions that seriously impeded the functioning of the Catholic Church. The confrontation escalated into a full-fledged war, known as the Cristero War, in central Mexico between 1926 and 1928.

9. The "awakening" of the intelligentsia to Mexico's landscape, to the reality of its social problems, and to the very notion of homeland is characteristic of this early period of cultural nationalism. See, for example, Alfonso Reyes's ambiguous story "El testimonio de Juan Peña," the poetic meditation of Ramón López Velarde in "Novedad de la patria," and the essay *1915* by Manuel Gómez Morín, all written in the 1920s.

10. Juan Flores, *Insularismo e ideología burguesa,* 74.

11. Manuel Aguilar, the Spanish editor, rejected the original title and requested alternatives. Guzmán proposed five new titles, including *El águila y la serpiente* (Carballo, *Diecinueve protagonistas,* 73).

12. In an interview Guzmán declared, "[It]is not a historical work as some have claimed; it is, I repeat, a novel" (ibid.).

13. Shaw, "*El águila y la serpiente,*" 5.

14. Christopher Domínguez, "Martín Luis Guzmán: El teatro de la política," 23–24. Performance certainly displaces "hard" politics in the section on the Convention of Aguascalientes, which, as Domínguez points out, appropriately takes place in the city's old theater (Teatro Morelos).

15. Martín Luis Guzmán, *Obras completas,* vol. 1, 98.

16. Guzmán's poetic awareness of the *rayo verde,* or green ray, probably came from reading Jules Verne's novel of the same name.

17. Carballo, *Diecinueve protagonistas,* 69, 70.

18. José Enrique Rodó, *Ariel,* 49–56.

19. Ibid., 94.

20. Ibid., 87–88.

21. Arielismo was an intellectual reaction to the historical crisis caused by the defeat of Spain in the Spanish-American War of 1898 and, more generally, the abrupt incorporation of the region into the capitalist world and modernity. Troubled by the ever-expanding influence of the United States on the continent and that country's attendant utilitarian values, Rodó warns that Latin America should resist the blind imitation of this new model (which he calls *"nordomanía"*). Capitalist transformation, however, is not to be rejected. Rodó acknowledges the importance of and even celebrates technological progress, science, and the materialist world, yet he views these signs of modernity as little more than the labor necessary to prepare the soil for humankind's greater task of cultivating the spiritual dimension of life. Without material wealth, he observes, the "realm of the spirit" is impossible (ibid., 87–90). Rodó's *Ariel* was the dominant influence in the intellectual life of Latin America in the early twentieth century. His highly rhetorical meditations attracted the attention and approval of the region's intelligentsia because he satisfactorily integrated and harmonized the turn-of-the-century philosophical conflict "between the idealistic and positivistic concepts of life" (Alfonso García Morales, *El Ateneo de México, 1906–1914*, 120). Moreover, Rodó's essay contributed to the prestige and advancement of modern subjectivity, whereby refinement and sensibility "would seem unequivocally on the side of the progressive middle class, as the aesthetic foundation of a new form of polity" (Terry Eagleton, *The Ideology of the Aesthetic*, 26). In Mexico, this "new form of polity" carried an implicit rejection of the mores of the rural population.

22. *Ateneísta* Antonio Caso was an advocate of the "philosophy of disinterest"; see *La filosofía como economía, como desinterés y como caridad*.

23. José Vasconcelos, *Memorias I*, 269–270.

24. Martín Luis Guzmán, "La vida atélica," *Caudillos y otros extremos*, 233–234. The article originally appeared in *Nosotros* in September 1913.

25. The *científicos* were a group of Liberal politicians who identified with the doctrine of positivism and claimed to have a "scientific" view of society. They were instrumental in implementing the industrial development program during the dictatorship of Porfirio Díaz, to whom they were closely associated (Alan Knight, *The Mexican Revolution*, vol. 1, 21–24).

26. Rodó, *Ariel*, 56–70.

27. Ibid., 67. The powerful influence of the Rodorian notion of "spiritual selection" is most visible in José Vasconcelos's utopian essay *La raza cósmica* (1925).

28. I condense here ideas expressed by three critics. David William Foster aptly discusses how the techniques Guzmán used to process information enabled him to scrutinize events carefully ("Escrutando el texto de la revolución: *El águila y la serpiente* de Martín Luis Guzmán"). Luis Leal ("La caricia suprema: Contextos de luz y sombra en *El águila y la serpiente*") shows how Guzmán associates darkness with tyranny, violence, brute force, and evil, and light with transparency,

idealism, freedom, peace, patriotism. Donald L. Shaw (*"El águila y la serpiente: Arielismo and Narrative Method"*) emphasizes the juxtaposition of episodes and the novel's moral dimension.

29. Alfonso Reyes, *Visión de Anáhuac*, 14–15.

30. Hence the distrust of and aversion to cities and urban culture of regional leaders Francisco Villa and Emiliano Zapata. When they met in the town of Xochimilco in December 1914, their dialogue captured this rural bias. Zapata complained, in typical country style, of Mexico City's sidewalks: "The men who have done most of the work are those who enjoy those sidewalks less. Only sidewalks. And I say for myself: the moment I get on one of those sidewalks, I start to fall down." Villa replies: "This ranch is too big for us. It is better to be out there" (Aguilar Camín and Meyer, *In the Shadow of the Mexican Revolution*, 56).

31. Villa opposed such centralization projects. As I discuss in Chapter 1, he favored autonomous local and regional politics and a decentralized state. See Katz, "El pensamiento social de Francisco Villa," 293–294.

32. *Ariel* is written in the form of a lecture given by Próspero, a wise and beloved teacher, to his students on the last day of class.

33. According to Elias (*The Civilizing Process*, 461ff), the behavioral code that repudiates expressive violence originates in the effort of the secular upper classes (the medieval court nobility) to differentiate themselves from the lower classes, a practice that eventually came to permeate the rest of society.

34. Ibid., 452.

35. Peter Stallybrass and Allon White, *The Politics and Poetics of Transgression*, 90.

36. Guzmán's judgmental application of the "civilizing code" in *The Eagle and the Serpent* is not limited to Villa and the uneducated masses, though they are his primary targets. He also uses it against Venustiano Carranza, Guzmán's enemy. He describes Carranza as a man who prefers to be photographed instead of asking "for a bath—soap and water to rid himself of the dirt and lice" after his long and difficult trek to Sonora (285).

37. John Reed records a different version of Villa's reaction to Western society's rules of war. When American general Hugh L. Scott sent a copy of the *Rules of War* (adopted by the Hague Conference) to Villa in 1914, the latter questioned the international legality of the pamphlet and found the content unbearably hypocritical. "What is this Hague Conference?" Villa asks. "Was there a representative of Mexico there? Was there a representative of the Constitutionalists there? It seems to me a funny thing to make rules about war. It's not a game. What is the difference between civilized war and any other kind of war? If you and I are having a fight in a *cantina* we are not going to pull a little book out of our pockets and read over the rules. It says here that you must not use lead bullets; but I don't see why not. They do the work" (Reed, *Insurgent Mexico*, 142–143).

38. Seen from the pragmatic rules of engagement enforced during the revolution by Villa, Obregón, Carranza, Zapata, and many other generals, however,

NOTES TO PAGES 92–94 ‖ 157

the original execution order is not only permissible, but expected, a sign not of moral insensitivity but of upholding a code of military conduct that is inflexible with regard to turncoats. Villa's own sense of justice distinguished between prisoners who previously had been revolutionaries (e.g., the *colorados*, or followers of Gen. Pascual Orozco) and those who were with the federal army. The former he would always have executed, because they were traitors to the cause. Prisoners from the federal army were separated by rank: officers were executed, but common soldiers were set free. See ibid., 143; Aguilar Mora, *Una muerte sencilla, justa, eterna*, 379–380.

39. In another story, "A Very Expedient Trial," no such formality exists, only the coldness, speed, and indifference with which Villa orders the execution of several counterfeiters from well-to-do families.

40. This lesson is repeated in the tragic story "The Death of David Berlanga," in which the spiritual and moral superiority of control of one's body, a symbolic triumph over arbitrary violence, is taken to the extreme.

41. To expose the appropriate code of conduct in a society ruled by the values of modern citizenship and denounce infringements of this code is part of a long tradition in Mexican literature. This particular aspect aligns Guzmán's work with the didactic narratives of José Joaquín Fernández de Lizardi (*El periquillo sarniento* [The Itching Parrot, 1816] and *La Quijotita y su prima* [The Girl Quixote and Her Cousin, 1818–1819]) and Ignacio Manuel Altamirano (*El Zarco* [1901]).

42. The contrast between the first description of Villa and that of Guzmán's friends in the border city of Nogales, Arizona, makes this clear: "They greeted us with affectionate warmth . . . smiled at us, hugged us, asked a thousand questions. . . . They represented *our first real contact with the Revolution*, and they were evidence to us that the struggle, at least on the border, was a reality" (*The Eagle and the Serpent*, 45; emphasis added). Guzmán's revolution is white-collar, "civilized," and more real for him than the one being won by Villa and his soldiers on the battlefield.

43. In the discourse of the social sciences, "denial of coevalness" is defined as "a persistent and systematic tendency to place the referent(s) of anthropology in a Time other than the present of the producer of anthropological discourse" (Johannes Fabian, *Time and the Other: How Anthropology Makes Its Object*, 31).

44. On distancing techniques and the aesthetic experience in historical narratives, see Mark Salber Phillips, "Relocating Inwardness: Historical Distance and the Transition from Enlightenment to Romantic Historiography."

45. Guzmán's nationalist identification with Mexico's Otherness is most explicit when he crosses the U.S.-Mexico border: "It made our hearts dance," he wrote, "as we felt the roots of our being sink into something we had known, possessed, and loved for centuries, in all its brutishness, in all the filth of body and soul that pervades the streets. Not for nothing we were Mexicans" (*The Eagle and the Serpent*, 38).

46. Elias, *The Civilizing Process*, 165. State formation and the phasing out of expressive violence are also discussed in Parts 3 and 4 of Elias's work.

47. Jorge Aguilar Mora offers the following insight regarding the depiction of Villa as a wild animal: "In fact, he [Villa] was an animal because he had internalized the animal point of reference in order to understand his surroundings, to attack and survive. However, to speak of him as an animal is not a value judgment, as many have made it out to be; it is simply a characterization of his perspective. . . . In Villa's case, his animalistic qualities were an essential function of his mode of life, because *survival* was his mode of living" (Aguilar Mora, *Una muerte sencilla, justa, eterna*, 380, original emphasis). For Aguilar Mora, then, animal-like attributes in Villa are not antithetical to human nature, as many of his enemies claimed. It follows that Aguilar Mora would not object to Guzmán's description of Villa as a "jaguar"; he would, however, disagree with the disparaging meaning Guzmán attaches to such a characterization.

48. Hugo Rodríguez-Alcalá, "Sobre las muchas 'especies de hombre' en *El águila y la serpiente*," 61

49. For a discussion of bandits and the corrido tradition in Mexico, see Nicole Girón, *Heraclio Bernal ¿Bandolero, cacique o precursor de la revolución?* For the U.S.-Mexico border region, see Américo Paredes, *"With His Pistol in His Hand:" A Border Ballad and Its Hero*.

50. Stallybrass and White, *The Politics and Poetics of Transgression*, 6.

CHAPTER 5

1. James W. Wilkie, *The Mexican Revolution: Federal Expenditure and Social Change since 1910*, 208.

2. Ibid.

3. "Datos estadísticos de las bibliotecas existentes en la República."

4. O'Malley, *The Myth of the Revolution*, 100.

5. Monsiváis, "Notas sobre la cultura mexicana," 1455.

6. The biographical information on Muñoz in the following paragraphs is based on four sources: Carballo, *Diecinueve protagonistas*, 265–280; Aguilar Mora, *Una muerte sencilla, justa, eterna*, 123–127; "Rafael F. Muñoz"; and Rafael Solana, "Rasgos bio-bibliográficos de Rafael F. Muñoz."

7. Carballo, *Diecinueve protagonistas*, 271.

8. Ibid., 273.

9. Gamboa de Camino, "The Novel of the Mexican Revolution," 270.

10. Carballo, *Diecinueve protagonistas*, 267.

11. Ibid.

12. Ibid. The newspaper editor needed space to begin serializing the memoirs of a revolutionary general.

13. Henry C. Schmidt, *The Roots of "Lo Mexicano": Self and Society in Mexican Thought, 1900–1934*, 97–138.

14. For the identification of Villa with the tradition of machismo in Mexico, see Katz, *The Life and Times*, 238–239.

15. The search for *lo mexicano* prominently included the concept of violence, which "was linked to that of the struggling masses . . . and their projected social redemption . . . [and] assumed a lyrical quality in Mexican identity" (Schmidt, *The Roots of "Lo Mexicano,"* 69, 70).

16. Rafael F. Muñoz, *¡Vámonos con Pancho Villa!* (1989), 11. This edition will be cited in the text and the notes.

17. Alonso, *Thread of Blood*, 76.

18. On the two systems of causality and the dual nature of the short story form, see Ricardo Piglia, *Formas breves*, 103–111.

19. "El puente" was dropped from the second edition of *El feroz cabecilla* (Ediciones Botas, 1936).

20. Alonso, *Thread of Blood*, 54.

21. In their eagerness to be at the front of the Villista forces, the *leones* resemble Villa's legendary Dorados, whose deeds probably inspired Muñoz. The Dorados were General Villa's personal entourage, soldiers of unquestionable bravery drawn from his home region of Durango and Chihuahua. With few exceptions, they were known to be intrepid on the battlefield and extremely loyal to Villa. A certain degree of vanity and theatrics was also involved, for, in some instances, they were motivated by the desire to stand out, to be recognized and appreciated by their superiors and their comrades-in-arms. The objective was to be remembered, to achieve fame in the ranks of the Division of the North. Most of them died fighting. Their exploits, it follows, were fertile ground for myth making and epic history. In *¡Vámonos con Pancho Villa!* the *leones* fit the profile of the Dorados: they are natives of Villista territory (San Pablo); fierce warriors who perform worthy deeds; and even under the most adverse circumstances, they remain faithful to the Villista cause. Near the end of Muñoz's novel, old Tiburcio is inducted into the Dorados. For an extensive account of this elite military group, see Vargas Arreola, *A sangre y fuego con Pancho Villa*, 27–111.

22. O'Malley, *The Myth of the Revolution*, 136.

23. In the chapter entitled "Así eran ellos" (That's the Way They Were), the threat of dishonorable death becomes a real possibility when Melitón Botello, Máximo Perea, and Tiburcio Maya, who are about to be hanged by federal soldiers, are almost killed by the approaching Villistas, who are trying to liberate them. For the *leones*, it is a traumatic moment, for being killed by friendly fire would make their sacrifice absurd, inconsequential. They would prefer a dignified death at the hands of the enemy.

24. "El círculo de la muerte" appears to be inspired by a game of chance occasionally played by members of Villa's Dorados (Vargas Arreola, *A sangre y fuego con Pancho Villa*, 87–88).

25. Carlos Monsiváis, *Amor perdido*, 31.

26. O'Malley, *The Myth of the Revolution*, 134. Later in the novel, Villa is

wounded in a skirmish with the Carrancistas. Tiburcio's emotional outburst, crying "like he did not [cry] when Villa killed his wife, when he killed his daughter, when his son died calling out for him" (167), confirms that his love for Villa is stronger than his love for his family.

27. Muñoz's specific anecdotes are inspired by popular myths; the vision he conveys of Villismo is grounded in historical reality. In one memorable incident, for example, Villa orders his brother Hipólito executed because he was negligent at his post, putting at risk the forces under his command. Villa is later persuaded by his aides not to carry out the sentence (Jaurrieta, *Con Villa (1916–1920)*, 138).

28. Friedrich Katz, "Introducción," in Osorio, *Villa, ese desconocido*, x.

29. Katz, *The Life and Times*, 238–239.

30. Anderson, *Imagined Communities: Reflections on the Origin and Spread of Nationalism*, 16.

31. Linda McDowell, *Gender, Identity and Place: Understanding Feminist Geographies*, 195.

32. O'Malley, *The Myth of the Revolution*, 136.

33. For the role of women in the revolution, see Shirlene Ann Soto, *The Mexican Woman: A Study of Her Participation in the Revolution, 1910–1940*.

34. O'Malley, *The Myth of the Revolution*, 136.

35. Franco, *Plotting Women*, 103.

36. A hyperbolic example of the connection between class liberation and sexual dominance in Muñoz's works, with Villa as the central character, is the short story entitled "La marcha nupcial" (The Wedding March), included in *Relatos de la revolución: Cuentos completos*.

37. Another example is Botello calling the young federal officer who is about to hang him, "señorita" (*¡Vámonos con Pancho Villa!* [1989], 48–49).

38. Katz, *The Life and Times*, 793.

39. Among them, José Clemente Orozco, Ermilo Abreu Gómez, and Gregorio López y Fuentes.

40. The harassment was directed against the members of the Contemporáneos group, some of whom lost their government positions (Carlos Monsiváis, "Los Contemporáneos: La decepción, la provocación, la creación de un proyecto cultural," 24).

CHAPTER 6

1. Alan Knight, "The Rise and Fall of Cardenismo, c. 1930–c. 1946," 282.

2. Hamilton, *The Limits of State Autonomy*, chap. 7.

3. James D. Cockcroft, *Mexico: Class Formation, Capital Accumulation, and the State*, 132.

4. Hamilton, *The Limits of State Autonomy*, 68.

5. For a review of the rise and development of anthropological research in

Mexico in the first half of the twentieth century, see Catalina Hewitt de Alcántara, *Anthropological Perspectives on Rural Mexico*.

6. Rafael Tovar y de Teresa, *Modernización y política cultural: Una visión de la modernización de México*, 42-43.

7. Other novels on rural themes written during this period include Gregorio López y Fuentes's *Arrieros* (Muleteers, 1937); Rosa de Castaño's *Rancho estradeño* (Estradeño Ranch, 1936); and Mauricio Magdaleno's *indigenista* novel *El resplandor* (The Shining, 1937).

8. Oliver Debroise, "Notas para un análisis del sistema de la cultura plástica en México," 163.

9. Emilio García Riera, *Historia documental del cine mexicano*, 90-91.

10. Rossana Cassigoli Salamón, "Educación e indigenismo en México: La gestión cardenista," 588.

11. Hamilton, *The Limits of State Autonomy*, 140; Knight, "The Rise and Fall of Cardenismo," 264-268.

12. Lázaro Cárdenas, *Obras: Apuntes 1913-1940*, 337-340.

13. For an account of the rise of this military dynasty, see Héctor Aguilar Camín, *La frontera nómada: Sonora y la revolución mexicana*.

14. Emiliano Zapata, the other popular revolutionary leader, had been co-opted in the early 1920s by the Obregonistas. See O'Malley, *The Myth of the Revolution*, 41-70.

15. In 1940, Campobello was no longer the marginal figure in the literary and artistic world of Mexico City that she had been in 1931, when the first edition of *Cartucho* appeared. She now had three books to her credit and was the director of the National Dance School. Among her friends and cultural allies were well-known and influential artists and writers such as muralist José Clemente Orozco (who painted sets and created custom designs for her ballets) and novelist and publisher Martín Luis Guzmán (who was responsible for the publication of the second edition of *Cartucho*). See Rodríguez, *nellie campobello*, 80-85. In 1940, when the second edition of *Cartucho* was published, Campobello had relocated in the intellectual and artistic field and was now far closer to Mexico's political and cultural establishment, which endorsed, or at least was no longer hostile to, her pro-Villa activities.

16. Chapters of *Memorias* appeared in the newspaper *El Universal* in 1936.

17. Curiel, *La querella de Martín Luis Guzmán*, 154-155.

18. According to Guzmán, Calles was so upset when *La sombra del caudillo* came out that he wanted to prohibit the novel's distribution in Mexico. Calles's cultural adviser persuaded him not to do so, but Espasa Calpe, Guzmán's Spanish publisher, under pressure from the Mexican government, had to agree not to print any book by Guzmán dealing with Mexico after 1910 (Carballo, *Diecinueve protagonistas*, 74-75).

19. Martín Luis Guzmán revealed this fact in a 1971 interview (Guzmán, *Iconografía*, 13).

20. One of these politicians, Adolfo López Mateos, would be elected president of Mexico in 1958 (Curiel, *La querella de Martín Luis Guzmán*, 173).

21. Archivo General de la Nación, Ramo Presidentes, Lázaro Cárdenas Papers, 530/30, Guzmán 7-22-37.

22. Guzmán acknowledged his debt to Campobello and Rentería by giving each woman 30 percent of the book's royalties (Katz, *The Life and Times*, 831). Luz Corral, another of Villa's widows, declared in an interview that the documents originally belonged to her, and that Guzmán and Campobello took advantage of her absence to remove the papers from her house in Chihuahua by making false promises to Marianita Villa, Corral's sister-in-law (Osorio, *Pancho Villa, ese desconocido*, 132).

23. Guzmán, *Obras completas*, vol. 2, 9-10; Carballo, *Diecinueve protagonistas*, 76.

24. Fellow *ateneísta* José Vasconcelos, however, recalls in his memoirs a Guzmán far more committed to Villismo than he was willing to admit in *El águila* (Vasconcelos, *Memorias I*, 608-609, 628-629, 649-650).

25. Knight, "The Rise and Fall of Cardenismo," 257.

26. Mary Kay Vaughan, *Cultural Politics in Revolution: Teachers, Peasants, and Schools in Mexico, 1930-1940*, 40.

27. Friedrich Katz in Rodríguez, *nellie campobello*, 332.

28. Guzmán describes the writing processes of *Memorias* in the prologue to the 1951 edition. See *Obras completas*, vol. 2, 9-13. This edition will be cited in the text and the notes.

29. Ibid., 11.

30. Ibid.

31. Ibid., 11-12.

32. This last book was included in the second edition of *Memorias de Pancho Villa*.

33. "In the *Memorias*," Guzmán declared, "there is not one word that is not supported by the firsthand testimony of an eyewitness, or by a document" (Carballo, *Diecinueve protagonistas*, 76; see also, Katz, *The Life and Times*, 830-831).

34. Guzmán uses redundant expressions such as "Me habló sus palabras...," "Le hablé las palabras de mi necesidad"; colloquial constructions like "Y lo cierto es que...," "pero lo cierto, señor, que...," "tomé mis providencias...," "según yo opino...," "según yo creo..."; archaic expressions such as "grande confianza"; and popular rural words like "masque" and "cuantimás."

35. Rodríguez, *nellie campobello*, 327.

36. For the life and death of Gen. Maclovio Herrera, and his views on Villa, see Isaac Grinaldo, *Apuntes para la historia*.

37. Ibid., 22-24. Celia Herrera's version suggests that Villa's henchmen killed Maclovio Herrera in a cowardly manner.

38. Jaurrieta, *Con Villa (1916-1920)*, 178.

39. Katz, *The Life and Times*, 761–768.

40. I have been unable to identify who in the Mexican government proposed the idea of building a monument to Villa.

41. Celia Herrera, *Villa ante la historia* (1939), 5. This edition will be cited in the text and the notes. The first edition (1939) has only 111 pages; two other editions, both twice the length of the original, were published in 1964 and 1981, respectively, by Costa-Amic Editores.

42. Soldiers who were close to Villa, such as José María Jaurrieta and Juan Bautista Vargas Arreola, sometimes concur with Herrera and sometimes provide a different version in their memoirs of events also described in Herrera's book.

43. According to Katz, in most "cases the wealthier inhabitants took over control over the defensa social" (*The Life and Times*, 644); for Villa's positions toward looting in the years 1917–1920, see 585.

44. Historical documents corroborate the classist content of the Villista movement. On one occasion, Villa forced a group of Parral merchants and well-to-do citizens into a stockade. No family visits were permitted, and they were allowed to eat only dried meat and corn. They would now have to live "as the poor were living," Villa told them (ibid., 596).

45. Ibid., 6.

46. Vasconcelos, "Timón" (May 11, 1940), reproduced in Herrera, *Villa ante la historia* (1981), 13.

47. In 1937, while living in the United States, Vasconcelos unexpectedly allied himself with General Calles and joined a conspiracy to overthrow the Mexican government. The conspiracy never materialized. A year later, Vasconcelos accepted the president's invitation to return to Mexico, where he continued his attacks on Cárdenas (José Joaquín Blanco, *Se llamaba Vasconcelos: Una evocación crítica*, 170–171).

48. Novo's review of Herrera's book was published in the newspaper *Últimas Noticias* (Jan. 18, 1940). It was later reproduced in the 3rd edition of Herrera's *Villa ante la historia*, 18–19.

49. Salvador Novo, *La vida en México en el período presidencial de Lázaro Cárdenas*, 25.

50. In a letter to Celia Herrera, Novo confesses that it would not be appropriate to talk about Villa in the weekly column he was writing for *Hoy*, one of the prime magazines of the period. The letter is included in Herrera, *Villa ante la historia* (1981), 17.

51. The first edition (1939) of *Villa ante la historia* does not indicate a publishing house. This suggests that publication costs were probably paid by the author or by the Herrera family.

52. See Rodríguez, *nellie campobello*, 327.

53. It is quite possible that Herrera's vehement anti-Villa book may have prompted changes in the second edition of *Cartucho*. While in the first edition Campobello's references to executions ordered by Maclovio Herrera and the hor-

rible death met by his brother Luis stress the cruelty of war, in the 1940 edition, the Herreras are accused of masterminding the death of popular revolutionary Abelardo Prieto (*Cartucho*, 81–83) and of ordering the execution of his friends (ibid., 51), leading the narrator to state, approvingly, that with the eventual death of the Herreras "Abelardo Prieto has been avenged" (ibid., 83).

CHAPTER 7

1. To divert attention from its growing authoritarianism and repression of grassroots movements, the Díaz Ordaz regime sought to cloak itself in the populist mantle by reclaiming the popular origins of the revolution and the postrevolutionary state (O'Malley, *The Myth of the Revolution*, 112, 173–174). O'Malley notes, however, that many people still opposed Villa. For example, Celia Herrera's *Villa ante la historia* was republished in 1964 in an effort to prevent the general's historical rehabilitation.

2. Katz, "Pancho Villa, Peasant Movements and Agrarian Reform in Northern Mexico," 59.

3. This is also true for Celia Herrera, although her case is unique because of her single-minded aim of attacking and discrediting Villa.

BIBLIOGRAPHY

ARCHIVAL SOURCES (MEXICO CITY)

Archivo General de la Nación (AGN). Ramo Presidentes. Lázaro Cárdenas Papers, 530/30, Guzmán 7-22-37.
Archivo Nellie Campobello. Fondo Reservado. Biblioteca de las Artes del Centro Nacional de las Artes (CNA). Patricia Aulestia, "Entrevista con Nellie Campobello," January 4, 1972.

WORKS CONSULTED

Aguilar Camín, Héctor. *La frontera nómada: Sonora y la revolución mexicana.* Mexico City: Siglo XXI, 1978.
———. *Saldos de la revolución: Cultura y política en México, 1910–1980.* Mexico City: Nueva Imagen, 1982.
Aguilar Camín, Héctor, and Lorenzo Meyer. *In the Shadow of the Mexican Revolution: Contemporary Mexican History, 1910–1989.* Austin: University of Texas Press, 1993.
Aguilar Mora, Jorge. "La despedida de Villa y la novela de la revolución mexicana." *Roa Bastos y la producción cultural americana,* ed. Saúl Sosnowski, 245–258. Buenos Aires: Ediciones de la Flor; Mexico City: Folios Ediciones, 1986.
———. *Una muerte sencilla, justa, eterna.* Mexico City: Era, 1990.
Alessio Robles, Vito. "Las memorias dictadas por el general Francisco Villa." *Todo* (July 28, 1936): 9–10.
Almada, Francisco R. *Diccionario de historia, geografía y biografía chihuahuense.* 4th ed. Chihuahua: Ediciones del Gobierno del Estado de Chihuahua, 1997.
———. *Diccionario de historia, geografía y biografía chihuahuense.* 2nd ed. Ciudad Juárez, Mex.: Universidad de Chihuahua, 1968.
Alonso, Ana María. "The Effects of Truth: Re-presentations of the Past and the Imagining of Community." *Journal of Historical Sociology* 1, no. 1 (1988): 33–57.
———. "'Progress' as Disorder and Dishonor: Discourses of Serrano Resistance." *Critique of Anthropology* 8, no. 1 (1988): 13–33.
———. *Thread of Blood: Colonialism, Revolution, and Gender on Mexico's Northern Frontier.* Tucson: University of Arizona Press, 1995.

Altamirano, Ignacio Manuel. *El Zarco*. Mexico City: Editora Nacional, 1979.

Anderson, Benedict. *Imagined Communities: Reflections on the Origin and Spread of Nationalism*. London: Verso, 1987.

Anderson, Danny. "Subjetividad y lectura: Ideología de la técnica en *El luto humano* y el cambio narrativo a medio siglo." *Perfiles: Ensayos sobre literatura mexicana reciente*, ed. Federico Patán, 113–125. Boulder: Society of Spanish and Spanish-American Studies, 1992.

Anguiano, Arturo. *El estado y la política obrera del Cardenismo*. Mexico City: Era, 1975.

Arriaga, Guillermo. *Relatos de los esplendores y miserias del Escuadrón Guillotina y de cómo participó en la leyenda de Francisco Villa*. Mexico City: Editorial Planeta Mexicana, 1991.

Azuela, Mariano. *Los de abajo*. Mexico City: FCE, 1974.

———. *Obras completas*. Vol. 3. Mexico City: FCE, 1958.

———. *San Gabriel de Valdivias, comunidad indígena*. Santiago de Chile: Ediciones Ercilla, 1938.

———. *The Underdogs*. Trans. E. Munguía Jr. New York: Signet Classics, 1963.

Bakhtin, Mikhail. *Problemas de la poética de Dostoievski*. Mexico City: FCE, 1986.

———. *Rabelais and His World*. Trans. Hélène Iswolsky. Bloomington: Indiana University Press, 1984.

Barthes, Roland. "Introduction to the Structural Analysis of Narratives." *Image-Music-Text*, trans. Stephen Heath, 79–124. New York: Hill and Wang, 1977.

Beer, Gabriella de. "Nellie Campobello, escritora de la revolución." *Cuadernos americanos* 223 (1979): 212–219.

———. "Nellie Campobello's Vision of the Mexican Revolution." *American Hispanist* 4 (1979): 34–35.

Benedicto, Luis. *Los guerrilleros*. Mexico City: Ediciones Populares de La Prensa, 1931.

Benjamin, Thomas, and Mark Wasserman, eds. *Provinces of the Revolution: Essays on Regional Mexican History 1910–1929*. Albuquerque: University of New Mexico Press, 1990.

Benjamin, Walter. "The Storyteller." *Illuminations*, 83–109. New York: Schocken Books, 1978.

Beverley, John. *Subalternity and Representation: Arguments in Cultural Theory*. Durham, N.C.: Duke University Press, 1999.

Bidault de la Calle, Sophie. *Nellie Campobello: Una escritura salida del cuerpo*. Mexico City: Instituto Nacional de Bellas Artes, Nueva Vizcaya Editores, 2003.

Blanco, José Joaquín. "Lecturas de *Los de abajo*." *La paja en el ojo*, 205–241. Puebla, Mex.: Universidad de Puebla, 1980.

———. *Se llamaba Vasconcelos: Una evocación crítica*. Mexico City: FCE. 1983.

Bruce-Novoa, Juan. "*El águila y la serpiente* en las versiones estadounidenses." *Plural* 193 (1987): 16–21.

―――. "Martín Luis Guzman's Necessary Overtures." *Discurso Literario* 4, no. 1: 63–83.

Calles, Plutarco Elías. *Plutarco Elías Calles: Pensamiento social y político. Antología (1913–1936)*. Mexico City: FCE, IEHRM, Archivos PEC, Fernando Torreblanca, 1988.

Campobello, Nellie. *Apuntes sobre la vida militar de Francisco Villa*. Mexico City: Edición y Distribución Ibero-Americana de Publicaciones, S.A., 1940.

―――. *Cartucho: Relatos de la lucha en el norte de México*. Xalapa: Ediciones Integrales, 1931.

―――. *Cartucho: Relatos de la lucha en el norte de México*. Mexico City: Edición y Distribución Ibero-Americana de Publicaciones, S.A., 1940.

―――. *Cartucho; My Mother's Hands*. Trans. Doris Meyer and Irene Matthews. Austin: University of Texas Press, 1988.

―――. "El combate de Tierra Blanca." *Todo* (July 9, 1935): 19–20.

―――. "Los hijos del General Villa necesitan que se acuerde de una vez la pensión solicitada." *El Universal Gráfico* (December 4, 1935): 4.

―――. "Martín Luis Guzmán, a propósito de 'El hombre y las armas.'"*Ruta*, 4ª época, 1, no. 6 (November 1938): 42–43.

―――. *Mis libros*. Mexico City: Compañía General de Ediciones, 1960.

―――. "La muerte de Tomás Urbina." *Todo* (February 20, 1934): 20.

―――. "Ocho poemas de mujer." *Revista de La Habana* 11 (1930): 133–139.

―――. "El Pancho Villa que no conoce el mundo: Dos cartas de amor del guerrillero." *Todo* (December 10, 1935): 11–12.

―――. "Perfiles de Villa." *Revista de Revistas* (August 7, 1932): 14–15.

―――. "La toma de Torreón por el gral. Villa." *Todo* (June 30, 1936): 9–10.

―――. "Villa siguió las normas de Napoleón en el ataque de Casas Grandes." *Todo* (June 25, 1935): 14–16.

Carballo, Emmanuel. *Diecinueve protagonistas de la literatura mexicana del siglo XX*. Mexico City: Empresas Editoriales, 1965.

Cárdenas, Lázaro. *Obras: Apuntes 1913–1940*. Mexico City: Universidad Nacional Autónoma de México, 1972.

Carr, Barry. *El movimiento obrero y la política en México, 1910–1929*. Mexico City: SepSetentas, 1976.

―――. "Las peculiaridades del norte mexicano, 1880–1927: Ensayo de interpretación." *Historia Mexicana* 22, no. 3 (1973): 320–346.

Caso, Antonio. *La filosofía como economía, como desinterés y como caridad*. Mexico City: Secretaría de Educación Pública, 1943.

―――, et al. *Conferencias del Ateneo de la Juventud*. Mexico City: Universidad Nacional Autónoma de México, 1984.

Cassigoli Salamón, Rossana. "Educación e indigenismo en México: La gestión cardenista." *Historia de la cuestión agraria mexicana*, coord. Everardo Escárcega López, vol. 5 (2ª pt.), 572–613. Mexico City: Siglo XXI, 1990.

Castaño, Rosa de. *Rancho estradeño.* Mexico City: Ediciones Botas, 1936.

Castellanos, Antonio. *Francisco Villa, su vida y su muerte: Sensacionales revelaciones y consideraciones sobre su vida y su asesinato.* San Antonio, Tex.: Librería Renacimiento, 1923.

Castro Leal, Antonio. *La novela de la revolución mexicana.* 2 vols. Mexico City: Aguilar, 1966–1967.

Catálogo del Archivo de la Palabra. Mexico City: Instituto Nacional de Antropología e Historia, 1977.

Cázares H., Laura. "Eros y Tanatos: Infancia y revolución en Nellie Campobello." *Escribir la infancia: Narradoras mexicanas contemporáneas,* ed. Nora Pasternac, Ana Rosa Domenella, and Luzelena Gutiérrez de Velasco, 37–58. Mexico City: El Colegio de México, 1996.

Cazés, Daniel. *Los revolucionarios.* Mexico City: Grijalbo, 1973.

Cervantes, Federico. *Francisco Villa y la historia.* Mexico City: Ediciones Alonso, 1960.

Cockcroft, James D. *Mexico: Class Formation, Capital Accumulation, and the State.* New York: Monthly Review, 1983.

Córdoba, Arnaldo. *La ideología de la revolución mexicana.* Mexico City: Era, 1985.

Cuesta, Jorge. *Poemas y ensayos.* Vol. 3. Mexico City: Universidad Nacional Autónoma de México, 1978.

Curiel, Fernando. *La querella de Martín Luis Guzmán.* Mexico City: Ediciones Coyoacán, 1993.

Chávez M., Armando B. *Diccionario de hombres de la revolución en Chihuahua.* Ciudad Juárez, Mex.: Universidad Autónoma de Ciudad Juárez, 1990.

"Datos estadísticos de las bibliotecas existentes en la República." *El Libro y el Pueblo* 3, no. 9 (1933): 7–8.

Debroise, Oliver. "Notas para un análisis del sistema de la cultura plástica en México." *Política cultural del estado mexicano,* coord. Moisés Ladrón de Guevara, 149–176. Mexico City: GEFE, 1983.

Dessau, Adalbert. *La novela de la revolución mexicana.* Mexico City: FCE, 1973.

Díaz Arciniega, Víctor. "Mariano Azuela y *Los de abajo:* Entre ser y parecer." *Investigaciones humanísticas* 3 (1987): 117–141.

———. *Querella por la cultura "revolucionaria," (1925).* Mexico City: FCE, 1989.

Díaz y de Ovando, Clementina. "Literatura popular contemporánea." *Anales del Instituto de Investigaciones Estéticas,* no. 21, 31–53. Mexico City: Universidad Nacional Autónoma de México, 1953.

Domínguez, Christopher. "Martín Luis Guzmán: El teatro de la política." *Vuelta* 131 (1987): 22–31.

Doñán, Juan José. "Entrevista con Friedrich Katz: Si Madero no hubiera muerto." *La Jornada Semanal* [Mexico City] (April 21, 1996): 10–11.

Dromundo, Baltasar. *Francisco Villa y la "Adelita."* Durango, Mex.: N.p., 1936.

Eagleton, Terry. *The Ideology of the Aesthetic.* Oxford: Basil Blackwell, 1990.

Elias, Norbert. *The Civilizing Process.* Oxford: Blackwell Publishers, 1994.

Engelkirk, John. "The Discovery of *Los de abajo.*" *Hispania* 17 (1935): 53–62.

Fabian, Johannes. *Time and the Other: How Anthropology Makes Its Object.* New York: Columbia University Press, 1983.

Fernández de Lizardi, José Joaquín. *El periquillo sarniento.* Mexico City: Porrúa, 1966.

———. *La Quijotita y su prima.* Mexico City: Porrúa, 1967.

Fitts, Dudley. *Anthology of Contemporary Latin American Poetry.* Norfolk, Conn.: New Directions, 1942.

Flores, Juan. *Insularismo e ideología burguesa.* Río Piedras, PR: Ediciones Huracán, 1979.

Florescano, Enrique. *El nuevo pasado mexicano.* Mexico City: Cal y Arena, 1991.

Foster, David William. "Escrutando el texto de la revolución, *El águila y la serpiente* de Martín Luis Guzmán." *Revista de Crítica Literaria Latinoamericana* 15, no. 30 (2nd sem. 1989): 79–90.

Franco, Jean. *Critical Passions.* Durham, N.C.: Duke University Press, 1999.

———. *The Modern Culture of Latin America.* Harmondsworth, Eng.: Penguin, 1970.

———. *Plotting Women: Gender and Representation in Mexico.* New York: Columbia University Press, 1989.

———. "Trends and Priorities for Research on Latin AmericanLiterature." *Ideologies and Literature* 4, no. 16 (1983): 107–120.

———, et al. *Cultura y dependencia.* Guadalajara, Mex.: Departamento de Bellas Artes, 1976.

Frías, Heriberto. *Tomóchic.* Mexico City: Porrúa, 1968.

Gamboa de Camino, Berta. "The Novel of the Mexican Revolution." *Renascent Mexico,* ed. Hubert Herring and Herbert Weinstock, 258–274. New York: Covici-Friede, 1935.

García Morales, Alfonso. *El Ateneo de México (1906–1914).* Seville: Escuela de Estudios Hispano-Americanos de Sevilla, 1992.

García Riera, Emilio. *Fernando de Fuentes (1894/1958).* Mexico City: Cineteca Nacional, 1984.

———. *Historia documental del cine mexicano.* Vol. 1. Mexico City: Era, 1969.

Gibson, Ian. *Federico García Lorca: A Life.* New York: Pantheon, 1989.

Gilly, Adolfo. "Memoria y olvido, razón y esperanza." *Brecha* 1 (1986): 7–15.

———. *La revolución interrumpida.* Mexico City: Ediciones "El Caballito," 1981.

Giménez, Catalina H. de. *Así cantaban la revolución.* Mexico City: CNCA, Grijalbo, 1991.

Girón, Nicole. *Heraclio Bernal ¿Bandolero, cacique o precursor de la revolución?* Mexico City: Instituto Nacional de Antropología e Historia, Departamento de Investigaciones Históricas, 1976.

Gómez, Marte R. *Pancho Villa: Un intento de semblanza.* Mexico City: FCE, 1974.

Gómez Morín, Manuel. *1915 y otros ensayos.* Mexico City: Jus, 1973.

González, Luis. *Introducción a la microhistoria.* Mexico City: SepSetentas, 1973.

————, et al. *Historia regional y archivos.* Mexico City: Archivo General de la Nación, 1982.

González, Manuel Pedro. *Trayectoria de la novela en México.* Mexico City: Ediciones Botas, 1951.

González, Manuel W. *Contra Villa: Relatos de campaña 1914–1915.* Mexico City: Ediciones Botas, 1935.

González León, José Ramón. *"La dama de las lilas": Apuntes biográficos de Nellie Campobello.* Gómez Palacios, Mex.: Legislatura del Estado de Durango, 1991.

Gramsci, Antonio. "Espontaneidad y dirección consciente." *Antología,* by Antonio Gramsci, 309–312. Mexico City: Siglo XXI, 1981.

Grimaldo, Isaac. *Apuntes para la historia.* San Luis Potosí, Mex.: Escuela Industrial Militar, 1916.

Guerra, François-Xavier. *México: Del antiguo régimen a la revolución.* 2 vols. Mexico City: FCE, 1991.

————. "The Spanish-American Tradition of Representation and Its European Roots." *Journal of Latin American Studies* 26 (1994): 1–35.

————. "Teoría y método en el análisis de la revolución mexicana." *Revista Mexicana de Sociología* 51, no. 2 (1989): 3–24.

Guerrero, Julio. *La génesis del crimen en México.* Mexico City: Porrúa, 1977.

Guha, Ranajit. *Elementary Aspects of Peasant Insurgency in Colonial India.* Delhi: Oxford University Press, 1992.

————, and Gayatri Chakravorty Spivak, eds. *Selected Subaltern Studies.* New York: Oxford University Press, 1988.

Guzmán, Martín Luis. *A orillas del Hudson.* Mexico City: Asociación Nacional de Libreros, 1984.

————. *El águila y la serpiente.* Mexico City: Porrúa, 1984.

————. *Caudillos y otros extremos.* Intro. Fernando Curiel. Mexico City: Universidad Nacional Autónoma de México, 1995.

————. *The Eagle and the Serpent.* Trans. Harriet de Onís. Gloucester, Mass.: Peter Smith, 1969.

————. *Iconografía.* Prol. Héctor Perea. Mexico City: FCE, 1987.

————. *Memorias de Pancho Villa.* 2nd ed. Mexico City: Compañía General de Ediciones, 1951.

————. *Obras completas.* 2 vols. Mexico City: Compañía General de Ediciones, 1974.

————. *La sombra del caudillo: Versión periodística.* Intro. Juan Bruce-Novoa. Mexico City: Universidad Nacional Autónoma de México, 1987.

Hamilton, Nora. *The Limits of State Autonomy: Post-Revolutionary Mexico.* Princeton, NJ: Princeton University Press, 1982.

Herrera, Celia. *Francisco Villa ante la historia (a propósito de un monumento que pretenden levantarle).* N.p.: N.p., 1939.

————. *Francisco Villa ante la historia.* 3rd ed. Mexico City: Costa-Amic, 1981.

Hewitt de Alcántara, Catalina. *Anthropological Perspectives on Rural Mexico.* London: Routledge & Kegan Paul, 1984.

Hobsbawm, Eric J. *Bandits.* New York: Delacorte, 1969.

———. *Primitive Rebels: Studies in Archaic Forms of Social Movements in the 19th and 20th Centuries.* New York: Norton, 1965.

Holguín, José de la O. *Rescate histórico de Villa Ocampo.* Durango, Mex.: Secretaría de Educación, Cultura y Deporte, 1994.

Jaurrieta, José María. *Con Villa (1916–1920), memorias de campaña.* Mexico City: Consejo Nacional para la Cultura y las Artes, 1997.

Joseph, Gilbert M., and Daniel Nugent, eds. *Everyday Forms of State Formation: Revolution and the Negotiation of Rule in Modern Mexico.* Durham, N.C.: Duke University Press, 1994.

Katz, Friedrich. *Ensayos mexicanos.* Mexico City: Alianza Editorial, 1994.

———. *The Life and Times of Pancho Villa.* Stanford: Stanford University Press, 1998.

———. "Pancho Villa, Peasant Movements and Agrarian Reform in Northern Mexico." *Caudillo and Peasant in the Mexican Revolution,* ed. D. A. Brading, 59–75. Cambridge: Cambridge University Press, 1980.

———. "Peasants in the Mexican Revolution of 1910." *Forging Nations: A Comparative View of Rural Ferment and Revolt,* ed. Joseph Spielberg and Scott Whiteford, 61–81. Lansing: Michigan State University Press, 1976.

———. "El pensamiento social de Pancho Villa." *Actas del Primer Congreso de Historia Regional Comparada, 1989,* 289–294. Ciudad Juárez, Mex.: Universidad Autónoma de Ciudad Juárez, 1990.

———. *The Secret War in Mexico: Europe, the United States, and the Mexican Revolution.* Chicago: University of Chicago Press, 1981.

———, ed. *Riot, Rebellion, and Revolution.* Princeton, NJ: Princeton University Press, 1988.

Keller, Gary D. "El niño en la revolución mexicana: Nellie Campobello, Andrés Iduarte y César Garizurieta." *Cuadernos Americanos* 170 (1970): 142–151.

Knight, Alan. "Los intelectuales en la revolución mexicana." *Revista Mexicana de Sociología* 51, no. 2 (1989): 25–65.

———. *The Mexican Revolution.* 2 vols. Lincoln: University of Nebraska Press, 1986.

———. "Peasant and Caudillo in Revolutionary Mexico 1910–17." *Caudillo and Peasant in the Mexican Revolution,* ed. D. A. Brading, 17–58. Cambridge: Cambridge University Press, 1980.

———. "Peasants into Patriots: Thoughts on the Making of the Mexican Nation." *Mexican Studies/Estudios Mexicanos* 10, no. 1 (1994): 135–166.

———. "Popular Culture and the Revolutionary State in Mexico, 1910–1940." *Hispanic American Historical Review* 74, no. 3 (1994): 393–401.

———. "The Rise and Fall of Cardenismo, c. 1930–c. 1946." *Mexico since In-*

dependence, ed. Leslie Bethell, 241–320. Cambridge: Cambridge University Press, 1994.

Langle Ramírez, Arturo. *El ejército villista*. Mexico City: Instituto Nacional de Antropología e Historia, 1961.

———. *Los primeros cien años de Pancho Villa*. Mexico City: Costa-Amic, 1980.

Latin American Subaltern Group. "Founding Statement." *Boundary 2* 20, no. 3 (1993): 110–121.

Leal, Luis. "La caricia suprema: Contextos de luz y sombra en *El águila y la serpiente*." *Five Essays on Martín Luis Guzmán*, ed., William W. Megenney, 71–82. Riverside: University of California, Riverside, Latin American Studies Program, 1978.

———. *Mariano Azuela*. New York: Twayne, 1971.

———, ed. *Cuentos de la revolución*. Mexico City: Universidad Nacional Autónoma de México, 1987.

Lister, Florence C., and Robert H. Lister. *Chihuahua: Storehouse of Storms*. Albuquerque: University of New Mexico Press, 1966.

López González, Aralia, coord. *Sin imágenes falsas, sin falsos espejos: Narradoras mexicanas del siglo XX*. Mexico City: El Colegio de México, 1996.

López y Fuentes, Gregorio. *Arrieros*. Mexico City: Ediciones Botas, 1937.

Magdaleno, Mauricio. *El resplandor*. Mexico City: Ediciones Botas, 1937.

Mallon, Florencia E. *Peasant and Nation: The Making of Postcolonial Mexico and Peru*. Berkeley and Los Angeles: University of California Press, 1995.

———. "The Promise and Dilemma of Subaltern Studies: Perspectives from Latin American History." *American Historical Review* 99, no.5 (1994): 1491–1515.

Mansour, Mónica. "Cúspides inaccesibles." *Los de abajo*, by Mariano Azuela. Critical ed. Jorge Ruffinelli, 251–274. Madrid: Archivos, 1988.

Martin, Cheryl English. *Governance and Society in Colonial Mexico: Chihuahua in the Eighteenth Century*. Stanford, Calif.: Stanford University Press, 1996.

Matthews, Irene. "Daughtering in War: Two 'Case Studies' from Mexico and Guatemala." *Gendering War Talk*, ed. Miriam Cooke and Angela Woollacott, 148–173. Princeton, N.J.: Princeton University Press, 1993.

———. *Nellie Campobello: La centaura del norte*. Mexico City: Cal y Arena, 1997.

Matute, Álvaro. "La revolución recordada, inventada, rescatada." *Memoria del Congreso Internacional sobre la Revolución Mexicana*. Vol. 2, 441–445. San Luis Potosí, Mex.: Gobierno del Estado de San Luis Potosí, Instituto de Estudios Históricos de la Revolución Mexicana, Secretaría de Gobernación, 1991.

McDowell, Linda. *Gender, Identity and Place: Understanding Feminist Geographies*. Minneapolis: University of Minnesota Press, 1999.

Megenney, William W., ed. *Five Essays on Martín Luis Guzmán*. Riverside: University of California, Riverside, Latin American Studies Program, 1978.

Mendoza, Vicente T. *El romance español y el corrido mexicano*. Mexico City: Universidad Nacional Autónoma de México, 1939.

Meyer, Doris. "Nellie Campobello's *Las manos de mamá:* A Rereading." *Hispania* 68, no. 4 (1985): 747–752.

Meyer, Jean. "Revolution and Reconstruction in the 1920s." *Mexico since Independence*, ed. Leslie Bethell, 201–240. New York: Cambridge University Press, 1994.

Monsiváis, Carlos. *Amor perdido*. Mexico City: Era, 1978.

———. "La aparición del subsuelo (Sobre la cultura de la revolución mexicana)." "La cultura en México," *Siempre* (supp.) 1122 (December 14, 1983): 36–42.

———. "Aproximaciones e reintegros." "La cultura en México," *Siempre* (supp.) 984 (May 3, 1972): x.

———. "Aproximaciones y reintegros: Notas sobre la novela de la revolución (II)." "La cultura en México," *Siempre* (supp.) 986 (May 17, 1972): xi.

———. "Los contemporáneos: La decepción, la provocación, la creaciónde un proyecto cultural." *Revista de Bellas Artes* 3ª época (1982): 17–26.

———. "Muerte y resurrección del nacionalismo mexicano." *Nexos* 109 (1987): 13–22

———. "Notas sobre la cultura mexicana en el siglo XX." *Historia general de México*. 3rd ed. Vol. 2, 1375–1548. Mexico City: El Colegio de México, 1981.

Montalvo, Enrique. *El nacionalismo contra la nación*. Mexico City: Grijalbo, 1986.

———, coord. *Historia de la cuestión agraria mexicana: Modernización, lucha agraria y poder político, 1920–1934*. Mexico City: Siglo XXI, 1988.

Moore, Ernest. *Bibliografía de novelistas de la revolución mexicana*. Mexico City: N.p., 1941.

Muncy, Michèlle. "La escritora a través de su obra." *La escritora hispánica*, ed. Nora Erro-Orthman and Juan Cruz Mendizábal, 121–130. Miami: Universal, 1990.

———. "Nellie Campobello: Anverso y reverso de la historia." *SECOLAS* 19 (1988): 54–61.

Muñoz, Rafael F. *El feroz cabecilla: Cuentos de la revolución en el norte*. Mexico City: Ediciones Botas, 1936.

———. *El feroz cabecilla, y otros cuentos de la revolución en el norte*. Mexico City: N.p. 1928.

———. *Obras incompletas, dispersas o rechazadas*. Mexico City: Ediciones Oasis, 1967.

———. *Pancho Villa, rayo y azote*. Mexico City: Populibros La Prensa, 1955.

———. *Relatos de la revolución: Cuentos completos*. Mexico City: Grijalbo, 1985.

———. *¡Vámonos con Pancho Villa!* 9th ed. Mexico City: Espasa Calpe Mexicana, 1989.

———, [and Ramón Puente]. *Memorias de Pancho Villa*. Mexico City: Universal Gráfico, 1923.

Nájera, Valeska Strickland. "La obra de Nellie Campobello." PhD diss., Northwestern University, 1980.

Novo, Salvador. *La vida en México en el período presidencial de Lázaro Cárdenas*. Mexico City: Consejo Nacional para la Cultura y las Artes, 1994.

Nugent, Daniel. "'Are We Not [Civilized] Men?' The Formation and Devolution of Community in Northern Mexico." *Journal of Historical Sociology* 2, no. 3 (1989): 206–239.

———. "Rural Revolt in Mexico, Mexican Nationalism and the State, and Forms of U.S. Intervention." *Rural Revolt in Mexico and U.S. Intervention*, ed. D. Nugent, 1–21. San Diego: Center for U.S.-Mexican Studies, 1988.

———, ed. *Rural Revolt in Mexico and U.S. Intervention*. San Diego: Center for U.S.-Mexican Studies, 1988.

O'Hea, Patrick A. *Reminiscences of the Mexican Revolution*. Mexico City: Fournier, 1966.

O'Malley, Ilene. *The Myth of the Revolution: Hero Cults and the Institutionalization of the Mexican State, 1920–1940*. Westport, Conn.: Greenwood Press, 1986.

Ong, Walter J. *The Presence of the Word*. Minneapolis: University of Minnesota Press, 1986.

Orellana, Margarita de. *La mirada circular: El cine norteamericano de la revolución mexicana 1911–1917*. Mexico City: Joaquín Mortiz, 1991.

Osorio, Rubén. *Pancho Villa, ese desconocido: Entrevistas en Chihuahua a favor y en contra*. Intro. Friedrich Katz. Chihuahua, Mex.: Ediciones del Gobierno del Estado de Chihuahua, 1990.

Oyarzún, Kemy. "Identidad femenina, genealogía mítica, historia: *Las manos de mamá*." *Sin imágenes falsas sin falsos espejos: Narradoras mexicanas del siglo XX*, coord. Aralia López González, 51–75. Mexico City: El Colegio de México, 1995.

———. "Mujer, memoria, Historia: *Cartucho*, de Nellie Campobello." *The Latin American Short Story: Essays on the 25th Anniversary of Seymour Menton's El cuento hispanoamericano*, ed. Kemy Oyarzún, 75–84. Riverside: University of California, Riverside, Latin American Studies Program, 1989.

Pacheco, Carlos. *La comarca oral*. Caracas: Ediciones La Casa de Bello, 1992.

Palacios, Guillermo. "Calles y la idea oficial de la revolución." *Historia Mexicana* 22, no. 3 (1973): 261–278.

Paredes, Américo. *Culture and Folklore on the Texas-Mexican Border*. Austin: University of Texas Press, 1993.

———. *"With His Pistol in His Hand": A Border Ballad and Its Hero*. Austin: University of Texas Press, 1958.

Parle, Dennis J. "Narrative Style and Technique in Nellie Campobello's *Cartucho*." *Kentucky Romance Quarterly* 32 (1985): 201–211.

———. "The Novels of the Mexican Revolution" Published by the Casa Editorial Lozano. *The Americas Review* 17, nos. 3–4: (1989): 163–168.

Parra, Max. "Memoria y guerra en *Cartucho* de Nellie Campobello." *Revista de Crítica Literaria Latinoamericana* 24, no. 47 (1st sem. 1998): 167–186.

———. "The Politics of Representation: The Novel of the Revolution and the

Zapatista Uprising in Chiapas." *Journal of Latin American Cultural Studies* 4, no.1 (1995): 65–71.

———. "Villa y la subjetividad política popular: Un acercamiento subalternista a *Los de abajo* de Mariano Azuela." *Foro Hispánico* 22 (2002): 11–26.

Paz, Octavio. *The Labyrinth of Solitude and Other Writings.* Trans. Lysander Kemp, Yara Milos, and Rachel Phillips Belash. New York: Grove Press, 1985.

Pérez Herrero, Pedro. "Regional Conformation in Mexico, 1700– 1850: Models and Hypotheses." *Mexico's Regions: Comparative History and Development*, ed. Eric Van Young, 117–144. San Diego: Center for U.S.-Mexican Studies, 1992.

Pérez Montfort, Ricardo. *Estampas del nacionalismo popular mexicano: Ensayos sobre cultura popular y nacionalismo.* Mexico City: Centro de Investigaciones y Estudios Superiores en Antropología Social, 1994.

Phillips, Mark Salber. "Relocating Inwardness: Historical Distance and the Transition from Enlightenment to Romantic Historiography." *PMLA* 118 (2003): 436–449.

Piglia, Ricardo. *Formas breves.* Barcelona: Anagrama, 2001.

Prakash, Gyan, "Subaltern Studies as Postcolonial Criticism." *American Historical Review* 99, no. 5 (1994): 1475–1490.

Puente, Ramón. *Hombres de la revolución: Villa (sus auténticas memorias).* Los Angeles: Spanish-American Print, 1931.

———. *Vida de Francisco Villa contada por él mismo.* Los Angeles: O. Paz y Compañía, 1919.

———. *Villa en pie.* Mexico City: Editorial México Nuevo, 1937.

"Rafael F. Muñoz." *Diccionario de escritores mexicanos*, ed. Aurora M. Ocampo de Gómez and Ernesto Prado Velázquez, 245. Mexico City: Universidad Nacional Autónoma de México, 1967.

Rama, Ángel. *La ciudad letrada.* Hanover, N.H.: Ediciones del Norte, 1984.

———. "Mariano Azuela: Ambición y frustración de las clases medias." *Literatura y clase social*, by Ángel Rama, 144–183. Mexico City: Folios Ediciones, 1983.

Ramírez, Guillermo. *Melitón Lozoya: Único director intelectual en la muerte de Villa.* Durango, Mex.: Herrera, n.d. [192?].

Rampersad, Arnold. *The Life of Langston Hughes.* Vol. 1: *1902–1941.* New York: Oxford University Press, 1986.

Reed, John. *Insurgent Mexico.* New York: International Publishers, 1978.

Reyes, Alfonso. "Pasado inmediato." *Obras completas.* Vol. 12, 182–216. Mexico City: FCE, 1983.

———. "El testimonio de Juan Peña." *Páginas escogidas*, by Alfonso Reyes, 524–537. Havana: Casa de las Américas, 1978.

———. "Visión de Anáhuac." *Obras completas.* Vol. 2, 13–34. Mexico City: FCE, 1956.

Robe, Stanley. *Azuela and the Mexican Underdogs.* Berkeley and Los Angeles: University of California Press, 1979.

Robleto, Hernán. *La mascota de Pancho Villa: Episodios de la revolución mexicana.* Mexico City: Libro-Mex, 1960.

Rodó, José Enrique. *Ariel.* Trans. Margaret Sayers Peden. Austin: University of Texas Press, 1988.

Rodríguez, Blanca. *nellie campobello: eros y violencia.* Mexico City: Universidad Nacional Autónoma de México, 1998.

Rodríguez-Alcalá, Hugo. "Sobre las muchas 'especies de hombre' en El águila y la serpiente." *Five Essays on Martín Luis Guzmán,* ed. William W. Megenney, 48–71. Riverside: University of California, Riverside, Latin American Studies Program, 1978.

Romance histórico villista: Diario en verso de un soldado de Villa. Chihuahua, Mex.: Edición de Antonio Delgado, 1975.

Rouaix, Pastor. *Diccionario geográfico, histórico y biográfico del Estado de Durango.* Mexico City: Instituto Panamericano de Geografía e Historia, 1946.

———. *Geografía del estado de Durango.* Mexico City: Talleres Gráficos de la Secretaría de Agricultura y Fomento, 1929.

Ruffinelli, Jorge. *Literatura e ideología: El primer Mariano Azuela (1896–1918).* Mexico City: Premiá, 1982.

———. "La recepción crítica de Los de abajo." *Los de abajo,* by Mariano Azuela. Critical ed. Jorge Ruffinelli, 185–213. Madrid: Archivos, 1988.

Rutherford, John. *Mexican Society during the Revolution.* Oxford: Clarendon Press, 1971.

Sánchez, Enrique W. *Corridos de Pancho Villa.* Mexico City: Editorial del Magisterio Benito Juárez, 1978.

Schmidt, Henry C. *The Roots of "Lo Mexicano": Self and Society in Mexican Thought, 1900–1934.* College Station: Texas A&M University Press, 1978.

Schneider, Luis Mario. *El estridentismo: O, una literatura de la estrategia.* Mexico City: Instituto Nacional de Bellas Artes, 1970.

———. *Ruptura y continuidad.* Mexico City: FCE, 1975.

Scott, James C. *The Moral Economy of the Peasant.* New Haven, Conn.: Yale University Press, 1976.

Shaw, Donald L. "*El águila y la serpiente*: Arielismo and Narrative Method." *Five Essays on Martín Luis Guzmán,* ed. William W. Megenney, 1–19. Riverside: University of California, Riverside, Latin American Studies Program, 1978.

Sheridan, Guillermo. *Los contemporáneos ayer.* Mexico City: FCE, 1993.

Sierra, Justo. *Evolución política del pueblo mexicano.* Caracas: Biblioteca Ayacucho, 1977.

Silva Herzog, Jesús. *Breve historia de la revolución mexicana.* 2 vols. Mexico City: FCE, 1972.

Solana, Rafael. "Rafael F. Muñoz, al medio siglo de su actividad literaria." *El Libro y el Pueblo,* época 4, no. 10 (1964): 1–3.

———. "Rasgos bio-bibliográficos de Rafael F. Muñoz." *El Libro y el Pueblo,* época 4, no. 10 (1964): 3–4.

Solares, Ignacio. *Columbus.* Mexico City: Alfaguara, 1996.

Sommers, Joseph. "Novela de la revolución: Criterios contemporáneos." *Investigaciones contemporáneas sobre historia de México,* ed. Juan de la Cueva, 737–749. Mexico City: Universidad Nacional Autónoma de México, 1971.

Soto, Shirlene Ann. *The Mexican Woman: A Study of Her Participation in the Revolution, 1910–1940.* Palo Alto, Calif.: R&E Research Associates, 1979.

Souza, María Isabel. *¿Por qué con Villa?* Mexico City: Instituto Nacional de Antropología e Historia, 1975.

Spivak, Gayatri Chakravorty. "Can the Subaltern Speak?" *Marxism and the Interpretation of Culture,* ed. Cary Nelson and Lawrence Grossberg, 271–313. Urbana: University of Illinois Press, 1988.

Stallybrass, Peter, and Allon White. *The Politics and Poetics of Transgression.* Ithaca, N.Y.: Cornell University Press, 1986.

Stavenhagen, Rodolfo. "Siete tesis equivocadas sobre América Latina." *Tres ensayos sobre América Latina,* by Rodolfo Stavenhagen, Ernesto Laclau, and Ruy Mauro Marino, 9–42. Barcelona: Anagrama, 1980.

Tannenbaum, Frank. *Peace by Revolution.* New York: Columbia University Press, 1933.

Terrazas, Silvestre. *El verdadero Pancho Villa.* Mexico City: Era, 1985.

Torres, Elías L. *20 vibrantes episodios de la vida de Villa (fragmentos de la vida revolucionaria del general Villa).* Mexico City: Editorial Sayrols, 1934.

Torres, Teodoro, Jr. *Pancho Villa: Una vida de romance y tragedia.* San Antonio, Tex.: Casa Editorial Lozano, 1924.

Tovar y de Teresa, Rafael. *Modernización y política cultural: Una visión de la modernización de México.* Mexico City: FCE, 1994.

Tuñón Pablos, Julia. *Mujeres en México, una historia olvidada.* Mexico City: Planeta, 1987.

Tutino, John. *From Insurrection to Revolution in Mexico: Social Bases of Agrarian Violence, 1750–1940.* Princeton, N.J.: Princeton University Press, 1986.

Van Young, Eric, ed. *Mexico's Regions: Comparative History and Development.* San Diego: Center for U.S.-Mexican Studies, 1992.

Vargas Arreola, Juan Bautista. *A sangre y fuego con Pancho Villa.* Mexico City: FCE, 1995.

Vargas V., Jesús. *Chihuahuismos: Dimes y diretes, modismos y malarazones de uso regional.* Chihuahua, Mex.: Ediciones Nueva Vizcaya, 1995.

Vargas Valdés, Jesús, and Flor García Rufino. *Francisca Yo! El libro desconocido de Nellie Campobello.* Mexico City: Nueva Vizcaya Editores, Universidad Nacional Autónoma de Ciudad Juárez, 2004.

Vasconcelos, José. *El desastre.* Mexico City: Jus, 1952.

———. *La raza cósmica.* Mexico City: Espasa Calpe Mexicana, 1992.

———. *Memorias I: Ulises Criollo: La Tormenta.* Mexico City: FCE, 1983.

Vaughan, Mary Kay. "Cambio ideológico en la política educativa de la SEP: Programas y libros de texto, 1921–1940." *Escuela y sociedad en el período cardenista,* ed. Susana Quintanilla and Mary Kay Vaughan, 76–108. Mexico City: FCE, 1997.

―――. *Cultural Politics in Revolution: Teachers, Peasants, and Schools in Mexico, 1930–1940.* Tucson: University of Arizona Press, 1997.

Vázquez de Knauth, Josefina. *El nacionalismo y la educación en México.* Mexico City: El Colegio de México, 1975.

Vázquez Valle, Irene, ed. *La cultura popular vista por las élites (antología de artículos publicados entre 1920 y 1952).* Mexico City: Universidad Nacional Autónoma de México, 1989.

Vera Estañol, Jorge. *Historia de la revolución mexicana: Orígenes y resultados.* 2nd ed. Mexico City: Porrúa, 1976.

Vida y hazañas de Francisco Villa: Su juventud audaz, su esplendor guerrero y su vuelta a la vida pacífica del campo. San Antonio, Tex.: Librería de Quiroga, 1921.

Wilkie, James W. *The Mexican Revolution: Federal Expenditure and Social Change since 1910.* Berkeley and Los Angeles: University of California Press, 1970.

Williams, Raymond. *The Long Revolution.* New York: Columbia University Press, 1961.

Womack, John, Jr. *Zapata and the Mexican Revolution.* New York: Vintage, 1970.

INDEX

Castellanos, Rosario, 140
Científicos, 84, 155n25
Civilizing code: 90, 93, 119, 156n36;
    and Villa, 20, 95. *See also El águila
    y la serpiente*
Colonias militares (military colonies),
    58–60
Contemporáneos (Los), 150n23,
    160n40
Córdoba, Arnaldo, 144n30
Corral, Luz, 150n32
Corrido, 53, 63, 69, 150n32
Cristero War, 13, 143n1, 154n8

Defensas sociales, 111, 131, 133,
    163n43
De la Huerta, Adolfo, 78, 79. *See also
    El águila y la serpiente*
Díaz, Porfirio, 21, 45, 59
Díaz Arciniega, Víctor, 145n11
Díaz Ordaz, Gustavo, 137, 164n1
Division of the North, 1, 2, 72, 126
Domínguez, Christopher, 81

Eagleton, Terry, 155n21
Ejido, 143n2
Elias, Norbert, 91, 95, 156n33
Elías Calles, Plutarco. *See* Calles,
    Plutarco Elías
Estrada Muñoz, Antonio, 149
Estridentista movement, 52

Fernández de Castro, José Antonio,
    51, 52
Fernández de Lizardi, José Joaquín: *El
    periquillo sarniento* and *La Quijotita
    y su prima*, 157n41
El feroz cabecilla (Muñoz), 100, 102, 105
Florescano, Enrique, 5
Foster, David William, 155n28
Francisca ¡Yo! (Campobello), 50, 149n8
Franco, Jean, 33, 116
Frías, Heriberto: *Tomóchic*, 145n3

Frontier culture, 59
Fuentes, Fernando de, 122

Gamboa de Camino, Berta, 53, 61, 100
García Lorca, Federico, 51
García Rufino, Flor, 149n8
Garro, Elena, 140
Gilly, Adolfo, 76
Gómez Morín, Manuel, 154n9
González, Manuel Pedro, 61
Gramsci, Antonio, 36
Guerrero, Julio, 146n21
Guha, Ranajit, 6, 7, 147n28; on popu-
    lar political consciousness, 36–37
Gutiérrez, Eulalio, 79, 87
Guzmán, Martín Luis, 10, 80, 86, 87,
    88, 89, 100, 124, 134, 135, 139;
    association with Villa, 161n24;
    Ateneo de la Juventud and, 84;
    evolving views on Villa, 20, 126;
    forced exile, 78–79; ideological
    contrast with Rafael F. Muñoz,
    99, 107, 114, 119; and ideology of
    Cardenismo, 9, 11, 130; middle-
    class liberal ideology, 8, 138;
    non-elitist literary influence, 130;
    and popular nationalism, 157n45;
    relation to Mexico's presidents,
    77–78, 125–127, 129, 153–154n1,
    162n20; research on Villa, 128;
    Rodó's influence on, 84–85; on
    Villa's colloquial language, 128;
    and Villista bravado, 107. *See also
    El águila y la serpiente*

Hamilton, Nora, 143n2
Henríquez Ureña, Pedro, 130
Herrera, Celia, 9, 10, 11, 124, 131,
    132, 134
Herrera clan (the): Jesús, 132; Luis,
    131; Maclovio, 91, 131; rivalry
    with Villa, 131–132, 133, 135. *See
    also Cartucho*